NOLO *and* USA TODAY

NOLO
YOUR LEGAL COMPANION

For more than 35 years, Nolo has been helping ordinary folks who want to answer their legal questions, create their own documents, or work with a lawyer more efficiently. Nolo.com provides quick information about wills, house buying, credit repair, starting a business—and just about anything else that's affected by the law. It's packed with free articles, legal updates, resources, and a complete catalog of Nolo books and software.

To find out about any important legal changes to this book's contents, check for free updates at Nolo.com. Under "Products," find this book and click "Legal Updates." You can also sign up for our free e-newsletters at Nolo.com/newsletters/index.html.

USA TODAY
The Nation's Newspaper

USA TODAY, the nation's largest circulation newspaper, was founded in 1982. It has nearly 3.9 million readers daily, making it the most widely read newspaper in the country.

USATODAY.com adds blogs, interactive graphics, games, travel resources, and trailblazing network journalism, allowing readers to comment on every story.

The **Judge** Who **Hated Red Nail Polish**

&

Other Crazy But True Stories of Law & Lawyers

Ilona Bray, Richard Stim and the Editors of Nolo

First Edition   APRIL 2010

Editor   ILONA BRAY

Book Design   SUSAN PUTNEY

Proofreading   SUSAN CARLSON GREENE

Printing   DELTA PRINTING SOLUTIONS, INC.

Bray, Ilona M., 1962-
   The judge who hated red nail polish : and other crazy but true stories of law and
lawyers / by Ilona Bray and Richard Stim ; and the Editors of Nolo. -- 1st ed.
      p. cm.
   ISBN-13: 978-1-4133-1191-4 (pbk.)
   ISBN-10: 1-4133-1191-1 (pbk.)
   1. Law--United States--Anecdotes. 2. Judges--United States--Anecdotes. 3. Lawyers--
United States--Anecdotes. I. Stim, Richard. II. Nolo (Firm) III. Title.
   K184.B73 2010
   349.73--dc22
                              2009046169

Acknowledgments

This book was a team effort, drawing on the knowledge, experience, and quirky obsessions of a wide range of people. It's hard to know where to begin with the thanks, but here goes.

First and foremost, we owe a big debt of gratitude to Nolo editors and authors Stephen Fishman, Lisa Guerin, Betsy Simmons, Diana Fitzpatrick, Emily Doskow, and Drew Wheaton, who contributed passages on topics such as canine crimes, M&Ms and Barbies in court, celebrity lawyers, and disputes over who caught the home run baseball.

We're also grateful to Forrest Booth, admiralty attorney at Severson & Werson (www.severson.com) in San Francisco, California, for clarifying the arcane and ever-changing law of sunken treasure.

Stan Jacobsen was our wonderful researcher, finding long-forgotten books within the California library system.

Nolo's production department exercised its usual artfulness, with Susan Putney designing the layout, and other great help coming from Jaleh Doane, Emma Cofod, and Ashley Garst.

About the Authors

We'll introduce you to the authors of this book with the first of a number of quizzes you'll find inside.

Ilona Bray:

    a. never went to law school

    b. didn't really write those ten-plus books with her name on them

    c. lives in an undisclosed location

    d. hasn't memorized all of the lyrics to *The Sound of Music*

ANSWER: None of the above

Richard Stim is:

    a. an attorney and author of a dozen Nolo books

    b. a Bay Area resident who lives on a houseboat not unlike the one in the 60s TV show, "Surfside 6"

    c. a big fan of Christmas movies

    d. a social networking denier

ANSWER: All of the above

Table of Contents

A Roadtrip Through Loony U.S. Laws

W e'll start with a reality check. The truth of the matter is, most loony laws that you've read about—over and over, after your great aunt forwarded that email for the umpteenth time—are fiction. Urban legends. May have existed once, but someone wised up and took them off the books.

That means you can, without fear of legal repercussions, grow a beard in Brainerd, Minnesota, take a bath less than once a year in Kentucky, and (if you're a moose) walk down a sidewalk in Alaska. (Sighs of relief all around.)

Nevertheless, if you happen to take a road trip across the United States, you might smack into a few remaining oddball laws. Remember, ignorance of the law is no defense! So unless you want to collect misdemeanor convictions, take our advice below.

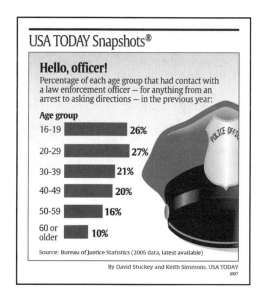

USA TODAY Snapshots®

Hello, officer!
Percentage of each age group that had contact with a law enforcement officer – for anything from an arrest to asking directions – in the previous year:

Age group

16-19	26%
20-29	27%
30-39	21%
40-49	20%
50-59	16%
60 or older	10%

Source: Bureau of Justice Statistics (2005 data, latest available)

By David Stuckey and Keith Simmons, USA TODAY 2007

In Kentucky:
Keep your chameleon under wraps at church

You'd better have at least $50 on hand for the fine if you decide to display, handle, or use "any kind of reptile in connection with any religious service or gathering" while in the Bluegrass State. Iguana worshipers, beware. (Kentucky Revised Statutes, § 437.060.)

In Oregon:
Don't hunt in a cemetery

Hmm, what if you're hunting for ghosts? (Oregon Revised Statutes, § 166.645.)

In West Virginia:
Don't taunt someone who refuses to duel

Let's say you know someone who's been challenged to a duel and says, "No." You may be thinking, "Come on, you lily-livered chicken, grab your sword and pistols and defend your honor!" In West Virginia, these are thoughts to keep to yourself. In particular, steer clear of any "reproachful or contemptuous language." Unless you'd like free board at a local jail for up to six months. (West Virginia Code, § 61-2-24.)

In New Mexico:
Don't expose yourself while waitering

Actually, this seems like a fairly sensible law. When we sit down to lunch or a drink, we like to see the waiter's hands and smiling face, but that's about it. Like so many laws, however this one makes you wonder what happened to bring "indecent waitering" to the attention of an entire legislature. (New Mexico Statutes § 30-9-14.2.)

In Virginia:
Don't hunt raccoons after 2 a.m. on a Sunday morning

Any other time of the day or week is fine for taking aim at little Rocky. But as for other wild birds or animals, Sunday is "declared a rest day," and you'll have to suppress any hunting urges. At least until Monday rolls around. (Virginia Code, § 29.1-521.)

In Massachusetts:
Make sure your sleigh-drawing horse wears three bells

Two bells won't do it; not if you plan to "travel on a way with a sleigh or sled drawn by a horse." Actually, we like this law so well we think it should be applied to all forms of transportation. Jingle all the way! (Massachusetts General Laws Annotated 89 § 3.)

In Little Rock, Arkansas:
Don't beep at a sandwich shop after 9 p.m.

Beeping at noodle shops or coffee shops may be alright, but check the menu first. The statute, a model of specificity, says that "No person shall sound the horn on a vehicle at any place where cold drinks or sand-wiches are served after 9:00 p.m." (Code; City of Little Rock, Arkansas 1961, § 25-74.)

New York:
Don't detain dead deadbeat debtors

We'll spell this one out for you: If someone owes you money, but dies, you have to curb your temptation to say, "Pay up, or you're not going anywhere." Don't try asking a police officer for help, either: It's illegal to arrest the dead debtor. (New York Public Health Law § 4219.)

In Washington, DC:
Don't play ball in the street

Geez, they're serious in DC. You're not allowed to play football, any other ballgame, or even "bandy, shindy, or any other game by which a ball, stone, or other substance is struck or propelled by any stick, cane, or other substance in any street, avenue, or alley" within the city. So where's a kid supposed to play shindy? (District of Columbia Code § 22-1308.)

In Ohio:
Don't let your horse have sex in public

For real. The law says: "No owner of a stallion or jack or the agent of such owner, shall permit it to serve a mare within thirty feet of a public street or alley in a municipal corporation." Say no more.
(Ohio Revised Code § 959.19.)

More Than You Ever Wanted to Know About Lawyers

W hether you love 'em, hate'em, or are one of them (or all of the above), you might know less about lawyers than you think.

Here's some fodder for your thoughts, theories, and niggling suspicions.

Just how many lawyers are there in the United States?

At last count, the United States had a total of 1,180,386 actively practicing lawyers. The entire U.S. population is around 307,280,418, so only .38% of the population are lawyers. That's one in every 260 people. If you have 259 Facebook friends, you might not even have a lawyer in the bunch!

Is anyone counting the outsourced lawyers in India?

By 2008, over 29,000 U.S. legal jobs had been "offshored" to Indian outposts, and that number is expected to increase to 79,000 by 2015. The loss in revenue for U.S. lawyers is estimated at $4.3 billion (though nobody has calculated the savings to clients).

Do any lawyers have the last name "Lawyer"?

Yes, fate seems to have pointed a number of people straight toward a legal career. As of 2009 (data from Martindale & Hubble at www.martindale.com), 18 U.S. lawyers had the last name "Lawyer," including a "Vivian Jury Lawyer." No fewer than 115 U.S. lawyers have the last name "Law," one of them sporting the can't-lose name of "Victor Law." Yet another 42 can claim the surname "Laws," (with two more "Victors" in the bunch). Sixty-six U.S. lawyers are named Justice (including one "Courtney" and one with the happy hyphenation "Hall-Justice"), 67 are named "Judge" or "Judges," nine are named "Court" or "Courts," and there's even one "Tort."

Of course, fate has a sense of irony. Forty-four lawyers have the last name "Lawless" (including one "Sue Lawless"), and eight are named "Doctor" or "Doctors."

How do people become lawyers?

Although some kids are said to be "born lawyers" (usually after arguing that they deserve the larger half of the candy bar), being a lawyer isn't a mere accident of birth.

After finishing college, wannabe lawyers must ordinarily attend law school, which will add three years to their schooling. Around 200 law schools operate in the United States. The competition for admission can be pretty stiff, particularly at top-rated schools like Harvard, Yale, and Stanford, each of which accepts around 10% of its applicants.

Of the nearly 50,000 people who enter law school every year, approximately 6,000 think twice about their decision and get the hell out.

USA TODAY Snapshots®

Becoming a lawyer
Overall passage rates of bar examination:

70% — 1996
65% — 2000
64% — 2005

Source: National Conference of Bar Examiners

By David Stuckey and Alejandro Gonzalez, USA TODAY 2007

How much does law school cost?

At state-run schools, tuition averages $16,800 for residents and $28,400 for nonresidents. Applicants lucky enough to get into a private school can look forward to tuition of around $34,300 per year.

No wonder surveys say law school debt prevents most lawyers from even considering a public interest or government career.

Is law school the only way?

No—just ask Abraham Lincoln, who became a lawyer by reading relevant books rather than going to law school. Of course, such a path was more common in his time.

Even today, however, people who want to be lawyers but can't stand (or afford) three years of law school can—in a few states such as California, Virginia, New York, and Washington—basically apprentice themselves to a practicing judge or lawyer in lieu of law school. This little-known method is rarely used—though Barry Melton, a cofounder of the band Country Joe and the Fish (popular during the 1960s), eventually became a California lawyer this way.

After completing law school (or alternate training), a prospective lawyer must pass a bar exam in the state where he or she plans to practice. The exam takes from one to three days to finish. The percentage of people who pass depends on the state, but it's usually around 70%.

What proportion of lawyers are women or people of color?

Although the profession is changing fast, it's still dominated by white males. About 25% of lawyers are women, and 12% are nonwhite.

How much do lawyers earn?

The median salary is approximately $102,000, with partners at big law firms taking home double that amount and more.

Can high salaries buy happiness?

Not necessarily, especially if you value home and family. Many lawyers often work absurdly long hours; 37% say they work 50 hours or more per week. While most lawyers report satisfaction with their jobs, no one seems to be keeping track of the number of lawyers who leave the profession altogether.

Do people *like* lawyers?

People in the United States like lawyers better than members of the real estate, automobile, and oil and gas industries. Unfortunately, that's not saying much. Only 25% of the U.S. population had a positive image of lawyers in 2009.

If it's any comfort to the lawyers out there, such sentiments go way back. Tacitus (56–117) said "Never was any item so openly sold as the perfidy of lawyers." Erasmus, who hails from the fifteenth century, said, "Lawyers are jackals." And an old German proverb says "Doctors purge the stomach, parsons purge the soul, lawyers purge the purse."

Do lawyers like each other?

That's something they'd probably argue over. But walk into any law firm, and you're likely to find that a good number of its lawyers are married to one another. With the long hours they work, how are they supposed to meet anyone else?

Actually, lawyers seeking other lawyers could check out this dating site: www.lawdate. com. It might be safer than risking love with a nonlawyer, if you believe Dr. Fiona Travis, author of *Should You Marry a Lawyer: A Couple's Guide to Balancing Work, Love & Ambition.* She says, "Lawyers have problems building and sustaining relationships," which she attributes to a combination of the lawyer personality and the lessons learned in law school. (Funny, we don't remember Relationship Destruction 101 being part of the curriculum.) •

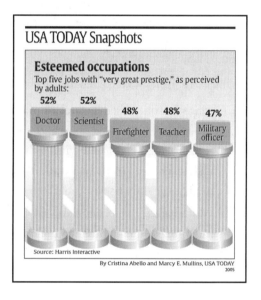

USA TODAY Snapshots

Esteemed occupations
Top five jobs with "very great prestige," as perceived by adults:

Doctor	Scientist	Firefighter	Teacher	Military officer
52%	52%	48%	48%	47%

Source: Harris Interactive

By Cristina Abello and Marcy E. Mullins, USA TODAY
2005

Barbie Goes to Court

I f you think of Barbie as a sweet girl who never gets into legal trouble, think again. No, it's not because she crashed her pink Corvette, neglected to renew her pilot's license, or has bust-to-waist measurements that should be illegal. Often, the trouble comes when creative people find, um, interesting ways to incorporate Barbie into their art—without Mattel's permission. Who knew innocent Barbie could be at the heart of such tumultuous legal battles?

Food Chain Barbie

A photographer used a series of photos he called "Food Chain Barbie" to comment on gender roles and consumerism. The photos show a naked Barbie juxtaposed with various kitchen appliances. For example, "Malted Barbie" features a nude Barbie in a malt machine and "Barbie Enchiladas" shows several Barbies wrapped in tortillas in an oven.

Mattel sued the artist, claiming that Barbie was used without permission and that the photographs tarnished her reputation. (What will Ken think?) However, the court found that the First Amendment made it okay and ordered Mattel to pay the artist's substantial attorney's fees.

Rockette Barbie

Radio City Music Hall designed a "Rockettes 2000 Doll" to celebrate the new millenium. The dolls were supposed to represent the famous Radio City Music Hall Rockettes, but Mattel thought they looked a little bit too much like Barbies. It claimed that Radio City and their doll makers used Barbie's facial features.

Radio City managed to fend off the lawsuit at the district court level. The court found no copyright infringement, repeating another court's finding that, "When it comes to something as common as a youthful, female doll, the unprotectible elements are legion, including, e.g., full faces; pert, upturned noses; bow lips; large, widely spaced eyes; and slim figures." However, the appeals court disagreed, saying that because Mattel had put a lot of work into figuring out which facial features appealed to the public, it was entitled to have Barbie's facial features protected by copyright.

Barbie Girl sings

Danish pop group Aqua's song "Barbie Girl" may have been a hit in the dance clubs, but not with Mattel. Perhaps it was the lyrics, in which Barbie croons "I'm a blond bimbo" and "undress me anywhere." In suing the record company, MCA Records, Inc., Mattel claimed that the song damaged the reputation of the brand.

Mattel lost that argument. The court found that the song was a parody within the rights of the First Amendment. Apparently, Mattel didn't have any hard feelings about the outcome, because it later licensed a modified version of the song for its own advertisements. It even chose to keep some of the lyrics, such as, "Life in plastic, it's fantastic."

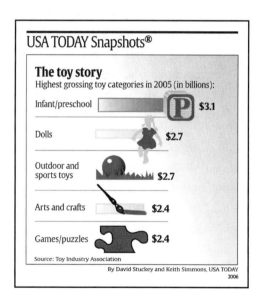

USA TODAY Snapshots®

The toy story
Highest grossing toy categories in 2005 (in billions):

Infant/preschool — $3.1
Dolls — $2.7
Outdoor and sports toys — $2.7
Arts and crafts — $2.4
Games/puzzles — $2.4

Source: Toy Industry Association

By David Stuckey and Keith Simmons, USA TODAY 2006

Barbie's telephone playhouse

An adult services website promoted "Barbie's Playhouse," where users could log in and pay by the minute to have an intimate video chat with a woman who called herself Barbie. The website used colors and fonts very similar to those used by Mattel. Mattel sued and won. The judge (now-Supreme-Court-Justice Sonia Sotomayor) found that the business purposely used the Barbie trademark to make money.

Barbie n' Bratz

When Barbie began to get some serious competition from some new girls on the toy shelf—the Bratz dolls—Mattel sued again. The Bratz dolls were hip, edgy, and multicultural, making Barbie seem plain and prudish by comparison. Sales in the billions of dollars cut into Barbie's profits and showed that girls loved Bratz. But after a long legal battle that racked up tens of millions of dollars in lawyer's fees, Barbie still came out on top. It turns out that the original designer of Bratz came up with the idea while working for Mattel and then took his idea to MGA, which produced the dolls. MGA was ordered to pay $100 million in damages and to stop producing and selling their sassy dolls. Predictably, that turned the existing dolls into eBay collectors' items.

Barbie and Nissan

You'd think the car company Nissan would have enough lawyers on staff to avoid this kind of trouble. But no, it created television commercials showing a GI Joe-like doll zooming in, riding his Nissan, to rescue a drowning Barbie-like doll, while a Ken-like doll looks on forlornly. The commercials, which featured the Van Halen version of "You've Really Got Me," were a hit with television watchers, but Mattel was not amused. It sued Nissan and settled out of court. ●

How One Woman Survived the Most Rigorous Law School Admission Process in History and Still Managed to Feed the Kids and Clean the House

On her first day at Hastings College of the Law in San Francisco, California, the male students taunted Clara Shortridge Foltz—mimicking her every move in one class, including coughing when she did. Foltz took the male taunts in stride; she was no shrinking violet. She had already changed California law with her "Women's Lawyer Bill" (in which she convinced the legislature to allow women to practice law). She had even become California's first woman lawyer, having passed the bar without attending law school.

So, if she was already an attorney, why bother with Hastings? Even though Foltz had won several cases, she believed that a formal law school education would enhance her stature as California's only lady lawyer. But the law school's all-male board of directors—after learning that Clara had paid the $10 admissions fee—secretly met and unanimously passed a resolution barring women from entering the law school. And on January 11, 1879, when Foltz arrived for her third day of classes, the school's doorman stopped her from entering.

Foltz wasn't the only woman barred from law school that day. A friend, Laura Gordon, had also sought admission. Gordon—a crusading women's journalist and the founder of two newspapers—had befriended Foltz during the battle over the Women's Lawyer Bill. Now, she, too, wanted to practice law, but was being denied an education.

Foltz and Gordon petitioned the courts to order the board of directors to admit them. The matter was sent to Judge R. F. Morrison in San Francisco. Morrison initially blocked Foltz from representing herself, refusing to honor her bar certificate and demanding she take a second bar exam. So, Foltz underwent her second three-hour inquisition by male attorneys and passed with flying colors.

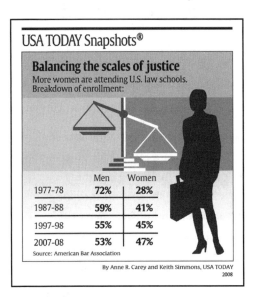

USA TODAY Snapshots®

Balancing the scales of justice
More women are attending U.S. law schools.
Breakdown of enrollment:

	Men	Women
1977-78	72%	28%
1987-88	59%	41%
1997-98	55%	45%
2007-08	53%	47%

Source: American Bar Association

By Anne R. Carey and Keith Simmons, USA TODAY 2008

The lawyers for Hastings took a less-than-courageous approach. They came up with various legal excuses for delays, hoping to render the case moot as the semester proceeded. The tactic backfired because, during the ensuing months, the state constitutional convention adopted a law stating that "no person shall on account of sex be disqualified from entering upon or pursing any lawful business, vocation, or profession." And then—aware of the Hastings lawsuit—California also passed a law saying that "no person shall be barred admission to any of the collegiate departments of the university on account of sex."

When it came time for trial, Hastings sent their greatest legal warriors into the fray, including two former California Supreme Court justices. They made two arguments. The first was that Hastings wasn't really part of the state school system, since its existence was due to a trust left by Judge Hastings. The second argument was that, let's face it, the business of law is really too nasty for ladies. "Law," they asserted, "has essentially and habitually to do with all that is selfish and extortionate, knavish and criminal, coarse and brutal, repulsive and obscene in human life." They then went down a laundry list of the "repulsive" aspects of law including, prostitution, sodomy, cohabitation, bastardy, impotence, and divorce.

Foltz responded by citing the new California laws and pointing out that knowledge of the law would make women better citizens. The case received a lot of attention from the newspapers, in whose journalistic judgment it was especially critical to give detailed accounts of the women's appearance. The *San Francisco Chronicle* reporter was apparently obsessed with the women's hair, writing that Foltz's "profuse hair" was "done in braids, which fell backward from the crown of her head like an Alpine glacier lit by a setting sun." Gordon "had curls enough to supply half the thin-haired ladies of San Francisco with respectable switches."

Ten days after the case was argued, Judge Morrison ordered Hastings to admit Foltz and Gordon.

Judge Hastings, the founder of the law school, agreed with Morrison's decision and recommended that the school's board of directors not appeal to the state supreme court. Unfortunately, the board wasn't ready to throw in the towel. It invoked a time-honored litigation strategy—keep pushing until the other side runs out of money. They appealed to California's Supreme Court.

Having taken the bar exam twice and passed both times, Foltz was now required by the California Supreme Court to take the bar exam a third time before she could argue her case

USA TODAY Snapshots®

Women and pay
Top occupation among women with the highest median weekly earnings:

Pharmacist	$1,432
Chief executives	$1,310
Lawyers	$1,255
Computer & information systems managers	$1,228
Computer software engineers	$1,149

Source: U.S. Department of Labor

By David Stuckey and Sam Ward, USA TODAY 2006

there. She passed again. And one spectator said of her Supreme Court argument, "I have never heard a better argument made by anyone."

In November 1879, almost a year after the two women had paid their admission fees to Hastings, the Supreme Court ordered the school to admit Foltz and Gordon.

Alas, after all that, Clara Shortridge Foltz never graduated from Hastings. During the legal battle, she'd been appointed as clerk to the Assembly Judiciary Committee, the first woman to achieve that legal position. She told friends she would later return to complete her formal legal education, but more exciting events intervened.

Aside from being the first woman lawyer in California (the third in the nation), she also became the first female district attorney in the United States and she advocated for and created the first public defender's office. She also instituted penal reform, including abolition of the "iron cages" that were used in San Francisco to contain criminal defendants in courtrooms. She helped draft and pass California's women's voting rights law, ran for governor, and was the first woman appointed to the State Board of Corrections, the first female licensed notary public, and the first woman director of a major bank. Oh, and did we mention that as a single mother, she raised five children?

Despite being ridiculed for her pioneering efforts, Foltz never lost her sense of humor. When a male attorney suggested her presence would be better served at home rather than in the courtroom, she responded, "A woman would better be almost any place than home raising men like you."

Clara Shortridge Foltz died in 1934 at the age of 85. As for Hastings and its board of directors, they seem to have buried the hatchet. The school's website now features an extensive biography of its first female law student.

Who is the youngest woman admitted to law school? We're not positive, but it could be Kate McLaughlin who in 2009 began Northwestern Law School at the age of 19. McLaughlin skipped six grades, graduated from the University of California San Diego at age 17 and scored a 174 out of 180 on the LSAT.

Reality TV in the Courtroom

A s if we didn't get enough reality in everyday life, reality TV now offers shows about every conceivable topic: from home repair to plastic surgery, dancing, multiple births, parolees who train pit bulls, weight loss, romance, jockeys, rich kids, rich adults, fishermen, and more. And what would real life be without the occasional lawsuit? No, we're not talking about reality TV shows with a legal angle (of which there are plenty, including shows about judges, lawyers, and law enforcement).

We're referring instead to the many show participants who've found themselves disappointed, injured, terrified, or bleeding—in other words, facing a little more reality than they could handle—and who then take the matter to court. Here are just a handful of the many, many lawsuits based on reality TV shows.

Smile! You won $300,000 from "Candid Camera"!

The grandparent of all reality TV shows, "Candid Camera" began airing in 1948 (believe it or not, it was formerly a radio program called "Candid Microphone"—apparently, the show's trademark exhortation to "Smile! You're on 'Candid Camera!'" was developed later).

The show, which catches people on film reacting to gag set-ups, was sued by Phillip Zelnick, who claimed that a fake airport security guard (played by host Peter Funt) instructed him to lie down on the conveyor belt and go through a fake X-ray scanning machine. He says he came out the other end—after getting stuck inside and punctured by a pen he had in his pocket—bruised and bleeding. After a trial, Mr. Zelnick was awarded $2,600 for injuries—and $300,000 in punitive damages.

"Kid Nation" needs a labor department

On "Kid Nation", 40 kids, ages eight to 15, spent 40 days in the New Mexico desert, trying to turn a "ghost town" (actually a movie set used for Westerns) into a functioning municipality run by kids. Apparently, before the kids got around to electing a health commissioner, several of them needed medical attention after they drank bleach; another was spattered by hot grease while cooking.

After complaints surfaced about the show, a parent complained to New Mexico officials. We're not sure whether a lawsuit was ever filed, but news reports indicated that lawyers had been retained. (This despite the extremely thorough contract all parents had to sign for their children to participate in the show, which absolved the network of liability for, among other things, their child's death, serious injury, or infection with a sexually transmitted disease.)

I thought it was a real alien

"Scare Tactics" is a show in which the unknowing victims, set up by their friends and relatives, are put in elaborately staged "horror" scenarios, designed to play on their worst fears. Well, it worked! Kara Blanc was set up and led to believe she was being taken to an exclusive Hollywood industry party, when the vehicle she was in stalled. Outside, she saw two people being chased by an alien, which led her to believe she had to run for her life or face death or injury at the alien's hands (or claws or tentacles).

In the personal injury lawsuit she later filed against the show, network, and others, Ms. Blanc made clear that, although she was led to believe the people she saw were under alien attack, she later learned that the "alien" was in fact a costumed actor, as were its victims. No word on what ultimately happened in the case.

Sometimes eight is not enough ... to save a marriage

The show "Jon & Kate Plus 8" followed the daily lives of the Gosselins: parents, Jon and Kate, their twin girls, and their younger sextuplets.

After several years (and many shows filled with on-air bickering and nagging), the Gosselins' marriage fell apart. And the divorce case wasn't the only lawsuit that came out of it.

TLC, the station that aired the show, sued Mr. Gosselin, alleging that he had breached his contract by, among other things, refusing to appear for filming, violating an exclusive arrangement with TLC by appearing regularly on "Entertainment Tonight," and selling photographic rights to pictures of the family. (Perhaps Gosselin was miffed by TLC's announced decision to give him a lesser role in the renamed version of the show, "Kate Plus 8.") The lawsuit also accused Gosselin of erratic public behavior, maybe referring to his very publicly dating the daughter of his wife's … plastic surgeon.

USA TODAY Snapshots®

Minding their media
Estimated number of hours the typical American will spend using various media this year:

Watching TV — 1,555
Listening to radio — 974
Using Internet — 195
Reading newspapers — 175
Listening to recorded music — 175

Sources: Communications Industry Forecast & Report; Statistical Abstract of the United States, 2007

By Robert W. Ahrens, USA TODAY 2007

Mr. Gosselin responded with a countersuit, claiming that TLC favored his wife, owed him money, and cut him off from media opportunities. In an affidavit accompanying the lawsuit, Mr. Gosselin said that the publicity attending the show made it impossible for him to find regular work—or, in the words of the *New York Post* headline on the case, "Jon Gosselin argues he's too famous to get a real job."

Every rose has its thorn: *The "Rock of Love" lawsuits*

Bret Michaels, front man for the 80s band Poison, has found a new calling as the host—and prize—of the VH1 show "Rock of Love." Each season, a group of women live together and compete, in ways organized and improvised, for Bret's attentions. Eliminations are made until the final lucky lady is asked to be Bret's rock of love. Awww.

Cue the lawyers: So far, the show has resulted in several lawsuits and a near miss. The owner of the "Rock of Love" house for the second season filed a lawsuit, claiming that $380,000 worth of damage had been done to his home. In another legal matter, producers of the show paid millions of dollars to settle claims arising out of a crash involving the "Rock of Love" tour bus. A spinoff show—"Rock of Love Charm School," in which the ladies from "Rock of Love" are taught how to be more … classy—resulted in a personal injury lawsuit against hostess Sharon Osbourne, who allegedly hit, scratched, and pulled the hair of a contestant who insulted her husband, Ozzie.

But there's at least one lawsuit that won't be filed: Bret Michaels told *Rolling Stone* magazine that he has no plans to sue over an incident in the 2009 Tony awards program, in which Michaels fractured his nose and split his lip when he was hit by a moving stage prop.

Rules, boundaries, and litigation

Cesar Milan, known from his television show "The Dog Whisperer" on the National Geographic channel, is famous for taming what he refers to as "red-zone" dogs (those who are aggressive and potentially danger-ous). Milan believes that dogs need exercise, discipline, and affection, but that many dog owners overdo it on the affection, praising their dog when it's anxious or fearful and thus reinforcing negative behavior.

Milan's training techniques are controversial—and have resulted in a lawsuit. A television producer sued Milan, claiming that Gator, his Labrador Retriever, was seriously injured by being put in a choke collar and forced to run on a treadmill. Hours after dropping the dog off, the producer claimed he was called and told that the dog had been rushed to the vet, bleeding from the nose and mouth and gasping for breath in an oxygen tent. (This probably didn't help the dog with one of the problems for which he was brought to Milan's facility: fear of strangers.) The lawsuit sought reimbursement for veterinary bills, including the cost of surgery on the dog's esophagus. Milan has said he wasn't at his facility at the time.

Biggest Beyond-the-Grave Control Freaks

Writing a will is a chance for somber personal reflection, for planning a legacy, and for a final act of beneficence toward family and friends. Or, it can be a prime chance to GET BACK AT ALL THE MISERABLE IDIOTS WHO'VE DRIVEN YOU CRAZY FOR THE LAST HEAVEN-KNOWS-HOW-MANY YEARS.

With a little money to dangle at them, perhaps one can even control their lives from the great beyond... .

Robert Allan Miller, 1995

This Bethlehem, Pennsylvania, man must have been seriously annoyed by people who double-parked. He bequeathed $5,000 to whichever police officer issued the most tickets to those who double-park. (Unfortunately, the town mayor overruled the bequest.)

Leona Helmsley, 2007

While Helmsley's Maltese got most of the headlines upon her death (the little dog received $12 million), let's not forget the two grandchildren to whom she did leave a little cash: $10 million apiece. (Lucky them—the other two grandchildren got zip, thus perhaps confirming Helmsley's nickname as "The Queen of Mean.")

But there's a catch: If the grandkids want to collect on the whole amount, they have to make twice-yearly visits to their father's grave (that being Helmsley's late son, Jay Panzirer). And how will anyone know they did so? Easy: They have to sign a registration book. Fail to sign in, and they lose half of what Helmsley left them. (Actually, at a per-hour rate, making those visits is a pretty profitable use of their time.)

Henry Budd, 1862

A bequest of 200,000 pounds was a small fortune back in nineteenth-century England, and Henry Budd left it all to his two sons; on one condition. They were not to grow mustaches. If either flouted this condition (and reports don't mention who was supposed to check their upper lips for excessive fuzz), the other brother would get his share.

Heinrich Heine, 1856

The German poet left his entire fortune to his wife—and the subject of much of his romantic poetry. Some say, however, there was one catch: she had to remarry immediately, so that, "there will be at least one man to regret my death." (It may be, however, that this was just a joke he expressed during life.)

Jeremy Bentham, 1832

Now here's a guy who hated to miss a meeting. The renowned philosopher and economist left a large sum to the University College in London on condition that his preserved (and fully clothed) corpse attend its annual board of directors' meetings. Apparently the preservation didn't work so well on his head, which had to be replaced with a wax replica. For many years, his ever-respectful colleagues recorded him as "present but not voting."

Charles Millar, 1928

A childless bachelor, this Canadian attorney and successful investor had an odd sense of humor, tied up with his theory that "Every man has his price." He used to get a kick out of leaving $1 bills on the sidewalk, then watching people's furtive expressions as they picked them up. (What, and women weren't falling all over themselves to marry this wild and crazy guy?)

With $568,106 to pass on (after some other, minor bequests), Millar had an opportunity for some big fun, prodding people to change their lives for money. He left it all to whichever mother gave birth to the most children in Toronto in the ten years following his death.

This prompted what Canadians called "the Great Stork Derby," as parents raced to fill their cradles before the deadline. (It's probably a good thing this predated the scientific possibility of having octuplets implanted in the womb.) The urgency became even greater as the Great Depression squashed most other forms of economic opportunity.

By 1938, there was a tie: Four mothers had given birth to nine babies apiece. They each received $125,000, while another two women, who'd been disqualified, each received $12,500 apiece, as a settlement—one had given birth to two stillborn children, and the other's births included illegitimate children.

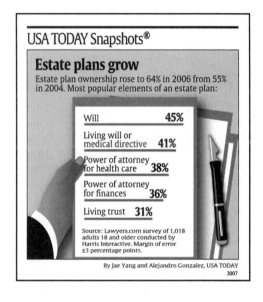

USA TODAY Snapshots®

Estate plans grow
Estate plan ownership rose to 64% in 2006 from 55% in 2004. Most popular elements of an estate plan:

Will	**45%**
Living will or medical directive	**41%**
Power of attorney for health care	**38%**
Power of attorney for finances	**36%**
Living trust	**31%**

Source: Lawyers.com survey of 1,018 adults 18 and older conducted by Harris Interactive. Margin of error ±3 percentage points.

By Jae Yang and Alejandro Gonzalez, USA TODAY 2007

T.M. Zink, 1930

Iowa attorney T.M. Zink was married and had a daughter. But this guy so hated women that, after leaving his daughter a lousy $5, he directed that the remainder of his estate (about $35,000) be placed in trust for 75 years, then be used to build the Zink Womanless Library. Yes, that's what it sounds like: a library with no books or magazine articles written by women, no feminine decorations, no artwork featuring women, and a sign over each entrance stating, "No women allowed." So, what does it say about Zink's legal skills that his daughter successfully challenged the will in court and got the money for herself?

Samuel Bratt, 1960

Samuel's wife never allowed him to smoke his beloved cigars around the house. He apparently suffered in silence, knowing he'd have the ultimate last word: In his will, he left his wife the enviable sum of £333,000. But, he made it conditional on her smoking five cigars a day for the rest of her life.

Five Things You (Probably) Didn't Know About Clarence Darrow

S ure, you may be aware that Clarence Darrow (1857–1938) was one of America's best-known attorneys and opponents of the death penalty, who, for example, defended thrill-killers Leopold and Loeb and represented teacher John Scopes in the 1925 Scopes Monkey Trial. You may also know that Darrow was an agnostic, a free thinker, and a champion of civil liberties and labor. You may even know some of the actors who portrayed him on stage and screen (Spencer Tracy, Orson Welles, Henry Fonda, Jack Lemmon, Melvyn Douglas, Kevin Spacey, and Jason Robards). But did you know these five facts about the greatest lawyer of the twentieth century?

1 He was barred from practicing law in California.

In 1910, Darrow had his hands full defending John J. McNamara, (head of the Bridge and Structural Workers Union) and his brother James, both accused of dynamiting the Los Angeles Times Building. Twenty employees of the *Times* had been killed in the blast and a suitcase full of dynamite had been found outside the home of the *Times*' publisher. A McNamara accomplice confessed and the case against Darrow's clients looked grim. (Eventually, they accepted a plea bargain to avoid the death penalty.)

Alas, the case might have just been a footnote in Darrow's career except that Darrow's chief investigator was caught trying to bribe two of the jurors and implicated the great lawyer. Darrow was tried separately for each bribery attempt. In the first trial, Darrow's closing argument lasted two days and moved many spectators to tears. The jury found Darrow not guilty and the judge congratulated Darrow on his acquittal. In the second case, the facts against Darrow were stronger and the jury deadlocked eight to four in favor of conviction. In 1913, Darrow accepted the D.A.'s plea bargain—no retrial if Darrow agreed to never practice law in California.

② He was a novelist.

Clarence Darrow was the inspiration for many novels—for example, *Inherit the Wind*, *Compulsion*, and *Clarence Darrow for the Defense*—but few people realize that Darrow was a novelist himself. In 1903, McClurg and Company published *Farmington*, Darrow's fictional account of his childhood. *The New York Times* called the book, "insidiously iconoclastic," advised some readers that they may find the whole thing to be "silly," and then pronounced, "Mr. Darrow has shown real art in the handling of one of the most difficult forms of literature."

Although Darrow wasn't a popular author—"Someday I hope to write a book where the royalties will pay for the copies I give away," he once said—he authored three other books, *Persian Pearl* (a book of essays), *The Story of My Life* (his autobiography), and *Resist Not Evil* (a criticism of the criminal justice system).

And speaking of lawyers and literature, Darrow later shared his law offices with attorney and poet Edgar Lee Masters, author of the *Spoon River Anthology*.

③ His best friend was an ordained Baptist Minister.

It seems strange that the lawyer who so disliked religion ("Some of you say religion makes people happy. So does laughing gas.") would become BFF with an ordained minister and a University of Chicago Divinity School theologian. But Clarence Darrow and George Burman Foster were not really such an odd pair of lifelong friends. Both men were considered rebels and iconoclasts in their own fields. Foster created controversy amongst the clergy for his "post modern" view of religious humanism. Two books that Foster published during his life—*The Finality of the Christian Religion* (1906) and *The Function of Religion in Man's Struggle for Existence* (1909)—resulted in his being expelled from the Baptist Ministers' Conference.

In some ways, both Foster and Darrow were approaching science and religion with the same cogent, intellectual fervor—both obsessed with what it means to be a "good" modern person among life's tragedies. Or as Darrow once put it, "The best that we can do is to be kindly and helpful toward our friends and fellow passengers who are clinging to the same speck of dirt while we are drifting side by side to our common doom."

④ He was a hopeless romantic who wrote over a hundred love letters to his wife.

Although a skeptic and a bit of a cynic ("The first half of our lives are ruined by our parents," he once said, "and the second half by our children"), Darrow never had a bad word to say of his wife, Ruby Hamerstrom Darrow. Ruby, a Chicago journalist, was Darrow's second wife. He fondly called her "Rube" and "Ruben" and referred to himself as "D." Since Clarence was on the road much of the time, their relationship was preserved in a collection of 176 love letters written by Clarence and discovered in 1998 by his grandniece.

According to one journalist who reviewed the letters, Darrow expressed his love for his wife in "a hundred different ways." In a 1910 letter he wrote, "It is all most bed time & I wish you were here." And even though he did not celebrate religious holidays, Darrow wrote on December 24, 1902, "Just a word tonight instead of a Christmas present to tell you that I think you are the dearest sweetest girl on earth & I love you with my whole heart & want you all to myself and I hope that this is the last Christmas so long as I live that I can not have you—have you as I want you—all for my own.... Good night dearest sweetheart & remember that you are always loved by your crazy old Clarence Darrow."

⑤ His ghost has been seen in Chicago's Museum of Science and Industry.

According to Darrow, once a person died, that was it. There was no God ("I do not believe in God because I do not believe in Mother Goose") or personal immortality ("The origin of the absurd idea of immortal life is easy to discover; it is kept alive by hope and fear, by childish faith, and by cowardice"). So it would have come as a surprise to him that some people claim to have seen the great man's ghost walking the streets of Chicago. Things really heated up in 1990 with reports that Darrow's ghost—a nicely dressed man in his sixties in a camel hair coat—had been spotted at Chicago's Museum of Science and Industry (located near where Darrow's ashes were spread and north of a bridge named after him). One museum employee alerted museum security, after seeing a strange man on the back steps who appeared to be in "another world." She later identified Darrow from his photographs. Ghost hunter Richard Crowe apparently also reported seeing the great orator on the museum's premises, and an Indiana man photographed a "smoky image resembling a face" just over the guardrails of the Clarence Darrow Memorial Bridge.

And here's something about Darrow that many people think is true ... but probably isn't

One of the most well-known rumors about Darrow is that he sometimes distracted the jury by employing a trick in which he hid a wire inside his cigar. The result was that he supposedly kept the ash from falling. Investigators can find no newspaper reports of the trick and Darrow never mentioned it in his writing. ●

Famous Prisoners' Last Meals

Nobody seems quite sure where the tradition of the last meal comes from, but it's alive and well in the United States. Prisoners who are about to be executed have the chance to put in a special meal request. In some states, prisoners can order out; in others, they must select something off the regular prison menu.

Sometimes, a prisoner's last meal request itself makes news—or sheds some new light on their crimes. Consider these final requests:

Robert Alton Harris:
Executed at San Quentin Prison, California, 1992

His last meal included a bucket of Kentucky Fried Chicken and two Domino's pizzas. Fast food played a significant role in his crime and conviction as well. Harris and his brother shot and killed two teenage boys, then took their car to use as a getaway vehicle in a planned bank robbery. The boys were eating hamburgers from Jack in the Box when they died; Harris finished the half-eaten burgers after murdering the boys, a widely reported fact that illustrated his attitude toward the crime.

Karla Faye Tucker:
Executed in Huntsville, Texas, 1998

Her last meal was a banana, a peach, and a garden salad with ranch dressing. This was a considerably healthier diet than she was consuming at the time she committed murder. She had just spent a wild weekend partying on alcohol, marijuana, methadone, heroin, speed, Valium, alcohol, and Percodan, among other things, when she and a male companion hacked two people to death with a pickax.

Ricky Ray Rector:
Executed at the Arkansas State Penitentiary, 1992

His last meal was steak, fried chicken, cherry Kool-Aid, and pecan pie—a dessert that later came to symbolize, to some, why Rector's life should have been spared. After killing a police officer he had known for years (the officer had come to Rector's house to take him into custody for another killing), Rector shot himself in the head. The gunshot caused brain damage so severe that he reportedly could not understand the concept of death, including that the people he killed were not still alive. Despite evidence of Rector's mental impairment, then-Governor (and presidential candidate) Bill Clinton refused to grant him clemency. The damning dessert evidence came out later: Apparently, Rector set aside his pie, telling the guards who came to take him to the execution chamber that he was saving it for later.

USA TODAY Snapshots®

Want fries with that? Heck, yeah!

Fueled by the popularity of fast-food fries, consumption of frozen potatoes has boomed. Per capita consumption in pounds per year[1]:

17.48

9.12

1970

2005

1 – Per capita availability adjusted for loss due to processing and waste from farm to table

Source: U.S. Department of Agriculture/Economic Research Service

By Tracey Wong Briggs and Veronica Salazar, USA TODAY 2007

Timothy McVeigh:
Executed at the Federal Penitentiary in Terre Haute, Indiana, 2001

The man convicted of the Oklahoma City bombing that killed 168 people had a last meal of two pints of mint chocolate ice cream. When compared to the most common last meal request (reportedly a cheeseburger and fries), asking for ice cream seems simple—not to mention animal friendly, as it's a meatless meal. But apparently that wasn't good enough for People for the Ethical Treatment of Animals (PETA), which wanted McVeigh to go vegan for his last meal in acknowledgment of all the lives he'd already taken. (That would have required him to forego all animal products, including dairy.) The group sent McVeigh a letter urging a vegan last supper, saying "I believe that your decision to go vegan would help the movement for compassion toward animals, and I am certain that if you made the decision prayerfully, it would profit your soul."

Thomas Grasso:
Executed at the Oklahoma State Penitentiary, 1995

Grasso's last meal request included steamed mussels, a double cheeseburger, a strawberry milkshake, pumpkin pie, a mango, and a 16-ounce can of Franco-American SpaghettiOs with Meatballs, served at room temperature.

Grasso killed two elderly people during robberies. Grasso's case had become an issue in the New York governor's race in 1994. Mario Cuomo refused to send Grasso to Oklahoma to face the ultimate penalty; on taking office, one of new Governor George Pataki's first acts was to send Grasso to Oklahoma to be executed. Perhaps used to all of the media attention, Grasso wrote a number of statements to the press in his final hours, including poetry by T.S. Eliot, his own poetry, a shout-out to Mr. Cuomo ("Mario Cuomo is wright" (sic)), and an urgent message regarding his last meal: "Please tell the media I did not get my SpaghettiOs, I got spaghetti. I want the press to know this."

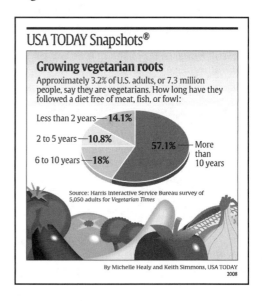

USA TODAY Snapshots®

Growing vegetarian roots
Approximately 3.2% of U.S. adults, or 7.3 million people, say they are vegetarians. How long have they followed a diet free of meat, fish, or fowl:

Less than 2 years—14.1%
2 to 5 years—10.8%
6 to 10 years—18%
57.1%—More than 10 years

Source: Harris Interactive Service Bureau survey of 5,050 adults for Vegetarian Times

By Michelle Healy and Keith Simmons, USA TODAY 2008

Velma Margie Barfield:
Executed at the Central Prison in Raleigh, North Carolina, 1984

Barfield was the first woman executed in the United States after the Supreme Court reinstated the death penalty, in 1976. Her last meal was

Cheeze Doodles and a Coke from the prison vending machine. Perhaps she didn't want anyone else preparing her food: She was convicted of murdering four people, including her mother, by poisoning their food with arsenic.

John Allen Muhammad:
Executed at Greensville Correctional Center, Virginia, 2009

The Washington, DC, sniper who killed ten people in 2002 and terrorized the area for weeks had an additional request beyond his last meal: He wanted his food choice kept private. Perhaps this reflected his obsession with the idea that the government was conspiring against him. In any case, word got out: Muhammad chose chicken with red sauce. (Death row prisoners in Virginia must select from items that have been on the prison menu within the last 28 days.) ●

Five Reasons Why John Donne Was Meant to Be a Poet, Not a Lawyer

It might comfort John Donne to know that he's considered a superstar poet today—given that "failed lawyer" might better describe how he and others saw him when he was alive, in sixteenth- to seventeenth-century Britain.

Who's John Donne? You know. He's the guy who wrote startlingly passionate poems in his younger days, with memorable bits such as, "Come live with me, and be my love, / And we will some new pleasures prove," as well as sermons of universal appeal (during his later life as a priest), like, "No man is an island, entire of itself; ... any man's death diminishes me, / because I am involved in mankind; and therefore never send to know for whom the bell tolls; it tolls for thee."

But writing poetry was, back then, even less of a lucrative career than it is now—just something you did to amuse your friends. Meanwhile, Donne's parents weren't rich, and he needed to earn a living.

So Donne started off doing the sensible thing. At age 20, he entered Lincoln's Inn, an exclusive college for legal studies on Chancery Lane in London. He was a smart kid and good at last-minute cramming for the moot court exercises and "oral disputation" that formed the core curriculum. (Almost no written work, wahoo!)

So what happened? Maybe the hand of fate took over, because Donne never finished law school and never formally practiced law. Even after the passage of centuries, we've isolated these five clues that Donne just wasn't meant to be a lawyer.

1 **If he'd written legal briefs, not poems, people centuries later wouldn't have borrowed his phrases for book titles.**

You've heard of *For Whom the Bell Tolls*, Ernest Hemingway's classic, and *Death Be Not Proud*, the memoir by John Gunther? Yup, those titles are taken from John Donne's writings. No one ever names their books after sixteenth-century legal briefs.

2 **Donne hated law school.**

He hated the studying part, anyway, which he described as having to "roughly chew, and sturdily digest; Th'immense vast volumes of our common law" (in a letter to a Mr. B.B.).

The hanging around with fellow students part, he liked just fine. Although Donne routinely set aside the hours between 4 a.m. and 10 a.m. for studying, friends were welcome to lure him away from his tiny dorm room at other times—and they did. For many of the young gentleman, law school was a chance to party. A contemporary noted, "Those that are disposed, studdie lawes," while "who so liketh, without checke, maye followe dalliance."

Nearby Lincoln's Inn Fields offered Elizabethan amusements like public executions, theatricals, and local taverns and brothels. In his second year, Donne's popularity led to his being appointed master of the revels, responsible for organizing entertainments and social events. (This turned out to be not as much fun as it could have been, since the Plague was ravaging London, and many law students left town to avoid becoming the next one "for whom the bell tolls.")

3 **Donne wrote his best love poems during law school.**

A contemporary described Donne during his years at the Inns as a "great visitor of ladies." In such ladies' honor, Donne wrote a trove of elegies and sonnets, like this one:

Come, Madame, come, all rest my powers defie; / Until I labor, I in labor lie. / . ... Off with that girdle, like Heaven's zone glittering, / But a far fairer world incompassing. / Unpin that spangled breastplate which you wear, That th' eyes of busie fooles may be stop't there. [Elegie XX: To His Mistress Going to Bed]

Although Donne's distractedness can't have helped his studies, it seems to have done great things for his poetry. The playwright Ben Jonson, who lived around the same time, claimed that Donne had "written all his best pieces ere he was 25 years old." In other words, Donne produced his best poetry right about the time he was in law school.

④ Donne messed up his first and only law job by pursuing a scandalous marriage.

Although Donne didn't formally graduate from law school, that was normal then. The final steps in the process were too arduous and time-consuming for most young men to bother with, and the fact that Donne had studied law for three years counted in his favor.

Donne's career took off to a promising start when he accepted a position as chief secretary to the Lord Keeper of the Great Seal and senior judge in the Court of Chancery, Sir Thomas Egerton. This was, in essence, a legal secretary position, but one that put Donne right in the heart of British government, in the Palace of Whitehall.

Donne also succeeded in seducing Egerton's young niece, Ann More. Knowing that he'd never get parental permission to marry Ann, Donne snuck off and did so in secret, when she was 16 or 17 (and apparently pregnant). Egerton summarily fired him.

⑤ Donne's powers of persuasion left his father-in-law unmoved.

A lawyer is supposed to be able to argue his way through anything, right? But after Donne secretly married Ann More, he faced the most important argument of his life: convincing his father-in-law, Sir George, to give up his wrath and accept the marriage.

In this, Donne made some pretty bad blunders—despite having procrastinated putting pen to paper for two months, from their marriage in December 1601 until the following February.

The letter Donne wrote starts off with some fairly straightforward confessions of fault (although he noted that Ann had "adventurd equally") and acknowledges that Donne knew perfectly well that Sir George wouldn't approve the match.

But then, as Donne's biographer John Stubbs points out, Donne manages to alienate his father-in-law by referring to his violent tendencies, saying "I humbly beg of yow that she may not to her danger feele the terror of yowr sudden anger."

He compounds his error by making a bad pun ("yt is irremmediably donne").

Donne then plays right into Sir George's suspicions that Donne is a money-grubbing ne'er-do-well by suggesting that if Sir George could just give the newly married couple a helping hand (i.e., money), Donne could make himself worthier of Ann. Oops.

The letter sent Sir George into a spitting rage. The man followed up by making sure that Donne was fired from his job, then marching into court to try to invalidate the marriage, and taking all other possible steps to ruin Donne's life before finally cooling off weeks later, after a personal meeting with Donne.

But the damage had been "donne." Donne next spent many penniless years raising many illness-prone babies and trying to recover his reputation. Sadly, Ann died in her thirty-third year, not long after giving birth. Donne never remarried.

How did Donne's career path wind up, you might ask?

Ironically, while the halls of law and government remained closed to Donne, the priesthood finally welcomed him. He took a position as divinity reader right back at Lincoln's Inn, where he gave sermons to young law students and lawyers.

Donne rose in the church, eventually being appointed Dean of St. Paul's in London. And, in a touch of closure, his legal training is said to have come in handy there, as he was called upon to make various judgments on ecclesiastical law.

Memorable Cases of False Advertising

W ith all the advertising we see every day, most savvy consumers have learned to laugh off outrageous or humorous claims. But every once in a while you'll see an ad that has stretched the truth to truly memorable lengths. Here are a few that stick in our minds (or craws).

This product wards off the common cold!

You've probably used it yourself or know people who swear by it: Airborne, that blend of vitamins and minerals that you let dissolve in water until it's fizzy, then drink. When it was launched onto the market in the late 1990s, the Airborne company advertised primarily to people who might be concerned about picking up airborne germs—such as travelers or teachers. The product was a hit, with sales zooming upwards into $100 million territory within the first six years.

Then came the "oops." In 2006, it was revealed that Airborne didn't have any reputable studies to back up its claims that the product could ward off or even cure a cold. A class action lawsuit followed shortly on the heels of this revelation.

Airborne continues to deny any wrongdoing, but it did agree to a $23 million settlement. If you're among Airborne's remaining devotees, don't worry, you can still buy it—but you'll notice it currently claims simply to "support your immune system."

It came out of the orange pasteurized!

In 1982, Tropicana aired a television commercial featuring Olympic athlete Bruce Jenner squeezing an orange and then pouring the juice into a Tropicana carton. He says, "It's pure, pasteurized juice as it comes from the orange." Coca-Cola (makers of a competing pasteurized orange juice) sued Tropicana for false advertising. It charged that, despite what the advertisement suggests, the reality is that the pasteurization process heats the juice up to 200 degrees Fahrenheit and that the juice is also sometimes frozen—hardly straight from the orange. Ultimately, the court agreed with Coca-Cola and prohibited Tropicana from airing the commercial.

Smoking is good for you!

As the most notorious of advertisers, tobacco companies have certainly had to own up to some false claims over the years. But perhaps no advertisements were as disconcerting—at least in retrospect—as the popular claim in the 1940s that not only do doctors support smoking, but that smoking is actually good for you. Ads abounded with distinguished-looking men in white coats holding cigarettes, spouting slogans like "made especially to prevent sore throats" and "more doctors smoke Camels than any other cigarette."

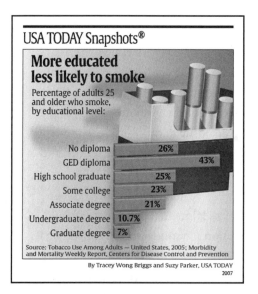

USA TODAY Snapshots®

More educated less likely to smoke

Percentage of adults 25 and older who smoke, by educational level:

No diploma	26%
GED diploma	43%
High school graduate	25%
Some college	23%
Associate degree	21%
Undergraduate degree	10.7%
Graduate degree	7%

Source: Tobacco Use Among Adults — United States, 2005; Morbidity and Mortality Weekly Report, Centers for Disease Control and Prevention

By Tracey Wong Briggs and Suzy Parker, USA TODAY 2007

By the early 1950s, the medical profession had cottoned onto the fact that smoking can kill you, and doctors began to distance themselves from the tobacco industry. Since then, the tobacco industry has come increasingly under attack for deceiving the public about the health risks of smoking. In the late nineties, the four largest tobacco companies agreed to pay more than $200 billion dollars over 25 years to settle a lawsuit brought by the attorneys general of 46 states. The settlement also put severe restrictions on the advertising of tobacco, including prohibiting advertising tobacco to young people. Despite this, tobacco use remains the number one preventable cause of death in the United States.

It shaves cartoon hairs like no other!

Razor maker Gillette has found itself on both sides of the false advertising battle. In the early 1990s, it sued Wilkinson Sword for false advertising in a commercial that showed the Wilkinson Sword razor shaving a basketball better than a Gillette razor. Gillette won that argument by convincing the court that suggesting that basketball shaving is similar to face shaving is misleading.

However, Gillette was later sued by Schick for its commercials that showed an animation of its razor as it lifted and cut hairs with almost magical precision. Gillette lost this time, and the court admonished Gillette by saying that the ads were "greatly exaggerated" and "literally false."

Miss Cleo knows your future! (better than her own)

If you watched late-night television in the late 1990s, you might remember Miss Cleo. She was the tarot card reader with the clichéd Jamaican accent who offered to read callers' futures. The first three minutes were "free," but were usually spent on hold. Subsequent minutes cost $4.99. Customers complained that they'd get charged way more than expected and then afterward be harassed for return business. Some people had phone records to prove they never made calls in the first place.

Both state and federal governments brought claims against Psychic Readers Network and Access Resource Services—the companies behind Miss Cleo. Florida even sued Miss Cleo herself. As a result of the lawsuits, the Miss Cleo enterprise shut down and was required to return millions of dollars to customers. Wouldn't you think she could have seen that coming?

Typhoid Mary Goes to Court

Q uick, how much do you know about Typhoid Mary? She spread typhoid, her name was Mary, and ... that's where most people stop.

In fact, no one had even heard of the now-infamous Irish immigrant, whose real name was Mary Mallon, until she brought her own case to court—a case in which she argued the unfairness of being the only one of thousands of typhoid carriers to have been basically imprisoned for life in a small island hospital near New York. Her confinement there was preceded by no trial, no hearing, not even any clear reason for such drastic and unusual measures.

Here's how it happened.

In the late nineteenth and early twentieth century, typhoid was a major killer (it's still a problem in the developing world, where antibiotics aren't always available). The bacteria, *Salmonella typhi*, is usually transmitted via water, so poor sanitation was a major cause of U.S. outbreaks.

To add to the trouble, the medical community was only just figuring out that germs, not other forces like "miasmas," cause disease—and, in one of its most cutting-edge discoveries, that people who had recovered from typhoid and seemed completely healthy could nevertheless carry and infect others with it. In particular, typhoid carriers who worked with food were likely to transmit the disease, via their not-entirely-clean hands.

Mary Mallon had the dubious honor of becoming the first U.S. typhoid carrier to receive serious scrutiny by health officials.

It all started in the summer of 1906, when she was working as a cook in the rented summer home of the Warren family, in Long Island, New York. Six out of the eleven people in the Warren household came down with typhoid fever. At that point, the home's owners, the Thompsons, figured they'd better trace the source if they hoped to ever rent the house again. They hired George Soper, a civil engineer known for epidemiological detective work.

After ruling out every other possibility, Soper turned his attention to the Warren's recently departed cook, Mary. The family remembered her as completely healthy—but also had fond memories of an ice cream dessert she'd made, which Soper knew would have been a prime way to transfer the typhoid bacillus. Before long, Soper discovered that Mary Mallon's working history coincided with between 22 and 26 cases of typhoid in houses where she'd cooked.

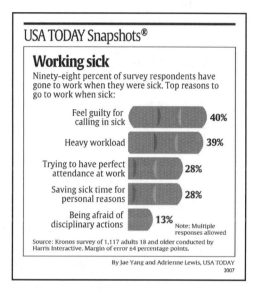

Soper showed up unannounced at the New York home where Mary lived in 1907, to ask for samples of her feces, urine, and blood. The course of that conversation may have determined much of what happened later. Mary Mallon, having never heard of the concept of a "healthy carrier," was understandably outraged at Soper's suggestion. In fact, she grabbed a carving fork and chased Soper all the way to the sidewalk.

Mary treated every other health official who showed up similarly, until New York health authorities finally sent an ambulance, more health officials, and a team of policemen to drag her to Willard Parker Hospital, "fighting and swearing," according to those who participated.

After tests confirmed that Mary Mallon was a typhoid carrier, the local health department shipped her off to North Brother Island, the site of a hospital used mostly to house people with tuberculosis. They put her in a small cottage with a dog, but no visiting privileges, and left her there.

This seems to have been more of a knee-jerk response than part of a considered policy. Many other known typhoid carriers (and there were thousands), such as Frederick Moersch, a confectioner from Brooklyn, were simply warned to find work that didn't involve food handling, and let go. The health officials seemed to be particularly lenient with men who were their family's primary wage earners. They were also well aware that they didn't have the resources to lock up every typhoid carrier in town. (Moersch eventually went back to selling ice cream, resulting in at least 60 new cases of typhoid and a few deaths.)

At first, Mary Mallon couldn't afford a lawyer to help her protest the unfairness of having been singled out in this way. But after over two years in her island exile, she somehow mustered up enough cash to hire young George Francis O'Neill, Esquire. He filed a writ of habeas corpus with the New York Supreme Court in 1909. (Habeas corpus is the legal means for a person to challenge an illegal detention. It's guaranteed under the U.S. Constitution and cannot be suspended, except in cases of rebellion or invasion, when "the public safety may require it.")

We'd like to say that the court duly considered the due process and precedent-setting implications of Mary Mallon's indefinite detention—but we can't. In an unpublished decision, the court simply returned her to her island cottage, basically agreeing with the health department lawyers that because she was infected and a danger to the public, she should be locked up.

The media seized on this story, issuing alternately damning and sympathetic accounts with headlines like, "'Typhoid Mary' Most Harmless and Yet the Most Dangerous Woman in America," and drawings of her cracking little skulls like eggs into a frying pan. A public health official finally released her in 1910.

Unfortunately for Typhoid Mary's legacy, she apparently never believed that she was a carrier. And she had trouble finding work outside kitchens. So in 1915, she was caught working under the name "Mrs. Brown" at New York's Sloane Maternity Hospital—a discovery occasioned by an outbreak of 25 cases of typhoid fever there.

The authorities sent Mary Mallon back to North Brother Island, and this time truly for life. She died there on November 11, 1938 at the age of 69.

Lawyers Who've Won Nobel Prizes for Literature

Who says lawyers can't write? Or can't construct a sentence that isn't weighed down by at least two unintelligible Latin phrases? The lawyers below have been honored for their literary prowess—and not just any old honor. They've won the freaking Nobel Prize.

Of course, some of them never actually practiced law—or even finished law school—but we won't hold that against them. They represent a happy indication that setting foot in a law school need not permanently taint one's ability to put pen to paper (or fingers to keyboard). Try not to think too hard about the fact that none of them went to law school in the United States.

1982 Gabriel Garcia-Marquez

As if winning the 1982 Nobel weren't enough, a 2009 survey of international writers named Marquez's *One Hundred Years of Solitude* as the work that has most shaped world literature over the past 25 years. It and his other works are widely credited with having opened readers' eyes to the style known as magical realism. The Colombian-born author and journalist has also written numerous other books (such as *Love in the Time of Cholera* and *Chronicle of a Death Foretold*), short stories, screenplays, and articles. He began studying law during his college days. However, he broke off his studies in order to work as a journalist, and never went back.

1979 Odysseus Elytis

A Greek poet, Elytis will be remembered (according to one obituary writer, after his death in 1996) as "a poet of the Greek summer and of the Aegean sea." Elytis attended the Athens Law School, but abandoned his studies in order to write. During World War II, he served on the frontlines against Nazi occupation, and later wrote "Heroic and Elegaic Song of the Lost Second Lieutenant of Albania" based on that experience.

1977 Vicente Aleixandre

Aleixandre was a Spanish-born surrealist poet who managed to maintain his creativity in the face of political turmoil and Spanish dictatorship. He studied and also taught law at the University of Madrid, until he developed a serious illness, after which he devoted himself to writing.

1967 Miguel Angel Asturias

Born in Guatemala in 1899, Asturias earned a law degree at the University of San Carlos. In 1923 he left for Europe, where he studied and became a correspondent for several Latin American newspapers. He wrote *Architecture of the New Life* (based on lectures he'd given while on a short stay back in Guatemala); *Legends of Guatemala*; and an anti-dictatorship volume called *Señor Presidente* (*The President.*)

1963 Giorgos Seferis

Born in Smyrna, Asia Minor, in 1900, Seferis moved to Paris with his family in 1918. He studied law at the University of Paris, but became interested in literature as well. After graduating, Seferis returned to Greece and became a foreign service officer. This lifelong career gave him ample material for poems and essays on themes such as alienation, wandering, and death. (Funny how no one writes poetry on torts, wills, and contracts.)

1960 Saint-John Perse (pen name of Alexis Léger)

This French-born poet studied law at Bordeaux and went into the diplomatic service in 1914. His brilliant career included serving in the

Peking embassy and later in the French Foreign Office. He left France for the United States in 1940, whereupon the Vichy regime stripped him of his citizenship and possessions. Much of his work was written after coming to the United States, such as *Exil* (*Exile*); *Poème l'Etrangère* (*Poem to a Foreign Lady*); and his abstract epic, *Chronique* (*Chronicle*).

1932 John Galsworthy

You know, he's the guy who wrote *The Forsyte Saga*, chronicling three generations of an upper-class Victorian family. Born in 1867, Galsworthy studied law at New College, Oxford, following in the steps of his solicitor father. He became a member of the bar at Lincoln's Inn in 1890, and practiced for several years. But at age 28, reportedly for his own amusement, Galsworthy began to write. The amusement soon became the career, and Galsworthy wrote numerous other novels as well as short stories and plays.

USA TODAY Snapshots®

International glory
Number of Nobel Prize winners since 1901:

725 — Men
33 — Women
18 — Organizations

Source: The Nobel Foundation

By David Stuckey and Robert W. Ahrens, USA TODAY
2006

1922 Jacinto Benavente

Born in Madrid in 1866, Benavente studied law until his father died. Realizing that he'd inherited a comfortable income, Benavente wasted no time in leaving school and traveling to France, England, and Russia. After returning to Spain, he wrote and edited for several newspapers and journals and published poems. But he became best known as a playwright, particularly of comedies of manners and one-act farces.

1919 Carl Friedrich Georg Spitteler

Born in 1845 in Baselland, in what's now known as Switzerland,

Spitteler pointedly stated that, "At my father's request I took up the study of law at the University of Zürich in 1863." Presumably, he was allowed to choose his next educational step for himself, and he studied theology. He then tutored and taught school in order to make money, but spent his free time writing an epic work of poetry, *Prometheus und Epimetheus,* which was largely ignored. But he kept at it, and won fame with *Olympischer Frühling (Olympic Spring).*

1911 Count Maurice (Mooris) Polidore Marie Bernhard Maeterlinck

With a name like that, he had to be a somebody! Born in 1862 to a well-to-do family in Ghent, Belgium, Maeterlinck (or can we call him "Mooris"?) was educated at a Jesuit college and read law. However, a short practice as a lawyer in his home town convinced him that he was "unfit for the profession." A stay in Paris was all it took for him to fall in love with literature. He started out writing poems, then turned to lyrical dramas noted for lack of action, fatalism, mysticism, and the constant presence of death. In later life, Maeterlinck wrote philosophical essays. He earned the title of "Count of Belgium" in 1932.

1904 Frédéric Mistral

Mistral, born in 1830 in Provence, is said to have read law; but after taking his degree devoted himself entirely to writing poetry, both epic and lyrical. (Anyone noticing a pattern here?)

1902 Christian Matthias Theodor Mommsen

Born in 1817 in Garding, Sleswick, Mommsen read law and classics at Kiel—and actually went on to become a professor of law at the University of Leipzig. However, his involvement in the revolution of 1848–1849 led to his dismissal in 1850. After holding various academic positions, he was appointed chair of Ancient History at the University of Berlin in 1858, and his many writings are said to have revolutionized the study of Roman history.

1901 Sully Prudhomme (pen name of René François Armand Prudhomme)

Born in 1839 to a French shopkeeper, Prudhomme studied literature, tried his hand at business, then took up law, "though without much conviction," says the Nobel committee. He forged on, however, working in a solicitor's office while writing poetry on the side. And perhaps some of his legal knowledge found its way into his epic poem *La Justice*. You be the judge: Its concluding line reads, "La Justice est l'amour guidé par la lumiére," or "Justice is love guided by enlightenment."

A Lexicon of Ne'er-Do-Wells

B ack around the nineteenth century, the law books were full of prohibitions on not only actual crimes, but on vague things like "vagrancy." Police were allowed to enforce basic morality, arresting people for things like wandering around without a job or (in the case of women) entertaining too many men in their home.

Such laws are mostly gone—but so is the colorful vocabulary that went with them. Does anyone today even remember how a rogue differs from a brigand or what's meant by a mountebank? We set forth to remedy that, below.

Adulterer

A man who has consensual sex with a woman other than his wife. Before the days of no-fault divorce, charging one's spouse with adultery was a common way to get out of the marriage. The wronged husband could also, at one time, sue the adulterer for alienation of his wife's affections.

Of course, it was important to be careful with the evidence because, as an Iowa court pointed out, "The woman who has admittedly been a faithful wife and mother for a quarter of a century, and then deserts her husband for the arms of an adulterer, is so rare an exception to her kind that the brand of infamy should not be placed upon her, even indirectly, unless the charge be supported by something more substantial than the highly wrought suspicions of a mind inflamed by jealousy." (*Belcher v. Ballou*, 124 Iowa 507, 100 N.W. 474 (1904).)

Brawler

One who takes part in a rough, noisy quarrel or fight. For example, Harley Atkinson, a Nebraska farmer, was indicted but later acquitted for shooting another man in the leg when it turned out that man had been part of a "howling mob of brawlers, masquerading under the name of 'Halloweeners,'" which was "parading the streets of his town," and trying to steal a buggy from Atkinson's property. (*Atkinson v. State*, 58 Neb. 356, 78 N.W. 621 (1899).)

Brigand

A bandit, usually allied with a roving band or even with pirates. For example, a New York court, explaining why innkeepers had a common law duty to insure their guests' possessions, pointed out that long ago, "there was little safety outside of castles and fortified towns for the wayfaring traveler, who, exposed on his journey to the depredations of bandits and brigands, had little protection when he sought at night temporary refuge…." (*Crapo v. Rockwell*, 17 N.Y.Ann.Cas. 112, 94 N.Y.S. 1122 (1905).)

Disorderly person

This term is broad enough to cover just about anything—for example, a Michigan appeals court didn't see any problem with convicting as a disorderly person a man who'd been "found loitering about in common barrooms, and wandering about the streets, by day and by night, without any lawful means of support, and without being able to give any satisfactory account of himself, at the city of Grand Rapids, for the period of two weeks." A whole two weeks! Well, he must have been up to no good. (*In re Stegenga*, 133 Mich. 55, 94 N.W. 385 (1903).)

Fornicator

One who engages in an illicit carnal connection or unlawful sexual intercourse, including between a man, whether married or single, and an unmarried woman. May also include someone who lives with an unmarried member of the opposite sex. At one time fornication was its own criminal offense, but these statutes have mostly been taken off the books or narrowed significantly.

Idler

A lazy person who wastes time and doesn't work. For example, in 1907, Mr. Enoch Lewis had a narrow escape after being convicted under a Georgia statute that criminalized "Persons wandering or strolling about in idleness, who are able to work, and have no property to support them." Luckily, he had witnesses to testify that he was a farm laborer who went from job to job, and that "instead of being an idler, he really was 'The man with the hoe.'" The appeals court reversed his conviction. (*Lewis v. State*, 3 Ga.App. 322, 59 S.E. 933 (1907).)

Mountebank

A medical quack or charlatan, who mounts a platform in a public place and attracts buyers of (useless) elixirs or remedies, through tricks or stories. In a pinch, laws against mountebanks could also be used against other ne'er-do-wells: For example, a New York court put its stamp of approval on the conviction of some circus performers whose act included pretending to pull someone's tooth. The court reasoned that the statute, which prohibited jugglers, mountebanks, and others, was "intended to prevent idle persons from inducing people to spend their time and money in practices of folly and dissipation," further opining that "a circus performance has as pernicious consequences following it, as has a wire or rope dance, or the slight [sic] of hand tricks of a juggler or the deceptions of a mountebank." (*Downing & Potter, overseers of the poor of Ithaca v. Lanchard*, 12 Wend. 383 (1834).)

Night-Walker

A thief, prostitute, or other person who goes about at night. Nora Stokes, in Alabama in 1891, discovered that it didn't matter whether she was soliciting men for money: The court upheld her conviction as a common night-walker, who "did walk and ramble in the streets and common highways at unreasonable hours of the night, without having any lawful business, and without any necessity therefor, for the unlawful purpose of picking up men for lewd intercourse." (*Stokes v. State*, 92 Ala. 73, 9 So. 400 (1891).)

Pilferer

One who steals small sums or petty objects. For example, Henrietta Curtis, in 1829, was arrested as a common pilferer for having stolen "two large silver spoons of the value of six dollars, and two silver tea spoons of the value of three dollars, of the goods and chattels of one William Fenno, in the dwellinghouse of Fenno." (*Commonwealth v. Henrietta Curtis*, 11 Pick. 134, Mass. 1831.)

Railer

One who breaches the peace with loud or argumentative behavior. Mr. Timothy Foley was convicted for being a common railer and brawler in Massachusetts in 1868, after it was found that he had "used loud and violent language, generally to some person or persons in or near his dwelling-house, and frequently to his wife when in the house; that the language consisted of opprobrious epithets and exclamations; that on several of these occasions, sometimes on Sunday, in the afternoon, and at other times in the night time of other days of the week, people passing and living in the neighborhood of the defendant's house (from twenty-five to fifty persons, and once as many as a hundred and fifty) gathered near it, having been attracted thither by his said loud and violent language...." (*Commonwealth v. Foley*, 99 Mass. 497 (1868).)

Rogue

A rascal, scoundrel, cheat, wandering beggar, or tramp. People once flung this term at each other with regularity, leading to many slander suits—like one in which the defendant proclaimed, "You are a thief and a rogue, you cheated me out of more than one hundred pounds of oats." (*Egan v. Semrad*, 113 Wis. 84, 88 N.W. 906 (1902).)

Swindler

One who gets property or money out of another on false pretenses; a cheat or fraud. A California court, noting that "such persons are a menace to the safety of the public," decided that it was fine to keep a man in prison on vagrancy charges based merely on his own confession to being a swindler and upon his having been caught "willfully and unlawfully loitering about and around a broker's office." (*Ex parte Hayden*, 12 Cal. App. 145, 106 P. 893, Cal.App. 2 Dist. (1909).)

Tramp

A hobo or vagrant who travels around, mostly on foot, begging or doing odd jobs for a living. An Iowa court even gives us a picture of what a tramp looks like, describing "a man who spent very little money on himself for the comforts of life, and ordinarily would be considered as a tramp. In the winter he would wear an old felt hat, with a red handkerchief wrapped over it. He wore no overshoes, and rather a shabby overcoat, if he had any at all. People would be more apt to give him money than to try to take any away from him." (*In re Barrett's Estate*, 167 Iowa 218, 149 N.W. 247 (1914).)

Vagabond

One who lives an unsettled, drifting, shiftless, irregular, or irresponsible life, wandering from place to place with no fixed abode. Or maybe even having an abode: Regularly lodging someplace wasn't enough to protect one Mr. Carter from being convicted as a vagrant in Georgia in 1906, where the court found that he was a "habitual loafer, idler, and vagabond," and "his loafing and loitering was about poolrooms, barrooms, dives, lewd houses, and other places of like character." (*Carter v. State*, 126 Ga. 570, 55 S.E. 477 (1906).)

Vagrant

One without a regular job, an idle rover who wanders from place to place, perhaps supporting him- or herself by begging—or, in the case of an old Washington statute, by telling fortunes. That's how a certain Mr. Neitzel got himself into trouble in 1921, after telling the sheriff he could tell his fortune for a dollar. The court had no sympathy for the fact that Neitzel was a regularly ordained minister in the National Astrological Society. (*State v. Neitzel*, 69 Wash. 567, 125 P. 939 (1912).)

Behind-the-Scenes Players in the U.S. Law Biz

P eople complain that there are too many lawyers out there—but the numbers start to look really scary when you add in the many other players who bring us The American Legal System. It's sort of like with theatre. We see only the actors, while a whole cadre of directors, stagehands, costume designers, and light operators madly runs around backstage.

Let's take a look at some of these oft-forgotten folks in the legal world.

Stenographers

This is the person who sits quietly at the front of the courtroom pounding away on a funny little machine, occasionally interrupting to replace a disk or take care of a mechanical glitch. But for the most part, the stenographer sits, listens, and types—very fast. Generally, stenographers type at the rate of 225 words per minute. Instead of a regular alphabet keyboard, they use a machine where combinations of letters represent words, sounds, and phrases.

Bailiff

Sort of the bouncer for the halls of justice, these folks provide security and order in the courtroom. Many are already trained in law enforcement.

Law clerk

Don't be fooled by the title—this is anything but a lowly clerk job. Law clerks are lawyers, usually right out of law school, hired by judges to help them in doing everything from researching and drafting opinions to assisting in settlement conferences. What does that leave for the judge to do, you ask? Well, there's still sitting at the front of the room looking judicious.

Legal secretaries

This is a secretary who works for a lawyer, with expertise in following the gnarly requirements of court documents, contracts, and so forth. They're also skilled at deflecting lawyers' requests to pick up laundry, buy a birthday gift for their spouse or child, and so forth.

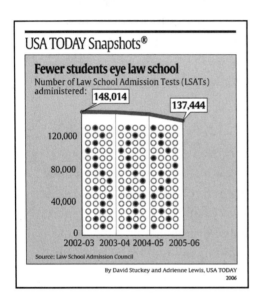

USA TODAY Snapshots®

Fewer students eye law school
Number of Law School Admission Tests (LSATs) administered: 148,014 ... 137,444

120,000
80,000
40,000
0

2002-03 2003-04 2004-05 2005-06

Source: Law School Admission Council

By David Stuckey and Adrienne Lewis, USA TODAY 2006

Paralegals

Why would lawyers do all the work alone, when they can pass some of it off to paralegals—also called legal assistants? While not authorized to give legal advice like lawyers, paralegals can do a lot of behind-the-scenes work, including legal research or routine paperwork.

Private investigators

Some law firms hire their own investigators, for example to do independent fact checking in a divorce or criminal case. We predict a trend of hiring more garbologists, too.

Law firm caterers

At some of the swankier law firms, lawyers receive a free lunch every day. And the law partners are not the ones doing the cooking.

Bar association staff

In every state, an entire organization is devoted to keeping lawyers in line, making sure they pass their bar exams, keep up with continuing education requirements, get disbarred when they bilk the clients out of too much money, and so on.

Legal publishers

Someone's got to publish the books of cases and analyses that lawyers refer to every day. And someone else has to publish books that actually make heads or tails of it all—hey, that's us!

Jury consultants

Wondering how O.J. got off or how IBM succeeded in its mammoth antitrust lawsuit? Behind many successful cases is a jury consultant, an expert who applies scientific principles of human behavior (and market research testing methods) to create a winning litigation strategy.

Malpractice insurers

Unhappy clients sue over 30,000 lawyers a year. What's a lawyer to do? Pay between $5,000 to $8,000 per year to an insurance company that specializes in defending attorneys, that's what.

Career planners for lawyers trying desperately to find another line of work

It's a fast-growing field! For example, corporate-lawyer-turned-Lego-sculptor Nathan Sawaya was quoted as saying, "The worst day being an artist is still better than the best day being a lawyer."

Lawyers Who've Won Darwin Awards

As lawyers ourselves, we can be a little sensitive to lawyer jokes. But even we can't resist the pairing of lawyers and the Darwin awards, which recognize the creative ways in which a few special members of our species manage to inadvertently end their own lives.

Is anyone else surprised there aren't a few more award winners? Or is it just that lawyers have been schooled to be so darned cautious about everything?

What strong glass you have!

At a reception for law students, a Toronto lawyer tried to show off the strength of the windows in his firm's twenty-fourth-floor office by throwing himself against the glass. The demonstration worked the first time, but on his second attempt, he broke through the glass and fell to his death. According to a partner at the firm, he was one of their "best and the brightest."

Palms, a pool, and power lines

A lawyer in Los Angeles was cleaning his pool with an aluminum pool skimmer when he noticed that a palm frond had gotten stuck in the power line above him. He attempted to dislodge the frond with the skimmer and was electrocuted when the metal pole came in contact with the live power line. His family, showing they'd learned a thing or two about the law, sued both the power company and pool supply company for not providing sufficient warnings.

See, he held the gun like this . . .

The night before he was to present his case in a murder trial, a famous lawyer, well known for his political leadership and opposition to the Civil War, met with colleagues in his hotel room. To prove his argument, he planned to demonstrate to the court how the victim had actually shot himself. However, in practicing this demonstration, he confused a loaded gun for an unloaded one and shot himself in the gut, causing his early demise.

Does this grenade work?

During a trial in Pakistan for possessing a hand grenade, the defendant first challenged police to produce the grenade, then, when they did, claimed it wasn't real. The judge, listening absentmindedly, picked up the grenade and pulled the pin. Though injured, the judge survived, thus reducing his 2002 Darwin Award to an honorable mention. In the future, we hope he plays with paperclips.

Longest Jury Deliberations

On people's lists of fun things to do, jury duty usually ranks somewhere between dental visits and tax audits. Yes, it's an important civic right and duty, we just hope no one died protecting our right to sit in uncomfortable chairs for menial daily pay, often yawning with intense boredom.

Still, there's a bright side. A stint of jury duty is normally over within four to five days. After that, you're free (unlike the defendant, perhaps) to go home and complain about it.

You'll notice we said that four or five days is "normal." We should also mention that not all cases go quite so normally.

Longest U.S. jury deliberation in a civil lawsuit

You know you're in for a long jury deliberation when the jurors request a refrigerator. That's what happened in *Association of Apartment Owners of Royal Palm Resort v. Mitsui Construction, Co., Ltd.*, a civil suit on the island of Guam. The actual trial was over, and we'll never know what went on behind those closed doors, but apparently the jurors wanted some serious time to think. They took all of 14 months to reach a verdict.

Granted, the case was complex, involving the collapse of two hotel towers during an earthquake. Nobody was killed, and the injuries were moderate, but the developer—Japanese conglomerate Kawasho—had lost a fortune on a hotel that had only been open for three weeks. The case was bigger, longer, and more expensive than any before on the island. To accommodate the spectacle, the parties chipped in $750,000, leased a warehouse near the airport, and built a state-of-the-art courtroom that included a computer monitor for each of the 20 jurors along with streaming digitized testimony. Kawasho's presentation included 700 graphics, 24 computer animations, and two videos to explain structural damage issues.

Did the jury really need 14 months to reach a verdict (an award of $146.8 million to Kawasho)? Some cynics claimed that the lengthy deliberations had something to do with the fact that Guam's 15% unemployment rate made the $35 a day payment—plus free lunch—an appealing day job.

Longest mainland U.S. jury deliberation in a civil lawsuit

Okay, not counting U.S. territories that are six times zones away, the longest U.S. jury deliberation in a civil case took place in a 1992 California trial in which a woman and her son sued the City of Long Beach for preventing the opening of a chain of residential homes for Alzheimer's patients. The case had a long tail, taking eleven years to get to trial. The jury sat through six months of testimony and then holed up for four and a half months before reaching a verdict (of $22.5 million to mother and son).

Though there's no record of them requesting a refrigerator, the case had a few other quirks. One juror was eliminated after suggesting that the court's name be changed from the U.S. District Court to the "U.S. Dairy Court" because, as he told fellow jurors, "you guys are milking this thing to death."

Reportedly, jurors treated deliberations much as they might treat a day job a la *Dilbert*, often starting late and ending early. One juror made a fake sick call in order to attend the track with some other jurors. Reports emerged of jurors ordering extra-large lunches at tonier restaurants so they could take home doggy bags for dinner.

Add to that the reports of drinking on the job and weekends, and it almost sounds like fun. Nonetheless, one juror told the local paper that being on the jury was "just like being incarcerated."

Longest U.S. jury deliberation in a criminal trial

Good thing they weren't filming this for an episode of "Law & Order." Three former Oakland, California, police officers known as "the Riders" were charged with roughing up suspects, planting drugs, and—what else—a cover-up. The trial took seven months and included 84 witnesses. Jurors had to read a mountainous 122 pages of instructions on 35 counts. They took four months to reach a verdict on eight counts (not guilty) but couldn't reach a verdict on the other 27 counts. The result: partial mistrial.

How long does it take to deliberate over a celebrity defendant?

Four hours for O.J. Simpson, 30 hours for Phil Spector (his second trial), seven and a half days for Scott Peterson, nine days for Charles Manson, nine days for Robert Blake, and twenty days for the Menendez brothers (their second trial).

What's the longest movie jury deliberation?

The jury in Sidney Lumet's groundbreaking directorial debut, *Twelve Angry Men*, deliberates for approximately 90 minutes, probably the longest screen time spent in a jury room in any film (with the exception of the two remakes of the film, described below). One marvel of *Twelve Angry Men* is that the film occurs in real time—that is, the length of the film is the actual length of the deliberations.

Twelve Angry Men was the first of three classic courtroom dramas by Lumet (the others were *The Verdict* and *Serpico*). He loved the genre, saying, "As soon as you get into a courtroom, you're ahead of the game because automatically you've got the conflict."

Ironically, the conflict in *Twelve Angry Men* all takes place outside the courtroom and inside a claustrophobic jury room—made even more so by an effect used by Lumet. As the film progressed, he decreased the camera's focal length, starting with a wide-angle lens and ending with a telephoto. The effect brings the actors' faces closer.

Even though 90 minutes isn't a long deliberation for a capital punishment case, it's too long for eleven of the jurors in this movie, one of whom has tickets for a baseball game. They know the defendant is guilty and just want to get out. But it's Juror #8, played by Fonda (we never learn the jurors' names) who takes it upon himself to single-handedly drag the other jurors into his world of reasonable doubt.

The dramatic irony, as Bergman and Asimow point out in their book, *Reel Justice*, is that the defendant in the movie probably was guilty (in fact, none of the jurors ever say he is innocent). Yet, they're willing to let him walk because the lawyers failed to do their jobs. Despite its dramatic liberties—Juror #8 should not, legally, have purchased the knife or run the experiment about how long it took the old man to get to the door—Bergman and Asimow believe the movie to be "the best film about jury deliberations ever made."

Twelve Angry Men was a commercial failure and a critical success. Today it's considered as one of the greatest films of the 1950s. It was remade in 1997 with Jack Lemon as Juror #8 and George C. Scott as Juror #1 (originally played by Lee J. Cobb). The story was also cleverly recast as *12*, a post-Communist Russian film by director Nikita Mikhalkov in 2007.

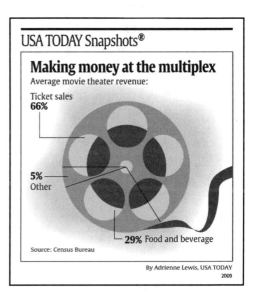

USA TODAY Snapshots®

Making money at the multiplex
Average movie theater revenue:

Ticket sales
66%

5%
Other

29% Food and beverage

Source: Census Bureau

By Adrienne Lewis, USA TODAY
2009

Can anyone pinpoint why some juries take so long to deliberate?

Three professors had a go at this in their study, "Time to Deliberate: Factors Influencing the Duration of Jury Deliberation." Professors Brunell, Dave, and Morgan reached several conclusions about the length of jury trials—for example, that criminal guilty verdicts generally take less time than nonguilty verdicts, but that in civil trials, juries that rule against the defendant take longer than those that find for the defendant. The professors examined seven hypotheses. Can you guess which are true?

1. A six-person jury will reach a decision more quickly than a twelve-person jury.

2. The more complex the case, the longer the jury will deliberate.

3. The more severe the charge against the defendant, the longer the jury will deliberate.

4. Nonunanimous decisions will take longer than unanimous ones.

5. Juries with members who have prior jury experience will tend to reach decisions more quickly than those comprising fewer experienced jurors.

6. Gender composition of the jury does not have a significant impact on the length of jury deliberations.

7. The more potential jurors who are excused before the trial starts, the longer the jury will take to reach a verdict.

Answers:

1. False 2. True 3. True 4. True 5. True in criminal trials; false in civil trials.
6. True 7. True

Finding M&Ms in Court, in Contracts, and in Compromising Legal Situations

es, they're delicious. True, they melt in your mouth, not in your hands. And then, there's that whole theory about the green ones. But did you also know that M&Ms have had more than a few days in court? Here are a handful of lawsuits and other legal matters involving M&Ms.

M&Ms in uniform

Did you know that M&Ms served in World War II? The Army included them in its soldiers' rations, apparently because of that whole "melts in your mouth, not in your hands" thing. The candy could withstand extreme temperatures, including the tropical conditions in which some of the fighting took place. This might explain the defense raised recently by an Army vet arrested for shoplifting in Florida: He told the officers that because he had served in Iraq, "he could steal all the M&Ms he wanted."

And out of uniform: *The naked cowboy lawsuit*

The "Naked" Cowboy (in quotes because he actually wears white cowboy boots, a white cowboy hat, and underpants while playing the guitar in Times Square) filed a $6 million lawsuit against the maker of M&Ms for trademark infringement. Apparently, the company created an ad campaign that featured the relatively new blue M&M wearing—you guessed it—white boots, hat, and underpants, while playing the guitar. A later ad featured the yellow M&M in the same getup.

In his lawsuit, the cowboy alleged that the company had used his likeness and persona without permission and gave the false impression that he endorsed the candy. (He also sued the agency that developed the ad; it was part of a larger New York campaign that also featured such Big Apple icons as the Statue of Liberty and King Kong.) After the Naked Cowboy fended off the company's efforts to dismiss his case, the parties settled for an undisclosed amount.

That sunflower seed looks a lot like an M&M

Kimmie Candy, a company based in Rocklin, California, had a rude entry into the candy manufacturing business: a trademark infringement lawsuit filed by M&M manufacturer, Mars. The Kimmie company's first product, Sunbursts—sunflower seeds coated in chocolate and dipped in a brightly colored hard candy shell—debuted at a trade show, where Mars executives grabbed up samples.

A month later, Mars sued for trademark infringement, claiming that Kimmie's character (a piece of candy with white gloves and arched eyebrows) looked too much like the M&M character. The case settled, and Kimmie toughed it out. The company now offers, in addition to Sunbursts, Corn Bits (salty corn nuts dipped in chocolate and a hard candy shell) and ChocoRocks (cocoa bits dipped in a hard candy shell and designed to look like stones).

M&Ms where they shouldn't be

In 1994, a jury awarded more than $7 million to Rena Weeks, a former legal secretary who claimed that she—and plenty of other women before her—had been sexually harassed by Martin Greenstein, a partner at the law firm of Baker & McKenzie. (The award was later cut in half.) The case got a lot of media attention, including on "Court TV." So where do the M&Ms come in? Apparently, one of Greenstein's sophomoric ploys was to drop the candies into Weeks's blouse pocket, en route to groping her breasts.

What's wrong with the brown ones?

Rock band Van Halen had a famous contract rider involving brown M&Ms. Their 1982 tour rider, a long list of requirements and requests, stipulated the food and supplies the band wanted backstage, including M&Ms—with the caveat "WARNING: ABSOLUTELY NO BROWN ONES." What's all this about? Apparently, the band wasn't hating on brown M&Ms; it was just a clever way of ensuring the band's safety and the quality of their performance. The rider also included a number of crucial specs regarding lighting, stage setup, security, and so on. The band figured that if they got backstage and saw brown M&Ms in the bowl, the powers that be probably hadn't read the contract carefully— and therefore the more important requirements of the band's elaborate show might not have been met.

USA TODAY Snapshots®

Biting into chocolate

Annual pounds per capita consumed in selected countries:

Switzerland 22.7
United Kingdom 18.5
Belgium 15
USA 12.1
Japan 4

Source: Business Monitor International

By Marcy E. Mullins, USA TODAY
2007

M&Ms phone home: *The peanut butter battle*

Reese's Pieces—peanut butter covered in a hard candy coating—are apparently highly prized by visitors from other planets. At least, that's the message of the movie *E. T.: The Extra-Terrestrial*. Remember how Elliot lured E.T. back to his house using Reese's Pieces as bait—those long bony fingers reaching out to grab the candy? The product placement boosted sales of Reese's Pieces by 65%.

Apparently, the Mars Company turned down the opportunity to have M&Ms featured in the movie instead—which makes what happened next interesting. Perhaps seeing the profits in peanut butter candy, Mars introduced Peanut Butter M&Ms, and was promptly sued by Hershey's, the maker of Reese's Pieces, over its packaging (called "trade dress" by the legal eagles). Hershey's argued that the shade of orange used on the packaging was the same as that used for Reese's Pieces. The judge nevertheless found in favor of Mars.

Relations between the two companies haven't always been rancorous. In fact, one of the Ms in M&Ms stands for Bruce Murrie, who joined forces with Forrest Mars to manufacture the first M&Ms. Murrie was the son of the president of Hershey's.

The infringement case that hasn't happened: *Eminem*

Rapper Marshall Mathers, known widely as "Eminem," used to go by the stage name M&M. As far as we can tell, Mars hasn't sued Eminem over using the same name—but that hasn't stopped others from noticing the overlap. In 2008, for example, artist Enrique Ramos created a portrait of Eminem out of M&Ms.

The Judge Who Hated Red Nail Polish

Supreme Court Justice James Clark McReynolds, who served from 1914 to 1941, hated a lot of things: tobacco (he was the first to install "No Smoking" signs at the Supreme Court), athletics (the only "sport" he participated in was duck hunting), women lawyers (whom he referred to "the female"), Franklin Delano Roosevelt (he, reportedly told his law clerk, "I'll never resign from the Court as long as that crippled son of a bitch is in the White House"), wristwatches worn by men (he considered it effeminate), and Jews (he refused to sit near, speak to, or be photographed with Justices Brandeis or Cardozo). But perhaps his most bizarre fixation was with red nail polish. He despised it—or more precisely, he despised women who wore it.

What could explain this nail lacquer aversion? Most men—at least according to a recent study—are attracted to women who wear red. But McReynolds—a confirmed misogynist—was not like most men. The color red is also associated with passion, embarrassment, or blood and, of course, with "scarlet women" a la Nathaniel Hawthorne's Hester Prynne. Perhaps something buried in Justice McReynolds' Kentucky childhood explains this cosmetic prejudice?

Perhaps ... but since no one has yet been able to pinpoint a "Rosebud" moment from his past, we might have to accept the fact that McReynolds' dislike for crimson fingertips was simply one more crazy prejudice from a man considered to be the most unpleasant individual ever to sit on the Supreme Court. (Chief Justice William Howard Taft labeled him a "continual grouch," "selfish to the last degree," and "fuller of prejudice than any man I have ever known.")

You might ask how such a dislikable, unpleasant, selfish person landed on the Supreme Court in the first place. The answer: Sometimes there's no other place to put somebody you can't stand.

It all started in 1912, when McReynolds—who had served as assistant attorney general under Teddy Roosevelt—campaigned vigorously for Woodrow Wilson. Once elected, Wilson made the mistake of appointing McReynolds as U.S. attorney general.

As AG, McReynolds was something of a trust buster, dissolving a major railroad merger and forcing AT&T to give up its monopoly over wire communications. But he also was an irritant to Wilson. McReynolds was accused of authorizing Justice Department spying on judges, mismanaging expenses on a new Justice Department building, and delaying prosecution of a politician's son-in-law. McReynolds' abrasive response to these charges embarrassed Wilson, so when a Supreme Court Justice died, Wilson saw his chance to ditch his AG. Bidding adieu to political life in 1914, McReynolds was "kicked upstairs" to the Big Bench.

No one could have been happy to see him arrive. For his law clerks, McReynolds would not accept "Jews, drinkers, blacks, women, smokers, or married or engaged individuals." McReynolds even fired one law clerk who asked for a few days off to take the bar. He was especially abusive to his staff and used one Court employee—an African-American named Harry Parker—as a retriever in the icy waters of the Potomac during the Justice's frequent duck-hunting expeditions. When

USA TODAY Snapshots®

Women and the law
Types of practice for female lawyers:

Type of practice	Percentage
Private practice	56%
Judicial clerkships	13%
Government	12%
Business	10%
Public interest	6%
Academia	2%

Source: American Bar Association

By David Stuckey and Marcy E. Mullins, USA TODAY
2006

a McReynolds' law clerk befriended Parker, McReynolds chastised the clerk for fraternizing with "darkies."

Apparently, being a selfish misogynist anti-Semite didn't get in the way of McReynolds writing two important decisions protecting personal liberties: *Meyer v. Nebraska* (1923), which guaranteed that states could not unreasonably regulate individual liberties, namely the teaching of German in schools; and *Pierce v. Society of Sisters* (1925), in which McReynolds struck down a law that required parents to send their children only to public schools. McReynolds' decisions apparently paved the way for some standards that McReynolds would likely find repulsive, including the Supreme Court's decision in *Roe v. Wade* (1973).

Court historians remember McReynolds best for his vehement opposition to Frank Delano Roosevelt's New Deal policies. Along with three colleagues dubbed "The Four Horseman," McReynolds voted down every New Deal proposal that was tested at the Court. Roosevelt's frustration was so great that he tried packing the Supreme Court with sympathetic justices. Although that move backfired, public support for FDR—along with the deaths of a few of the Four Horseman—eventually led to the Court's approval of New Deal policies and McReynolds' further embitterment. He became so disgusted by the reelection of FDR that he broke his promise to remain on the court until the man was gone (see above) and in 1941 announced, "any country that elects Roosevelt three times deserves no protection."

When McReynolds died five years later, not one Supreme Court Justice attended his funeral. Not too surprising, considering he had alienated everybody at the Court. He insulted Harlan Fisk Stone for presenting dull opinions, so enraged John Hessin Clarke that Clarke resigned from the Court in 1922, never spoke a word to Louis Brandeis or Benjamin Cardozo, and refused to attend Felix Frankfurter's swearing in, claiming, "My God, another Jew on the Court." McReynolds infuriated Chief Justice William Howard Taft by taking off on announced vacations once whenever duck season opened, often causing important decisions to be delayed. (In an example of poetic justice, six Supreme Court Justices attended the funeral of Harry Parker, the Court employee who'd been forced to go splashing in the Potomac after dead ducks.)

McReynolds never married (perhaps out of concern he'd have to look at the dreaded red nail polish) and—despite his curmudgeonly nature—left most of his estate to charity.

World's Longest Prison Sentences

How long should a person convicted of murder or another heinous crime be sentenced to prison? Since everyone has only one life, you might think that a single life term would be enough. But far longer sentences have been handed out. What's the point? Retribution, symbolism, and the desire to make sure the convicted person will be long dead before he or she could possibly come up for parole.

It's impossible to say for certain what is the longest prison sentence ever, but the following are surely among them.

43,000 YEARS: Two Moroccans and one Spaniard were each sentenced to 43,000 years in prison for their participation in the bombing of four commuter trains at a Madrid train station in 2004. The bomb blasts killed 191 people and injured more than 1,800. However, these sentences were purely symbolic, because under Spanish law no one can serve more than 40 years in jail.

10,750 YEARS: Darron Anderson, of Oklahoma, was found guilty in 1994 of a variety of crimes including rape, kidnapping, larceny, robbery, and kidnapping. He was initially sentenced to 2,200 years. He appealed, and won a new trial. Unfortunately for him, things didn't go so well the second time around. He was convicted again and resentenced to a total of 10,750 years: 4,000 years each for rape and sodomy, 1,750 years for kidnapping, and 1,000 years for burglary and robbery. It could have been worse. The jury also gave him 500 years for grand larceny, but the state Court of Criminal Appeals held that this charge was double jeopardy on the robbery conviction and dismissed it. Anderson will be eligible for parole in the year 12,744.

10,000 YEARS: Dudley Wayne Kyzer, an Alabama college student, murdered his wife, mother-in-law, and another student. He was sentenced to two life sentences for two counts of first degree murder.

But this wasn't enough for the jury. It also sentenced him to 10,000 years in prison for one count of second-degree murder for the killing of his wife. All the sentences were upheld on appeal due to a legal technicality—Kyzer waited too long to file his appeal.

7,109 YEARS: In another grand symbolic gesture, a Spanish court sentenced letter carrier Gabriel March Grandos to 7,109 years in prison for fraud after he was convicted of failing to deliver 42,768 letters. Under Spanish law, Grandos will have to be released after a mere 40 years. But at least he'll have the satisfaction of having officially been given one of the longest prison terms ever.

1,200 YEARS: Richard Speck, one of the most notorious mass murders in U.S. history, was sentenced to 1,200 years in prison. In a case that shocked the nation, Speck systematically tortured, raped, and murdered eight student nurses at a student dormitory in Chicago, Illinois. Curiously, Speck's fellow prisoners gave him the nickname "birdman," after the film *Birdman of Alcatraz*, because he kept a pair of sparrows that had flown into his cell.

845 YEARS: The longest sentence ever meted out in the United States for a white-collar crime was the 845-year prison term given to Sholam Weiss in 2000. Weiss was convicted of 78 counts of fraud and money laundering for looting $125 million from the National Heritage Life Insurance Company. He has a projected release date of November 23, 2754. Weiss's sentence makes the 150-year prison term given to Bernie Madoff, convicted of stealing $65 billion in the largest investment scam ever, look miniscule by comparison.

Sure, it's easy to sentence someone to 10,000 years in prison, but what's the longest anyone has actually spent in the big house? Again, it's difficult to know for certain. The famed Birdman of Alcatraz, Robert Stroud, was given life without parole for murdering a prison guard while in prison for manslaughter. He stayed in prison until his death at age 73, having served 54 years. But things could have been worse. Unlike most convicted murderers, the Birdman had a movie made about his life, with Burt Lancaster in the title role.

A far grimmer case is that of Illinois man named Richard Honeck who was convicted of murdering his former schoolteacher and sentenced to life in prison in 1899. He was 20 years old at the time. He was finally paroled in 1963 after serving 64 years in prison. During his entire time in jail he received one letter and two visitors. No movie was ever made about him.

However, it's likely that the longest time ever spent in prison by an American is the 68 years and 245 days served in various New York state prisons by Paul Geidel. In 1911, when he was 17, Geidel was sentenced to 20 years to life for killing a wealthy broker during a robbery

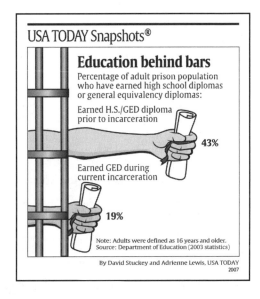

USA TODAY Snapshots®

Education behind bars

Percentage of adult prison population who have earned high school diplomas or general equivalency diplomas:

Earned H.S./GED diploma prior to incarceration

43%

Earned GED during current incarceration

19%

Note: Adults were defined as 16 years and older.
Source: Department of Education (2003 statistics)

By David Stuckey and Adrienne Lewis, USA TODAY 2007

at a hotel where he worked as a bellboy. Sixty-three years later, he was granted parole. However, the now-80-year old did not want to leave jail. This was not as crazy as it sounds. Geidel had spent his entire adult life in prison and had no family in the outside world. He didn't think he would survive on the outside—after all, there aren't many jobs for 80-year-old bellboys. Geidel spent six more years in prison, but was finally released in 1980. He is believed to have lived out the rest of his days peacefully in a New York nursing home.

As we all know, records are made to be broken, and it's likely that Geidel's 68-plus-year record will be exceeded one day. Today, there are at least 9,700 prisoners in the United States serving life sentences for crimes committed before they were eighteen years old. Several children as young as thirteen have been convicted of murder and sentenced to life in prison without the possibility of parole. Given today's longer life expectancies, one of these could end up serving 80 years or more in prison. Of course, this is one record no one wants to hold.

Literary Lawyers Quiz

H ere's a test that will probe your knowledge of law school grads who have achieved literary fame. It's not as hard as a bar exam, but you may have a tricky time identifying some of these legal wordsmiths. (And no, none of the answers are John Grisham, Scott Turow, or Lisa Scottoline.)

1 This Scottish novelist and poet earned his law degree from Edinburgh University. To appease his father, he studied engineering and law, but what he really wanted to do was write and travel. He's written some classics, one of which is named after the unlawful act of capturing and carrying away a person against his or her will.

2 This author received his law degree in 1906 and later worked investigating insurance claims. He published a few short stories during his lifetime and his executor was directed to destroy the remainder of his writings after his death. (His executor disobeyed the instructions and published the works posthumously.) One of this author's greatest works is a courtroom novel featuring subservient clients and existential justice.

3 This German author detested his time in law school. (He especially hated memorizing the law.) He later served as a civil servant and occupied a variety of court positions. But it was as a writer that he blossomed—some consider him to be the finest German writer in history. He invigorated the Teutonic legend of Faust and made *Sturm und Drang* part of the literary lexicon.

4 He was a lawyer, governor, and general in the Union Army (he even negotiated to pardon Billy the Kid—an effort that failed). Some critics believe that his greatest novel (filmed four times) is actually a thinly disguised tale of his own Civil War adventures (even though the novel took place in ancient Rome).

5 This writer received his law degree from the University of Chicago in 1934 but never practiced and instead pursued a series of odd jobs—concierge, actor, and radio announcer. He became famous for his efforts to preserve American oral history, and many of his books are based on conversations with everyday working people. He won the Pulitzer Prize in 1985.

6 He published his first novel at age 58. One of his books was adapted into a movie starring Jack Nicholson (and features a nude Kathy Bates in a hot tub!). Another, *Wartime Lies*, was the subject of an uncompleted film by director Stanley Kubrick. A Holocaust survivor and hard-working attorney—he was a partner and of counsel to Debevoise & Plimpton until 2007—he won the PEN/Hemingway award as well as the French literary award, Prix Medicis.

7 This author helped to draft Scotland's model criminal law, is an expert on medical ethics, and is a professor of medical law at the University of Edinburgh. In addition to numerous children's books and several mystery series, he wrote the libretto for an opera of *Macbeth* set among a group of baboons. His most well-known series deals with a detective agency located in the city of Gaborone.

8 The books by this American wordsmith are all in puzzle format—he's the editor for *The New York Times* crossword puzzle page and has authored or edited over 100 word puzzle books. He received his law degree from the University of Virginia School of Law, but never took that great legal puzzle known as the bar exam.

9 He trained as a barrister but ditched that profession after befriending novelist Joseph Conrad. He had an affair with the wife of one his cousins and then married her—exactly the sort of family drama that he depicted in his three family saga trilogies—one of which was made into an award-winning BBC series. He was awarded the Nobel Prize for literature in 1932.

10 Due to his failure as a rainmaker—he averaged five clients a year—this British barrister had to supplement his income by writing satirical stories, reviews, and humorous illustrations. His popular poetry led to a series of well-received plays in nineteenth century London. But his real legacy began with a theatrical collaboration entitled *Trial By Jury*. He and his collaborator created the most successful operettas in history … until their battling and mistrust ended the partnership in 1896.

11 A tireless advocate for children's rights—his clients are all under 18—this eye patch-adorned New York attorney has also directed children's services in Biafra, written a book on juvenile law, and when not advocating for youth, he's supporting efforts to protect dangerous dog breeds. His 22 gritty, hard-boiled novels focus on the underbelly of society, particularly child abuse (the hero of many of his books is a career criminal who was abused as a child). He was also commissioned to write a Batman graphic novel.

12 This French blueblood studied law before entering a career as a civil servant. At the age of 67, after being removed from his final government post, he embarked on a career as a children's writer and published *The Tales of Mother Goose*. His children's writing—he specialized in conversions of folk legends into readable stories—included *Puss in Boots*, *Sleeping Beauty*, and *Little Red Riding Hood*. Many of his works were later retold by the Brothers Grimm.

13 This former lawyer has made a career out of popularizing the American legal practice—no wonder he still uses yellow legal pads to write first drafts of his television screenplays. He was one of the guiding writers for "L.A. Law," and the creator and writer of "The Practice", "Ally McBeal", and "Boston Legal."

14 This author attended school with future-attorney and author, James Russell Lowe, and was a student of Ralph Waldo Emerson. The year he passed the bar (1840), he also published a tale based on his two years spent as a merchant seaman—later made into a film starring Alan Ladd and Brian Donlevy. He served as U.S. attorney, argued before the Supreme Court, and lost his bid to become ambassador to Britain over a plagiarism dispute related to a legal treatise he had edited.

15. He earned his law degree from Lycée Louis-le-Grand in 1642 but abandoned his legal interests (and social standing) for a career in the theater, first as an actor, and later as one of the most famous playwrights in history—he's considered the father of French comedy. Although the law forbade burial of actors in the "sacred ground" of a cemetery, his wife was able to obtain a legal exception from the King.

Bonus Question: Can you name at least one movie director who studied law?

Answers

1. Robert Louis Stevenson: Scottish novelist and poet, 1850–1894. Author of *Kidnapped, The Strange Case of Dr. Jekyll and Mr. Hyde*, and *Treasure Island*.

2. Franz Kafka: Czechoslovakian short story writer and novelist, 1883–1924. Author of *The Trial, The Castle*, and *The Metamorphosis*.

3. Johann Wolfgang von Goethe: German poet, novelist, and playwright, 1749–1832. Author of *Faust, The Sorrows of Young Werther*, and *Wilhelm Meister's Apprenticeship*.

4. Lew Wallace: American author and novelist, 1827–1905. Author of *Ben-Hur: A Tale of the Christ* and *The Boyhood of Christ*.

5. Studs Terkel: American activist and author, 1912–2008. Author of *Giants of Jazz, Hard Times*, and *Will the Circle Be Unbroken?*

6. Louis Begley: American novelist and attorney, 1933–. Author of *Wartime Lies, As Max Saw It, About Schmidt*, and *Matters of Honor*.

7. Alexander McCall Smith: Scottish medical-legal ethicist and author, 1948–. Author of several fictional series, including *The No. 1 Ladies' Detective Agency* series.

8. Will Shortz: American enigmatologist and author, 1952–. Author or editor of over 100 puzzle-related books.

9. John Galsworthy: English novelist and playwright, 1867–1933. Author of *The Forsyte Saga*, *Skin Game*, and *One More River*.

10. William (W.S.) Gilbert: English dramatist, 1836–1911. Author of numerous plays and lyricist of Gilbert and Sullivan fame.

11. Andrew Vachss: American attorney and author, 1942–. Author of the Burke series, numerous novels and graphic novels.

12. Charles Perrault: French attorney, 1628–1703. Author of *Mother Goose*.

13. David E. Kelley: American attorney and screenwriter, 1956–. Author of numerous screenplays and TV shows including "Chicago Hope," "Picket Fences," "Ally McBeal," and "Boston Legal."

14. Richard Henry Dana, Jr.: American attorney, seaman, and author, 1815–1882. Author of *Two Years Before the Mast*.

15. Jean-Baptiste Poquelin, aka Molière: French playwright, 1622–1673. Author of *Le Misanthrope*, *Tartuffe ou L'Imposteur*, and *L'Ecole des femmes*.

Bonus Question: Directors who studied law include Otto Preminger (*Anatomy of a Murder*, *Laura*, and *Exodus*); Frederick Wiseman (*Titicut Follies* and *Juvenile Court*); and Federico Fellini (*La Strada* and *Juliet of the Spirits*).

Must-Visit Travel Destinations for Law Buffs

Tired of the usual treks to amusement parks, resorts, and fishing holes? Here's a collection of places to visit, both traditional and offbeat, at which big events in legal history took place.

Greenbrier Government Relocation Facility—White Sulphur Springs, West Virginia

Without the men and women of the U.S. Congress, there'd be no one to pass more laws. That's why, during the Cold War (of the 1950s and 1960s), the U.S. government constructed this massive underground bunker. Measuring over 100,000 square feet, with concrete walls up to five feet thick, it was meant to protect up to 1,100 senators, representatives, and their aides in the event of nuclear fallout. (Oops, no room for their families. Sorry.)

The bunker was never used, except by President Dwight Eisenhower and his staff for a test run. The site was kept secret until the 1990s, but now is available for public tours. Check out those metal bunk beds and freeze-dried food packets! Then, as now, it's connected with a luxury resort.

For more information, see www.greenbrier.com (under "Activities," look for "Bunker Tour").

Dexter Avenue King Memorial Baptist Church—Montgomery, Alabama

Dr. Martin Luther, King, Jr., preached here and helped initiate such law-changing civil rights efforts as the 1950s Montgomery bus boycott. That was the protest launched in opposition to Montgomery's policy of racial segregation on buses and public transit, catalyzed by the arrest of Rosa Parks for refusing to sit in the back of a bus. Ultimately a U.S. District Court struck down segregation on transit systems, in the case of *Browder v. Gayle*, 142 F. Supp. 707 (1956).

The church is still operating and also houses a museum. For more information, see www.dexterkingmemorial.org.

U.S. Supreme Court—Washington, DC

The U.S. Supreme Court has the last word on matters of U.S. constitutional, federal, and international law—and you can watch it in action. Picture yourself in the shoes of the attorneys presenting oral arguments. It's probably the fulfillment of their lifetime dream. Look closer and you might see their adrenalin-pumped hearts trying to pound through their chest walls.

The court is in session between the first Monday in October until late April; check the "Oral Arguments" link on its website for the exact calendar. Even when the court is not in session, you can visit the building, constructed in 1935.

For more information, see www.supremecourtus.gov.

Inns of Court—London, England

From medieval times onward, the Inns of Court and Chancery have been the sole place where British barristers (lawyers who can practice in court) receive their training. They can also live, dine, and keep offices there. Back in the 1300s, their training included not only law, but history, music, and dancing.

Nearby are the Royal Courts of Justice and the Old Bailey, where cases are tried to this day. Keep an eye out for barristers clad in gowns and the traditional white wigs (made of horsehair). Hint: It's not considered good form to blurt out, "Hey, he looks like Rumpole!"

For more information, see www.fodors.com/world/europe/england/london and click "Bloomsbury and Legal London" and www.cityoflondon.gov.uk/Corporation (on the A-Z list, choose "Central Criminal Court").

The Forum—Rome, Italy

Though mostly containing white-marble ruins now, this area was once the center of Rome's legal, religious, social, and commercial activities. In 450 BC, the Romans inscribed their first written laws on the "Twelve Tables," and displayed them in the Forum for all to see. (Unfortunately these were on bronze or wood, and have since been destroyed.)

Roman law is considered the basis for European and, by extension American law. Of course, we've dropped or altered a lot of it; like this bit from the Twelve Tables: "He whose witness has failed to appear may summon him by loud calls before his house every third day."

For more information, see www.britannica.com and search for "Roman law;" and www.lonelyplanet.com (search for "Rome").

Salem Village and witch trials site—Massachusetts

In one of the creepiest reminders of how the law can be misused, the sites of the late-1600s witch trials in historic Salem and Danvers, Massachusetts, have become popular tourist spots, especially around Halloween. Favorite places to visit include:

- The Jonathan Corwin House, also known as the Witch House, where one of the judges lived and interrogated some of the accused. (See www.salemweb.com/witchhouse/.)
- The Witch Dungeon Museum, containing a replica of the dungeons in which accused people were held before trial, and a live reenactment of the trials adapted from actual transcripts. (See www.witchdungeon.com.)
- The Salem Witch Museum, with tours and historical exhibits. (See www.salemwitchmuseum.com.)
- Gallow's Hill, a public park where the "guilty" were publicly hung. You might gather your own evidence that it's haunted.

Alcatraz Island and historic penitentiary—San Francisco, California

Located right in the San Francisco Bay, Alcatraz is such a popular tourist attraction that it's easy to overlook. The prison was in operation from 1934 to 1963 and housed notorious inmates like Al "Scarface" Capone and the "Birdman," Robert Stroud. Cruise tours (run by a private company) let you visit the now-uninhabited prison, view historical exhibits, and enjoy the natural surroundings and views of the Golden Gate Bridge and beyond.

For more information, see www.nps.gov/alca/index.htm and www.alcatrazcruises.com.

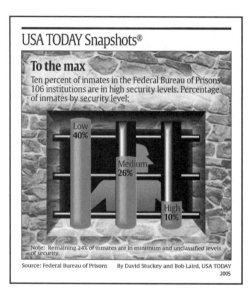

USA TODAY Snapshots®

To the max

Ten percent of inmates in the Federal Bureau of Prisons' 106 institutions are in high security levels. Percentage of inmates by security level:

Low 40%

Medium 26%

High 10%

Note: Remaining 24% of inmates are in minimum and unclassified levels of security.

Source: Federal Bureau of Prisons   By David Stuckey and Bob Laird, USA TODAY 2005

Nellie Mitchell, Age 96, Takes on a Tabloid

s you stand in line at the supermarket scanning the headlines about which celebrity has three months to live, which two are having an affair, and which three were abducted by aliens, you're probably skeptical—but figure maybe there's a grain of truth in there somewhere. Or that it doesn't matter, because, hey, they're celebrities, and their lawyers can sue over the details, right?

Tell that to Nellie Mitchell. She was anything but a celebrity, having spent most of her 96 years selling newspapers in Mountain Home, Arkansas. Then one day she saw a picture of herself in *The Sun* newspaper, with the headline, "SPECIAL DELIVERY: World's oldest newspaper carrier, 101, quits because she's pregnant!" The article featured a story about an Australian "papergal" named Audrey Wiles who became pregnant by a millionaire on her paper route. And why didn't they use a photo of the real Audrey Wiles? Because no such person exists. The entire story was fictitious, false, made up.

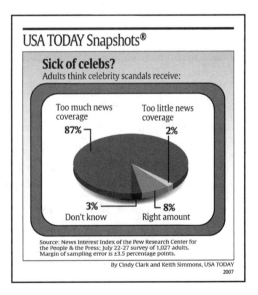

USA TODAY Snapshots®

Sick of celebs?
Adults think celebrity scandals receive:

Too much news coverage
87%

Too little news coverage
2%

3%
Don't know

8%
Right amount

Source: News Interest Index of the Pew Research Center for the People & the Press; July 22-27 survey of 1,027 adults. Margin of sampling error is ±3.5 percentage points.

By Cindy Clark and Keith Simmons, USA TODAY
2007

Absurd though the article was, Nellie was devastated by it. She stayed in her home for days, and even talked about buying up the remaining papers so that no one else would see the story. A witness testified, "[No] matter where you went, people were talking about it because, you know, this was Nellie they were talking about. And everybody recognized her as being Nellie, the newspaper lady."

Nellie sued the newspaper. And then the story gets even weirder. *The Sun* admitted that including the photo of Nellie was a mistake—but not an "Oops, it was an accident," mistake; more like an, "Oops, we had the photo sitting around in our archives from ten years ago and figured by now she must be dead anyway so why not use the picture?" kind of mistake. The paper said that normally they use photos of people from other countries who wouldn't be damaged by circulation in the United States. (Well, that's comforting.)

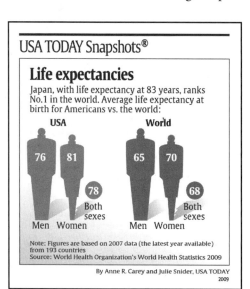

And now, for the newspaper's clever defense: It argued that since that the article was obviously false, no one could reasonably believe it was about Nellie, so what was the harm? In particular, the paper noted that it's not physically possible for a person of Nellie's age to get pregnant. (Glad they cleared that up for us.) And by the way, they further argued, newspapers have a First Amendment right to make up stories and print them, for people's entertainment.

The court wasn't overwhelmed by sympathy for the paper. It found that other aspects of the printed story were believable and potentially detrimental—for example, the suggestion of sexual impropriety and Nellie quitting her lifelong profession.

The court also found that even though the paper admitted to printing mainly fiction, it blurred the lines between real stories and false stories—leaving it up to the reader to figure out what was truth and what wasn't. For example, the paper put disclaimers on some advertisements that warned the reader that the product hadn't been vetted by the newspaper. However, it didn't put any such disclaimers on articles, suggesting that those had all been properly vetted.

Ultimately, the court found that the newspaper recklessly failed to anticipate the impact that the article would have on Nellie. It awarded her $650,000 in compensatory damages for her injuries and $850,000 in punitive damages against the newspaper. Later, the compensatory damages were found to be excessive and were reduced to $150,000, but that still left Nellie with a total of $1 million in damages—not a bad addition to a 96-year old's retirement pot! And we're happy to report that Nellie had several more years in which to enjoy the award, as she lived until the age of 103.

Times May, in Fact, Have Changed: Old Court Opinions

orget time capsules—if you want a window into the obsessions, standards, sources of discomfort, and outright prejudices of a previous generation, take a gander at its court decisions. Better yet, read them out loud. Did people really used to talk like this?

By the way, you'll notice that the judges quoted below are often puffing about the greatness of laws long since thrown onto the trash heap of history.

Judge Wagner of the New York Supreme Court—writing in 1924

With a title like *Casanova's Homecoming*, it's not hard to imagine that the book under this court's consideration was at least a little racy. The prosecutor called it "obscene, lewd, lascivious, indecent, and disgusting." Here's how Judge Wagner concludes that the book was sufficiently obscene that defendant Thomas Seltzer's case (he was caught in possession of it and indicted), should be put before a jury for consideration:

> *"Neither literary artistry nor charm and grace of exquisite composition may cloak protectively those obnoxious impulses that subtly creep unaware to a point of approval, which on patent appearance would be abhorred. We ... cannot accept a book's adoption by another land or the approval of critics as conclusive of nonobscenity under the statute, for we may assert with pride—though not boastfully—that we are essentially an idealistic and spiritual nation and exact a higher standard than some others."*

(*People v. Seltzer*, 122 Misc. 329, 203 N.Y.S. 809, N.Y.Sup. 1924.)

Judge Walton, of the Maine Supreme Court—writing in 1895

As near as we can tell, the worst thing done by the man who incurred Judge Walton's displeasure below was to call a street car conductor a "damned liar." The conductor then threw the man, named Clarence Robinson, out of the street car, whereupon Mr. Robinson sued the street car company for damages—and won! Until he met Judge Walton, that is, who pronounced the following in overturning the win:

USA TODAY Snapshots®

Big drop in audience outrage
Number of consumer complaints regarding radio and television programming indecency/obscenity:

2004
1.4 million

2005
233,471

Source: Federal Communications Commission
By David Stuckey and Sam Ward, USA TODAY
2006

"In this state, the use of indecent or profane language in a street-railroad car is a breach of the peace. And if, in a car filled with passengers, nearly one-half of whom are ladies, a man in earnest conversation undertakes to emphasize his statements, as some men are apt to do, by saying, "By God," it is so, or "By God," it is not so, the law makes it the duty of the conductor to check him; and, if the latter denies his guilt, and, upon being assured by the conductor that he was guilty, flies into a passion, and calls the conductor a "damned liar," it is the opinion of the court that he may rightfully be removed from the car; not as a punishment for his insult to the conductor as an individual, but to vindicate the authority of the law, which forbids the use of such language in a street car, or any other public place, where women and children have a right to be."

(*Robinson v. Rockland*, T. & C. St. Ry. Co., 87 Me. 387, 32 A. 994, Me. 1895.)

Judge Smith of the Court of Civil Appeals of Texas, San Antonio—writing in 1923

Here, Judge Smith refuses to allow young Charles Robert James to inherit his father's estate, on grounds that the law wouldn't recognize the parents' common-law marriage—despite the fact that the parents had married after Charles was born:

> *"A mere secret agreement, stealthily followed by clandestine cohabitation, is not all that is necessary in this country to constitute a legal, or the true, marriage state… When the 'wedding day' of the parent ceases to be revered by the offspring, there will be a weakening of the family ties and a lowering of the standard of marriage and home."*

> *(James v. James*, 253 S.W. 1112, Tex.Civ.App. 1923.)

Judge Roy, of King's County Court, New York—writing in 1915

There are plenty of ways to show a man you don't like him. But once this defendant started making a habit of, in the words of the judge, "greet[ing] another by placing the end of his thumb against the tip of his nose, at the same time extending and wiggling the fingers of his hand," he probably should've expected a disorderly conduct conviction. And that's what he got.

> *"What meaning is intended to be conveyed by the above-described pantomime? Is it a friendly or an unfriendly action; a compliment or an insult? … Among boys it serves as a harmless vent for injured feelings, which lack the proper vocabulary to relieve themselves through audible speech. But when boys become men they should 'put away childish things.' In the case at bar the circumstances attending the enactment of the nasal and digit drama aforesaid tend to show a design to engender strife…. I am satisfied the magistrate was fully warranted in reaching the conclusion he arrived at, and I therefore affirm the conviction."*

> *(People ex rel. Shannon v. Garstenfeld*, 34 N.Y.Crim.R. 86, 92 Misc. 388, 156 N.Y.S. 991.)

Judge Bryan of the North Carolina Supreme Court— writing in 1903

In this case, Mr. Albert Jones had been living with another woman, but attempted to enter his former home, which was wholly owned by his wife. She alleged trespass, but Judge Bryan cast aside that notion as follows:

> "Can it be that a wife may, whenever she sees fit, leave her home, and take up her residence in another place, refuse the society of her husband, and indict him as a trespasser if he puts his foot upon the wife's abandoned property, the place he has made his home? Have we reached that stage of social progress when the sacred relation of husband and wife and the hallowed influences of the home are converted into mere traditions without power to influence, and dreams instead of relations? ... The ease and frequency of divorce and separation in this state has become a matter of unenviable notoriety and of just contempt among decent people."

(*State v. Jones*, 132 N.C. 1043, 43 S.E. 939, N.C. 1903.)

Judge Frick, of the Utah Supreme Court—writing in 1919

When was the last time you sat in a restaurant booth and thought to notice—much less measure—the dividers between you and the next patrons? You might have been more conscious of it if you'd lived in Ogden City, Utah, in 1919, where a municipal ordinance made it illegal for such dividers to be any higher than three feet, six inches. And that was just fine with Judge Frick:

> "We confess our entire inability to discover anything in the ordinance that is unreasonably oppressive ... We have a right to assume that the purpose of the ordinance is merely to prevent persons of both sexes who have regard for neither the law nor good morals from meeting at late and unusual hours of the night and entering those booths where they can avoid detection and can indulge their propensities for violating both the law and good morals."

(*Ogden City v. Leo*, 54 Utah 556, 182 P. 530, Utah 1919.)

Judge Threadgill, of the Oklahoma Supreme Court—writing in 1924

The scary thing is, Judge Threadgill wasn't the only one to hold opinions like the one he expresses below, in refusing to allow an African-American man to inherit the property of his Choctaw Indian wife, based on state laws prohibiting "marriage of the descendants of the African race with any other race:"

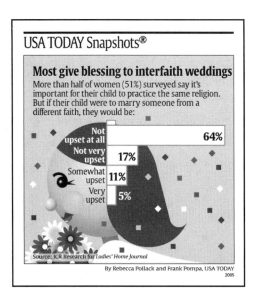

USA TODAY Snapshots®

Most give blessing to interfaith weddings
More than half of women (51%) surveyed say it's important for their child to practice the same religion. But if their child were to marry someone from a different faith, they would be:

Not upset at all **64%**
Not very upset **17%**
Somewhat upset **11%**
Very upset **5%**

Source: ICR Research for *Ladies' Home Journal*
By Rebecca Pollack and Frank Pompa, USA TODAY 2005

"Statutes forbidding intermarriage by the white and black races were without doubt dictated by wise statesmanship, and have a broad and solid foundation in enlightened policy, sustained by sound reason and common sense. The amalgamation of the races is not only unnatural, but is always productive of deplorable results. The purity of the public morals, the moral and physical development of both races, and the highest advancement of civilization, under which the two races must work out and accomplish their destiny, all require that they should be kept distinctly separate, and that connections and alliances so unnatural should be prohibited by positive law and subject to no evasion."

(*Eggers v. Olson*, 104 Okla. 297, 231 P. 483, Okla. 1924.)

Consider Yourself Warned!

Have you ever gone and bought something new, only to discover that the pamphlet of instructions and product warnings took up more package space than the product itself?

Blame the lawyers for this one—or at least the American tendency to, immediately after hurting oneself, look for someone to sue.

Product liability law is its own specialty—some lawyers spend their life on this stuff. The basic idea is that, when someone gets hurt by using a product that was either manufactured or marketed in a defective or dangerous way, that person can recover damages from whomever was responsible. But, the person suing has to have been using the product for its intended or expected purpose—in other words, you shouldn't be able to use an aerosol can to pound in nails and then sue when it explodes.

USA TODAY Snapshots®

Fit is first
What women find most important when buying a swimsuit:

Fit 70%
Style 16%
Color 7%
Latest trend 1%
Other 6%

Source: Caravan telephone survey of 1,021 women for TJ Maxx (Jan. 12-16). Margin of error ± 3 percentage points.

By Mary Cadden and Sam Ward, USA TODAY 2006

Aha, reason the manufacturers (and their lawyers): We'll just warn people away from doing practically every possible thing you could do with this product! Or doing anything with it all!

Below are some of the results of this advanced legal analysis. (You'll soon find yourself wondering, if it's so important for companies to protect themselves in this way, shouldn't they pay more attention to translation and proofreading?)

Let's start with this warning found in the package for a camera neck strap:

Never use neck strap so that it is in contact with the throat or any other part of the neck which would expose the user to a choking hazard.

(So, where are you supposed to use it?)

On a yellow pages directory:

Please do not use this directory while operating a moving vehicle.

(Don't use your landline phone while operating a vehicle, either.)

Attached to some Sesame Street holiday ornaments:

This is a decoration not a child.

(That probably came as a relief to some buyers.)

In an ad for an "off-road commode"—essentially, a toilet seat that people out fishing or camping can hook to the back of their car to momentarily approximate an outhouse:

Not for use when vehicle is in motion.

(Don't even try to imagine that.)

On a food package:

Product made in a nut free area, but nuts elsewhere.

(Perhaps that's simply an accurate description of the state of the world.)

On a swimsuit label:

Severe damage may be caused by rough surfaces, suntan lotion, oil, fingernails, by extra stains, or by abnormal use. Salt water deteriorates fabrics. Expect some change in color with sun exposure. Spandex fabrics will give limited service when used for physical fitness activities, in pools of above average chlorine content, or in water of above average temperature.

(Better to just admire your new swimsuit hanging in your closet.)

In the cautions accompanying a step-counting meter:

Under the following condition, the stepping meter can't count correctly: (i) Moon Walking, Wearing Sandal; (ii) When walking in the tricky condition; (iii) Vibration without walking.

In the packaging to a can opener:

Caution: Avoid contact with rim of can which may have a sharp edge.

(This would have been a fine warning if the packaging hadn't also advertised, "No More Sharp Edges On Lids!")

With a heating pad:

Do not use on any unexplained pain or swollen muscles, or following muscular injury, before consuming your physician.

Instructions for installing an antenna:

Warning: Do not attempt to install if drunk, pregnant or both. Do not throw antenna at spouse.

Check your own blow dryer; it may contain this warning:

Do not use in bathtub.

(Just in case the problem of getting electrocuted in the bathtub while using appliances was an urban legend, the Discovery Channel show *Mythbusters* actually ran a test where it tossed an electric fan into a bathtub with a test dummy. This one's no legend: The dummy got fried. In fact, it appears that people aren't reading the labels; 15 or more people each year get themselves electrocuted while using blow dryers.)

And finally, here's a set of instructions for a global-positioning system device that sounds like it *should* have been a warning:

You may need to be held down for a period of time to start a secondary function, when the instructions tell you to, do so.

Top Ten Songs That Are Really, Truly About Lawyers

The trouble with most "Top Ten Songs about the Law" lists is that they're unfocused. You'll find tales of legal woes ("I Fought the Law" by Bobby Fuller) mixed in with brushes with legal authority ("Alice's Restaurant" by Arlo Guthrie or "I Shot the Sheriff" by Bob Marley), along with true tales of legal injustice ("Hurricane" by Bob Dylan), litigation metaphors ("Sue Me" from the musical *Guys and Dolls*), tales of incarceration ("Jailhouse Rock" by Elvis or "Folsom Prison Blues" by Johnny Cash), ... and let's not forget old-fashioned heavy metal insanity ("Breaking the Law" by Judas Priest).

What we're looking for are songs that are *just* about lawyers. We understand that songwriters are generally not inclined to sing about their legal representation (although we did find one composition simply titled, "I've Got a Lawyer"). That's not to say composers have avoided the subject completely. A search of the repertoire at BMI and ASCAP—the two major song licensors—uncovered over 100 songs with the word "lawyer" or "attorney" in the title. These include songs with an agrarian angle ("The Lawyer and the Cow" and "The Lawyer and the Farmer"), an antilawyer stance ("Lawyers Suck," "Lawyers Screw It Up," "Lawyers and Leeches," and "Lawyer Liar Blues"), romance ("Lawyer's Love Song"), gratitude ("A Lawyer Saved My Life"), absurdity ("Lawyers Are Like Bananas," "Lawyers and White Paper," and "Lawyers on Acid"), dancing ("Lawyer's Hoedown"), wishful thinking ("I Would Have Made a Good Lawyer"), religion ("Lawyer's Prayer"), antagonism ("Lawyer Up"), and an all-American love of spectacle, "Lawyers on Parade."

We've sorted through them all. Below are our ten favorites. Sure, some of them may not be as well known as "Thriller," and the artists might not be as popular as Britney or Bruce, but don't let that stop you from appreciating the sharp legal analysis and deep appreciation for the legal profession that these tunes possess. In no particular order:

❶ "My Attorney Bernie"

A bebop pianist with a knack for humorous lyrics and jazzy melodies, composer/singer Dave Frishberg created the ultimate paean to the legal profession with this oft-covered composition. Bernie the attorney has a lot going for him, including "Dodger season boxes and an office full of foxes." He may not be a perfect lawyer ("Sure we blew a couple ventures with a counterfeit debenture") but when it comes down to the important stuff, "Bernie tells me what to do, Bernie always lays it on the line. Bernie says we sue, we sue; Bernie says we sign, we sign."

❷ "Talk to My Lawyer"

Chuck Brodsky is known amongst folk literati for his barbed wit, his groove-oriented guitar style, and his songs about baseball players (eleven Brodsky songs are in the Baseball Hall of Fame). Brodsky's "Talk to My Lawyer" is accurate, businesslike, and a bit one-sided in its focus on personal injury ("I'm gonna talk to my lawyer. I think I've got a pretty good case. All I need are some crutches; maybe put on a neck brace. I've got a witness to put a hand on the Bible. Jury jury, hallelujah you might be liable.") Whether or not he gets it exactly right, Brodsky's tongue-in-cheek lyrics probably reflect the reality of contingency fee practice.

USA TODAY Snapshots®

Music industry downbeat
Hours and spending on recorded music per person, per year:

Hours listening: 259 (2000), 180¹ (2010)
Spending: $61.20 (2000), $51.08¹ (2010)

1 – projected

Source: Veronis Suhler Stevenson, *Communications Industry Forecast & Report*

By David Stuckey and Sam Ward, USA TODAY 2008

❸ "Lawyers in Love"

For sheer weirdness, Jackson Browne's 1983 composition, "Lawyers in Love" seems to baffle everyone who hears it. ("Among the human beings in their designer jeans, am I the only one who hears the screams, and the strangled cries of lawyers in love?"). Browne convincingly belts out this folk-rock classic, complaining about eating from TV trays while watching "Happy Days," and in the final verse, discourses on how the U.S.S.R. will soon be a "vacationland for lawyers in love." Hmm? Although Browne himself hints that the song is a critique of political complacency, we prefer to focus on its verification that attorneys are capable of amore.

④ "The Philadelphia Lawyer" (also known as "Reno Blues")

Speaking of lawyers in love, in 1949, folk musician Woody Guthrie wrote a ballad loosely based on a true story. A romantic Philly attorney attempts to talk his paramour (a Hollywood maid) into leaving her husband, a cowboy named Bill. Alas, Bill overhears the pair talking and the result is Murder One. Guthrie concludes his song, "Now tonight back in old Pennsylvania, among those beautiful pines, there's one less Philadelphia lawyer in old Philadelphia tonight."

⑤ "Legal Man"

Belle & Sebastian, a Scottish band whose music was featured in the film *High Fidelity*, released "Legal Man" in 2000. With its retro sound reminiscent of sixties groups such as Love, "Legal Man" analogizes to contract law as a means of enforcing a romantic commitment ("Notwithstanding provisions of Clauses 1, 2, 3, and 4; Extend contractual period, me and you for evermore.") The song ends with the repeating advice to Legal Man, "Get out of the office and into the springtime." All in all, that's solid advice—unless one has a summary judgment brief due in the springtime.

⑥ "California Sex Lawyer"

This one's a tale of wish fulfillment from Fountains of Wayne (a band that got its name from a New Jersey lawn ornaments store). The song portrays a young man named Doug who plans to become a California "sex lawyer," a specialty that's apparently not covered in most law school curriculums. According to Doug, he's got the makings of this particular discipline: "I've got big ideas. I've got backup plans. I've got the cha-cha-charisma. Got the sleight of hand. I'm gunna do some damage. Gunna bust some heads. I'm gunna go the distance. Then I'm going to bed." Sounds like a plan; we're just not sure how Doug's malpractice carrier will respond.

⑦ "We Love Our Lawyers"

We may have misheard the lyrics but the only vaguely decipherable phrase in this bouncy Latin-flavored jazz song appears to be the repeating phrase "cosign." Inscrutability is nothing new for Cibo Matto, the creators, as the bulk of their songs are about food (the band's name is Italian for "crazy food"). Even though singing about lawyers is a bit far afield for this group (and the song lacks any serious legal content), the exuberance of "We Love Our Lawyers," combined with its devoted title, ultimately sends an upbeat message that wins this one top ten placement.

⑧ "One Million Lawyers"

In 1985, folk singer Tom Paxton released "One Million Lawyers," based on the prediction that the United States would have that many lawyers within a decade. Apparently, Paxton viewed this as a bad thing (the title of the album was *One Million Lawyers and Other Disasters*) and wrote, "Lawyers around every bend in the road. Lawyers in every tree. Lawyers in restaurants. Lawyers in clubs. Lawyers behind every door. Behind windows and potted plants, shade trees, and shrubs. Lawyers on pogo sticks. Lawyers in politics. In ten years, we're gonna have one million lawyers. How much can a poor nation stand?" Paxton may have had some justification for his paranoia, but twenty years later, we know one thing: He was wrong about the pogo sticks.

⑨ "My Dad's a Lawyer"

Some might find this track a bit overbearing—what with bad-boy folkie Geoff Berner's taunting tenor and the honking accordion he uses for accompaniment. But those elements actually add to the song's message as Berner goads listeners, "You don't like the way I sing. Go ahead take a swing … cause my dad's a lawyer." This track has us conflicted. On the one hand we don't like the mocking encouragement to litigation; on the other hand, we're glad to see family pride in the legal profession.

⑩ "Will Your Lawyer Talk to God For You?"

With its old-timey steel pedal guitar and Kitty Wells' classic country vocal, this track poses a cosmological dilemma for many in the legal business—or as Kitty puts it when asked to sign the divorce papers, "Man-made laws set you free on earth but is God satisfied? Will your lawyer talk to God for you?" This simple country and Western tune is the only one on our list to make BillBoard's Top Ten (1962). By the way, Wells' attorney never had to discuss divorce with the Almighty. She may have had the longest celebrity marriage in history, having been married to country singer Johnnie Wright for over seventy years.

Test Your Knowledge of Impeachment

f you've ever said, "He ought to be impeached!" about a U.S. president, you're not alone.

But what if you suddenly found yourself sitting in the U.S. Senate (after a surprise write-in campaign, maybe)? Would you know the basic ground rules and historical context of the impeachment process?

Use this self-test to start getting ready, just in case.

True or False: The word "impeachment" derives from the Greek practice of throwing rotten fruit at corrupt officials.

False. The word derives from Latin roots meaning to catch, entangle, or fetter. Other modern words from the same root include the French verb "empêcher" (to prevent) and the English verb "impede."

True or False: Any federal official can be impeached.

True. The Constitution provides that federal officials shall be removed "on Impeachment for, and Conviction of, Treason, Bribery, or other high Crimes and Misdemeanors." In other words, it can be used to remove any federal official from office, including judges, all the way up to the Supreme Court.

True or False: Impeachment is really a twentieth century phenomenon.

True. Although the principle comes from the U.S. Constitution art. II, §4, impeachment was almost never used before the 1960s. The tide turned in 1960 when the John Birch society began pushing for the impeachment of Supreme Court Chief Justice Earl Warren, angry at his presiding over court decisions ordering desegregation in the South and allowing members of the Communist Party to "take the Fifth." They put up billboards saying "Impeach Earl Warren" along roadsides all over the United States.

USA TODAY Snapshots™

Do you discuss politics at work?

Just listen and keep my opinions to myself **49%**

Discuss politics **47%**

Don't know **4%**

Source: Ajilon Finance survey of 1,027 respondents. Margin of error ±3

By Darryl Haralson and Bob Laird, USA TODAY 2004

Justice Warren was not impeached; he retired of his own volition in 1969. But impeachment became more common thereafter as a political tool.

True or False: Committing a felony automatically results in impeachment.

False. After Vice President Aaron Burr killed Alexander Hamilton in a dual, he was promptly indicted for murder in both New Jersey and New York. By staying away from both states, he managed to avoid arrest and trial. But the majority Democrats in Congress weren't eager to go after one of their own, so he remained in office.

True or False: The standard for impeachment—"high crimes and misdemeanors"—has never been clearly defined.

True. Nobody is really sure what the phrase means. Some say it should refer to any violation of the law, others prefer to limit it to abuse of power or violation of the public trust. President Gerald Ford once said it's "whatever a majority of the House of Representatives considers it to be at a given moment in history."

True or False: The entire Supreme Court can be impeached.

True. In fact, Senator Strom Thurmond once urged that it be done. He was that mad about the Court's repeated upholding of due process rights for members of the Communist Party (during the McCarthy era of the late 1950s). His recommendation was basically ignored and seems not to have hurt his career any—he left office in 2002, at the age of 100.

True or False: The majority and minority leaders of the Senate jointly preside over impeachment hearings.

False. The Chief Justice of the Supreme Court presides. It's an unusual alliance between the Supreme Court, the House of Representatives (which drafts the impeachment resolution), and the Senate (which holds hearings and makes the decision to impeach by a two-thirds majority).

True or False: President Nixon was impeached.

False. He was certainly headed down that road, after it was revealed that the so-called "Watergate burglars" who broke into the headquarters of the Democratic National Committee in 1972 were employed by the Committee to Reelect President Nixon and were planting listening devices.

After months of Senate hearings, and Nixon's famous assertion that, "I'm not a crook," he finally saw the writing on the wall and resigned in August 1974, before his impeachment could come to a Senate vote.

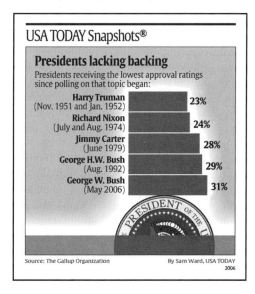

USA TODAY Snapshots®

Presidents lacking backing
Presidents receiving the lowest approval ratings since polling on that topic began:

Harry Truman (Nov. 1951 and Jan. 1952) — 23%
Richard Nixon (July and Aug. 1974) — 24%
Jimmy Carter (June 1979) — 28%
George H.W. Bush (Aug. 1992) — 29%
George W. Bush (May 2006) — 31%

Source: The Gallup Organization   By Sam Ward, USA TODAY 2006

True or False: President Clinton was impeached.

Almost, but in the end, no. Impeachment proceedings were started against Clinton over the Whitewater controversy. The investigations quickly turned from the alleged financial scandal toward his personal life. The four articles of impeachment that the House of Representatives ultimately sent to the Senate all had to do with lies Clinton told during investigations of his extramarital relationship with Monica

Lewinsky and his alleged sexual harassment of Paula Jones. The Senate did not, however, reach the required two-thirds majority, and Clinton was acquitted in 1999.

True or False: President George W. Bush was impeached.

False. Congressman Dennis Kucinich introduced 35 articles of impeachment to the U.S. House of Representatives, alleging crimes to do with Bush having ignored warnings of terrorist threats that led to the events of September 11, 2001; created a secret propaganda campaign to justify illegally going to war with Iraq; failed to provide troops with body armor; exposed classified information concerning CIA agent Valerie Plame Wilson; mistreated prisoners of war; conducted spying and wiretapping of U.S. citizens; used signing statements to alter legislation; failed to respond to Hurricane Katrina and threats of global climate change; and much more.

The House voted to refer the matter to the Judiciary Committee, which took no further action.

Celebrities With Law Degrees

s there a lawyer in the house? That's a question you don't hear very often; yet the answer is likely to be "Yes." You just never know who's going to have a law degree rolled up in their back pocket.

John Cleese, actor:
Law degree from Cambridge, 1963

Before *Monty Python*, *A Fish Called Wanda*, and *Harry Potter*, John Cleese ambled his way across the stage to receive a law degree from Cambridge. While Cleese never practiced law, his time at Cambridge allowed him to meet future *Python* members Graham Chapman and Eric Idle. He also got to use his attorney background in some roles: He plays Mr. Toad's attorney in *The Wind in the Willows* (1996) and attorney Archie Leach in *A Fish Called Wanda*.

Howard Cosell, sportscaster:
Law degree from New York University School of Law, 1941

Cosell went into law to please his parents, but luckily encountered clients who were sports and entertainment figures and got him to do a short radio show interviewing sports pros. The rest is journalism history. Known for his catchphrase "I'm just telling it like it is," Howard Cosell covered boxing legends Muhammad Ali, Joe Frazier, and George Foreman. Cosell also covered Monday night football, and he famously broke the news of John Lennon's murder on the night on Monday, December 8, 1980.

Peter Garrett, musician, and politician:
Law degree from the University of New South Wales, 1976

In 1976, Pete Garrett took a break from the commercially undiscovered band Midnight Oil to finish his law studies. Starting in Sydney, Midnight

Oil slowly captured the minds and ears of Australians, and in the late 1980s, they became an international success. With a focus on social progress and environmentalism, Garrett began his political career in 1984, and he has served as president of the Australian Conservation Foundation as well as minister for the environment, heritage, and the arts.

Julio Iglesias, singer:
Law degree from Madrid Complutense University, 2001

A popular and accomplished musician for over 40 years, Julio Iglesias has sold more than 250 million albums. While studying law in Spain in 1963, Iglesias was in a car crash that left him partially paralyzed. During his recovery, Iglesias learned to play the guitar, and the rest is music history. In 2001, he returned to Madrid Complutense University to fulfill a graduation promise he made to his father.

Tony La Russa, professional baseball player, and manager:
Law degree from Florida State University, 1978

Tony La Russa spent a majority of his baseball playing career in the minor leagues. In 1978, he landed his first managerial job for the Knoxville Sox, a Double-A team affiliated with the Chicago White Sox. As of this writing, he has managed 4,773 games, which ranks him second all-time. He has said, "I decided I'd rather ride the buses in the minor leagues than practice law for a living."

Geraldo Rivera, talk show host, reporter, and journalist:
Law degree from Brooklyn Law School, 1969

While he's better known for his "Trash TV" talk show, Rivera practiced law in New York in the late 1960s. He worked with a New York Puerto Rican activist group, the Young Lords, and this association soon attracted the attention of "Eyewitness News" executive Al Primo. Currently, Geraldo has his own television show, "Geraldo at Large," on "Fox News.

William Sanderson, actor:
Law degree from University of Memphis, 1971

Best known for his role as progeria-suffering genetic designer J.F. Sebastian in Ridley Scott's *Blade Runner*, Sanderson began acting during his time at the University of Memphis. His recent roles include E.B. Farnum on *Deadwood* and Sheriff Bud Dearborne on *True Blood*.

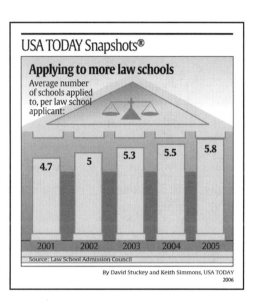

USA TODAY Snapshots®

Applying to more law schools

Average number of schools applied to, per law school applicant:

2001	2002	2003	2004	2005
4.7	5	5.3	5.5	5.8

Source: Law School Admission Council

By David Stuckey and Keith Simmons, USA TODAY 2006

Jerry Springer, talk show host, reporter, and politician: Law degree from Northwestern University, 1968

Before the tawdry talk show antics of "The Jerry Springer Show," Springer graduated from Northwestern University and began work as an aide to Robert Kennedy's 1968 presidential campaign. During the 1970s, he spent time on Cincinnati's city council, and from 1977 to 1978, Springer served as mayor of Cincinatti. In 1991, he debuted "The Jerry Springer Show," which is still in syndication.

Steve Young, professional football player:
Law degree from Brigham Young University, 1994

Seven consecutive Pro Bowl selections? Check. Three Super Bowl rings? Check. Two NFL MVPs? Check. A 96.8 career passer rating? Check. Impressively, Steve Young obtained a law degree from BYU in the same year he led the San Francisco 49ers to a Super Bowl victory over the San Diego Chargers. After receiving his seventh official concussion in 1999, the scrambling lefty retired from professional football.

Seven Rules You'd Think Every Bank Robber Would Know

here's a certain elegance to a well-executed bank robbery. We've all seen them in the movies: The criminal gang rushes into the bank, fires a few shots into the air, collects the money, and then gracefully sprints out to a waiting car to make a fast getaway. It all goes like clockwork.

Unfortunately, real life isn't like the movies. A shockingly large number of bank robberies go awry due to the robbers' failure to follow a few simple rules.

RULE #1: Wait until the bank opens.

Unlike 7-Eleven stores, banks aren't open 24 hours a day. The goal of an efficient robber is not to break into the bank, but to walk in and then run out with the money. An Elmira, New York, man ignored this rule when he showed up at a bank late in the day wearing a mask and wielding a shotgun, but couldn't open the already-locked doors. Luckily for him, the bank had an outdoor ATM he was able to rob. Unluckily for him, some people still inside the bank got his license plate number. Police were able to track down and arrest the man.

RULE #2: Write a legible stickup note.

It's not absolutely mandatory that the teller be presented with a written note demanding the money. But, for traditionalist robbers using a note, they'd better make it legible. That's what the woman who attempted to rob a bank in Hillsboro, Oregon, discovered after handing a teller a note that said, "Need $300 or I'll kill you. I'm serious." The teller—apparently a stickler for good penmanship—told the robber she couldn't read the writing. While the robber stepped away to rewrite her note on a bank slip, the teller hit a silent alarm and police and FBI agents soon arrived to make the arrest.

By the way, this is no time for robbers to show a commitment to paper recycling. One robber walked into a bank in Jacksonville, Illinois, and handed the teller a stickup note saying he had several pounds of explosives. The note was apparently legible enough—the robber got away with some cash. Unfortunately, the note was written on the back of a police arrest report the robber had received a few weeks earlier, in which he'd been charged with opposing a police officer. The report contained his full name and home address.

RULE #3: Wear a good disguise.

All banks have video cameras, so robbers have learned to use disguises. A mask seems to work best. Attempts to use duct tape, shaving cream, and drywall (yes, drywall) have all gone awry. Not even the classic stocking over the head can be counted on. One would-be robber forgot to cut eyeholes in the stockings. When he donned the cap, he couldn't see and was quickly arrested.

RULE #4: Don't leave incriminating evidence at the crime scene.

A successful bank robber must be meticulous and not leave incriminating evidence behind—such as a wallet, driver's license, fingerprints, or peanuts. That's right, peanuts. A man who robbed an Orlando, Florida, bank was snacking on peanuts just before committing the crime and dropped some at the scene. Police searched the area and found him. They knew they had their man because, not only did he match the description of the perp, but he also had a bag of peanuts on him.

RULE #5: Make a clean getaway.

After getting the money, any robber with an ounce of sense should leave the bank and its environs—immediately. In criminal parlance, this is called "making a getaway." Typically, bank robbers use a car or other motorized vehicle. However, this is not without risk. For example, when two robbers in the United Kingdom left a bank with their stolen loot, they found their getaway car had been stolen. Foolishly, one of them had left the keys inside. They then attempted to carjack a passing vehicle. Unfortunately, it was a police car.

Of course, robbers don't necessarily have to use a car to make a getaway. There's always public transportation, though it didn't work too well for the Georgia bank robber who was nabbed by the cops while waiting at a bus stop.

What about going green and using a bicycle? Maybe not. One Chicago robber who attempted to flee a bank using pedal power was tackled by the cops.

It's possible to avoid the complexities of using wheeled transportation entirely by electing to make a getaway on foot. But a little physical training is probably in order first. After a 300-pound Washington-state bank robber attempted to flee on foot with his loot, he soon tired and had to stop to catch his breath. That gave the bank security guard all the time he needed to catch up to, handcuff, and arrest the huffing and puffing robber.

USA TODAY Snapshots®

Prime times for bank crimes

Of the 7,272 bank crimes that occurred in 2006, the most incidents happened between 9 a.m. and 11 a.m. Occurrences of crimes by time of day:

6-9 a.m.	203
9-11 a.m.	1,901
11 a.m.-1 p.m.	1,656
1-3 p.m.	1,574
3-6 p.m.	1,613
6 p.m.-6 a.m.	321
Not determined	4

Note: Bank crimes encompass robberies, burglaries and larcenies
Source: U.S. Department of Justice

By David Stuckey and Adrienne Lewis, USA TODAY 2007

RULE #6: Don't count the loot until getting home.

Sure, it's only natural to be curious about how much cash one got away with. But such curiosity did in one bank robber in Bridgeport, Connecticut, when he was discovered behind the bank counting his take—all of $857—and was quickly arrested.

RULE #7: Don't brag about the exploits.

One Chicago robber found this out when he phoned a local radio call-in program on the theme of "confessions" and boasted that he and his fellow robbers tied up bank workers and got away with $81,000. FBI agents eventually traced the call to his cell phone and arrested him.

Another bank robber was caught because he blogged about his crimes on MySpace. The message read, "On tha run for robbin a bank Love all of yall." He also put "just robbed a bank" on the top of his "25 Things You Don't Know About Me" list on his Facebook page.

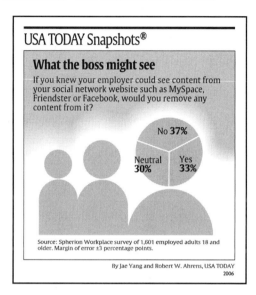

USA TODAY Snapshots®

What the boss might see

If you knew your employer could see content from your social network website such as MySpace, Friendster or Facebook, would you remove any content from it?

No **37%**

Neutral **30%**

Yes **33%**

Source: Spherion Workplace survey of 1,601 employed adults 18 and older. Margin of error ±3 percentage points.

By Jae Yang and Robert W. Ahrens, USA TODAY
2006

Who Did You Say Went Bankrupt?

Whether you view bankruptcy as the ultimate failure or a chance at a fresh start, you might be surprised at who among the rich and famous have had to resort to this legal remedy.

From presidents to professional athletes, one day they're ordering the limo driver to take them to the fanciest restaurant in town, the next day they're in court begging for their debts to be forgiven—or at least postponed.

What's going on here? The lesson seems to be that no matter how much money you have, there's always a way to overspend or mismanage it. (We'll do better than these folks when we make our first million, right?)

Mike Tyson, Heavyweight champion boxer *(Bankrupt, 2003)*

Tyson earned hundreds of millions during his boxing career—and spent it almost as fast as it came in. Jewelry, mansions, nice clothes, motorcycles, parties, and Siberian tigers (whose care and feeding adds up!) were among his extravagances.

It all came to a crashing end in 2003, when Tyson's debt level reached more than $27 million at the same time his fighting career was reaching its close. Tyson's bankruptcy petition reportedly contained the simple statement, "I am unable to pay my bills."

Cashing in the goodies he'd bought wasn't going to help. His major debts included a $9 million divorce settlement to his exwife, Monica Turner; a $13.4 million IRS bill; another $4 million owed to the British tax authorities; and bills for legal, financial, and other services. It almost made his $51,949 child support debt look like small change.

By 2009, Tyson was claiming to be living a more positive and structured lifestyle and making noises about a comeback.

Dorothy Hamill, Figure skater (*Bankrupt, 1996*)

No, not Dorothy Hamill, the Olympic figure skater with the cute wedge haircut that was soon named after her? Yes, she filed for bankruptcy 20 years after her 1976 gold-winning performance at the U.S. Olympic Games, citing poor investment and financial advice. She once said, "Money is very evil. You find out anyone and everyone tries to take it away from you."

Kim Basinger, Actress (*Bankrupt, 1993*)

As a former model with several movie roles to her name (for example, in *The Natural, 9 ½ Weeks, My Stepmother Is an Alien,* and *Batman*), Kim Basinger was doing just fine financially. Her per-movie salary was in the range of $8 million.

But that was before she pulled out of the title role of the 1993 movie *Boxing Helena*. Anyone might have gotten cold feet about the role: Basinger was supposed to play a girl injured in a hit-and-run motor accident in front of the home of a lonely Atlanta surgeon who then kidnaps and treats her in his house, amputating both of her legs as well as her healthy arms. Aside from some cult fan-dom, the reaction of many audience members (after the movie was eventually produced, with Sherilyn Fenn playing Helena), was "Ick."

The moviemakers sued Basinger for breach of contract. After a jury verdict, she was ordered to pay $8 million—at which point, she filed for bankruptcy. Fortunately, the verdict was later set aside on appeal, and Basinger continues to be in high demand as an actress.

John James Audubon, Naturalist and illustrator of *Birds of America* (*Bankrupt, 1819*)

John James Audubon's name today is synonymous with birds and conservation. Yet he endured multiple business failures before turning these passions into a livelihood. He tried his hand at a dry goods store, a steam grist, and a lumber mill, but instead of showing up for work could usually be found wandering the woods, working on a growing portfolio of bird drawings.

Not surprisingly, his business career ended precipitously in bankruptcy —landing Audubon briefly in jail. All he had left were his clothes, his gun, and his drawings. He credits this total failure for leading him back to his true passion—those bird drawings. After raising enough money for a trip to England, he found a publisher for *Birds of America*. The book, with its life-size, dramatic pictures of birds, was an immediate success.

For all his knowledge of birds, Audubon was never able to build up a nest egg. After he died at the age of 66, Lucy, his widow, was forced to resort to selling some of Audubon's copper plates for scrap (the ones used to print his bird images), and she died poor.

Abraham Lincoln, sixteenth president of the United States (*Bankrupt, 1833*)

Since 1909, shoppers have been seeing President Lincoln's image on the U.S. penny—and probably never imagined that opening a shop once drove Abraham Lincoln himself into bankruptcy.

Before embarking on his political career, Lincoln and a partner bought a general store in New Salem, Illinois. Sales didn't go well, and when Lincoln's partner died, he became liable for $1,000 in back payments. After the sheriff seized Lincoln's last remaining assets, a horse and surveying gear, Lincoln declared bankruptcy in 1833—one year after opening the store.

USA TODAY Snapshots®

Abolishing the penny
Do you favor or oppose abolishing the penny?

Favor
24%

Oppose
56%

Not Sure
20%

Source:
Harris Interactive survey of 2,513 adults 18 and older.
Weighted to represent actual population.

By Jae Yang and Sam Ward, USA TODAY
2009

Honest Abe spent the next 17 years of his life paying off the debt he owed to friends and creditors. After suffering through further hard times as well as political defeats, Lincoln was elected president in 1860.

Ulysses S. Grant, eighteenth president of the United States and Civil War general (*Bankrupt, 1884*)

After retiring as president, Ulysses S. Grant had no income. He'd given up his military pension when he became president, but at the time, retired presidents didn't earn a pension. Grant decided to invest all his money in an investment banking partnership—which, wouldn't you know it, swindled Grant and the other investors of all of their money and went bankrupt. At the same time, Grant learned he had throat cancer.

To avoid leaving his family destitute, Grant hurriedly started working on his memoirs, which he managed to complete one week before he died. Although he died deep in debt, his writings eventually earned his wife and family hundreds of thousands of dollars.

Mark Twain, American writer and humorist (*Bankrupt, 1893*)

Mark Twain (born Samuel Clemens) is best known for his great American classics, *The Adventures of Huckleberry Finn* and *The Adventures of Tom Sawyer*. Throughout his lifetime, he earned a substantial amount of money through his prolific writing. But Twain had a weakness for inventions and risky business ventures, such as a new typesetting machine that was beautifully designed and engineered but quickly became obsolete. Twain invested $300,000 in the machine—equivalent to over $7 million today.

A friend eventually stepped in to help Twain sort out his finances, advising Twain to file for bankruptcy and transfer all his copyrights to his wife to protect his works from creditors. By following this advice, Twain recovered financially. He earned enough money touring and lecturing worldwide to finally pay off all his creditors, even though the bankruptcy laws didn't obligate him to do so.

The Lawyer Who Invented Copying

Snazzy inventions aren't just for science geeks and movies about time travel—they also changed the way that law offices did business in the twentieth century. The ballpoint pen made it easier to sign contracts, by eliminating attorney's fountain pens and inkwells. Post-Its made it possible to flag legal errors and provide handy "sign here" notes. Liquid Paper enabled secretaries to make corrections (instead of retyping whole briefs), the Rolodex simplified keeping client information, and, of course, Scotch tape enabled lawyers to tape together legal bills after clients ripped them to shreds.

But one invention—the Xerox 914—turned out to be the most profitable device to drop into the law office. And surprise, surprise, it was invented by an attorney.

Like many people who worked with legal documents, Chester Carlson was frustrated by inefficiency. Back in the early 1930s before he became a lawyer, Carlson worked in the patent department of Bell Laboratories. He quickly tired of copying patents using carbon paper. The reproductions were time-consuming and prone to errors. (For those too young to remember, copies used to be made by jamming sheets of carbon paper between sheets of paper, stuffing them into a typewriter, and typing firmly enough so that the carbon made imprints—then swearing up a storm if there was a typo.)

At about the same time, Carlson's hypercritical mother-in-law moved into his apartment. To avoid her unpleasant nightly tirades, Carlson enrolled in law school. While hand-copying passages from law books one night, Carlson again ran into the same frustration. Why wasn't there a simple method of reproducing copies on paper? Carlson began to pursue an obscure idea—a process that would fuse fine black powder to paper using electrostatic charges. Carlson originally called his process "electron photography," and then nicknamed it xerography (from the Greek words *xeros* (dry) and *graphein* (writing).

In 1937, by which time he was a patent attorney, Carlson perfected his theory and used his legal drafting skills to patent his revolutionary process. But he still had no actual proof that it worked. He offered his patent to IBM for a $10,000 advance and 5% royalty—in hindsight, one of the best offers of the twentieth century—but IBM passed. (Twenty years later, IBM still failed to see the potential when it reviewed the first Xerox copier and concluded that the device "has no future in the office copying market." *Ouch!*)

It wasn't until 1945 that Carlson partnered up with a nonprofit R&D firm in Ohio, which improved on the invention and licensed manufacturing rights to the Haloid Company, a tiny photographic paper manufacturer in Rochester, New York. Things dragged on until the mid-1950s when—just as Carlson's initial patents were expiring—the Haloid Company (now renamed Xerox) perfected Carlson's process and tested it in nearby offices. Xerox knew it had a hit when the testing companies asked to keep their demo machines.

The debut of the Xerox 914 was one of those rare moments in inventing history when a device transforms the environment in which it is placed. Xerox believed that businesses would use the 914 primarily to make duplicates of outgoing correspondence. They never imagined that employees—no longer encumbered by messy and time-consuming copies—would use it for internal document reproduction, such as memos, reports, newsletters, and even personal documents or their faces and other body parts. The result was an explosion of office and personal

USA TODAY Snapshots®

The world's inventors
U.S. patents for inventions granted in 2006:

36,807

Japan 10,005
Germany 6,360
Taiwan 5,908
South Korea 3,585
United Kingdom

Source: Census Bureau

By David Stuckey and Adrienne Lewis, USA TODAY
2008

copying. Within seven years of its introduction, Xerox was the 15th largest publicly owned company in the United States.

It's said that the business of law is really about selling paper to clients; and the Xerox machine put that principle into overdrive. The law firms devised a clever system of markups. Initially, they leased copiers and paid per copy, allowing them to mark up and pass along those charges to clients. But even after law firms began to own their photocopiers, they retained the per-copy charges for clients. A few cents per copy may not seem like much at first, but hey, what if everyone is suddenly buried in paper?

And buried they are. Consider, for example, when one business sues another. As a normal part of the pretrial discovery process, in which each side asks to see evidence held by the other, attorneys review the other side's relevant memos, phone records, financial records, and other documents. With piles more photocopied documents at each business, however, it creates an exponential increase in the size of discovery requests—literally boxes, and sometimes trucks of documents being sent back and forth. To deal with this paper explosion, law firms added more staff, thereby increasing the billing. In short, Xerox had created a cash machine for law firms.

The copier also triggered illegal activity (always a boon for lawyers). For example, there was office espionage, loss of trade secrets, and even fraud (for those who understood how to create fake photocopied documentation). The Xerox machine launched many copyright lawsuits: for example, a series of cases where authors and publishers protested the fact that people—students and teachers, in particular— were no longer buying their books and scholarly journals, but simply slapping a borrowed original onto a copy machine. Legislators took the device into consideration when creating the 1976 Copyright Act, by including provisions on academic photocopying. Although we now take the photocopier for granted, it was essentially the original VCR or Napster—a device that, for the first time, put infringement into the hands of ordinary Americans.

Carlson earned millions from Xerox, but never measured success by money. He had spent his childhood in poverty—during his last year in high school he lived in a converted chicken coop—and had a goal to rid himself of his wealth before he died. He spent his final years getting rid of his royalties via charitable contributions and pursuing spiritual goals. His process—which remains virtually unmodified from his 1937 patent—continues to supply copies to his legal brethren via photocopiers, laser printers, and fax machines.

Haunted History:
The Salem Witch Trials

If you've ever wondered why the term "witch hunt" has such a bad rap, look no further than the series of infamous trials that took place in Salem, Massachusetts, in the late 1600s. The Salem witch trials created a kind of "witch hysteria," resulting in 25 deaths, many imprisonments, and various tortuous punishments (dunking, anyone?).

To charge someone with witchcraft, didn't you have to believe in witches? Yes. And during the seventeenth century—a little over 200 years ago—almost everyone did. Witches, according to contemporary beliefs, were people who were in league with the Devil; and practicing the "devil's magic" was a capital offense.

The hysteria began with the seemingly inexplicable behavior of two young girls in Salem Village during the winter of 1692. Betty, the nine-year-old daughter of the village's minister, Reverend Samuel Parris, and her eleven-year-old cousin Abigail, started having fits. They contorted themselves into strange positions, cowered under chairs, threw things, and shouted strange words.

The town doctors, finding no natural explanation for the girls' behavior, logically concluded that the two were bewitched. Under the prodding of the Reverend Parris and others, the girls blamed three women for afflicting them. All were outcasts: Tituba, the Parris's Caribbean slave; Sarah Good, a disheveled beggar; and Sarah Osborne, an elderly impoverished woman.

Local magistrates interrogated the three women over several days. Osburn and Good claimed they were innocent. But, after being whipped by her master, Tituba "confessed," saying that "The Devil came to me and bid me serve him." She described frightening images of black dogs, red cats, yellow birds, and a "black man" who wanted her to sign the devil's book. She admitted that she signed the book and said there were other witches who wanted to do in the Puritans. All three women were thrown in jail.

Soon, hunting witches became a paranoid crusade. Over the next several months, dozens of people were accused, and the governor created a special court to try them. All twenty-six accused who went to trial before this court were convicted. Of these, 19 were hanged.

What kind of "trials" were these? They're not like you'd expect to see on "Court TV". For one thing, none of the accused was represented by a lawyer. Nor did they have much time to prepare their defense—many were tried the same day they were indicted.

Most damning, however, was that much of the evidence used against the accused was "spectral evidence"—testimony from the afflicted persons about their dreams and visions involving the alleged witches.

Other evidence included presence of "witch's teats" on the body of the accused—a mole or blemish insensitive to touch; discovery of which was considered certain evidence of witchcraft. In reality, the examiners used secretly dulled needles so the accused could not feel the prick of a pin.

One of the accused, an 80-year-old farmer named Giles Corey, refused to enter a plea and, therefore, could not legally stand trial. But this didn't dissuade his judges. They subjected him to an

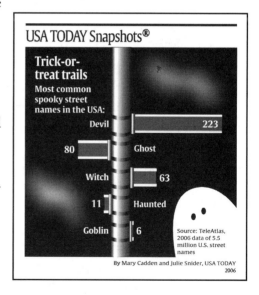

USA TODAY Snapshots®

Trick-or-treat trails

Most common spooky street names in the USA:

Devil — 223
Ghost — 80
Witch — 63
Haunted — 11
Goblin — 6

Source: TeleAtlas, 2006 data of 5.5 million U.S. street names

By Mary Cadden and Julie Snider, USA TODAY 2006

ancient form of torture in which heavy stone weights were placed upon his chest until he could no longer breathe. Amazingly, he survived for two days before dying.

Eventually, the governor's own wife was accused of witchcraft, which was too much for her husband. He prohibited further arrests, released many of the accused from jail, and dissolved the special court. The governor later pardoned all who were in prison on witchcraft charges. Unfortunately, by this time 19 people had been hanged and seven others had died in prison. Almost 200 people had been accused of practicing witchcraft.

In 1702, the witch trials were declared unlawful, and the accused later had their rights fully restored and were granted restitution. But it wasn't until 1957—more than 250 years later—that Massachusetts formally apologized for the events of 1692.

The Salem witch trials have long fascinated artists, historians, and tourists. Most famously, playwright Arthur Miller, in his 1953 play *The Crucible*, used the trials as an allegory for the McCarthy anticommunist paranoia during the 1950s. The trials have also been the subject of at least four films. They've even found their way into popular music— for example, the song "The Eye" from the heavy metal singer King Diamond is about the Salem witch trials.

In 1992, the 300th anniversary of the trials, the Witch Trials Memorial was dedicated in Salem by Nobel Laureate Elie Wiesel. The original court documents can be found in the Peabody Essex Museum, also in Salem.

Most people don't believe in witches anymore. So, what really caused the hysteria, fits, and other strange behavior back in 1692? One widely known theory is that it was all due to a fungus called ergot that's found in rye bread made from infected grain. Eating this fungus, which is the substance from which LSD is derived, can lead to muscle spasms, vomiting, delusions, and hallucinations. Rye bread was a staple food in Salem Village. Other theories implicate Lyme disease, encephalitis, and even post-traumatic stress disorder (several of the afflicted had been victims of Indian attacks).

However, many historians reject such scientific explanations and instead focus on psychological factors such as the accusers' desire for attention; spite; and jealousy. Some of the accusers may have also had an economic incentive. Most of the accused witches were unmarried or recently widowed land-owning women. According to the law in effect at the time, upon their death their land would go to the previous owner or, if none could be found, to the state. This made witch hunting a way to obtain valuable real estate.

Would the Law Protect You From Buying a Haunted House?

"Honey, what was that noise?"

Nearly every new homeowner spends a sleepless first night or two, wondering where those bumps, creaks, and howls are coming from. Usually the source is no more sinister than the plumbing or the neighbor's cat. But what if the noises were really supernatural? What if the new home you bought was haunted?

Apparently that's the situation in which Jeffrey Stambovsky found himself in 1990 when he purchased a turreted turn-of-the-century Victorian in Nyack, New York. Being from New York City, Stambovsky wasn't familiar with local legends, and the seller hadn't disclosed to him that the lovely riverfront home came with its own family of Caspers. According to reports regarding the previous owner, Mrs. Helen Ackley:

- The ghosts periodically left gifts of baby rings for the owner's grandchildren (and then took them back).

- One ghost woke the owner's daughter every morning by shaking her bed (until the girl loudly informed the poltergeists that she wanted to sleep in because it was spring break).

- While she was painting the home, Mrs. Ackley (according to what she told *The New York Times*) saw a ghost, sitting in midair, rocking and back forth. "I was on an 8-foot stepladder. I asked if he approved of what we were doing to the house, if the colors were to his liking. He smiled and he nodded his head."

- Another ghost was a Navy lieutenant during the American Revolution who confronted the owner's son "eyeball to eyeball outside the basement door."

Once Stambovsky learned that he'd be sharing his home with the cast of *Poltergeist*, he wanted out of the purchase contract. Rather than bring in the exorcist—apparently New York eviction procedures did not apply to apparitions—he took the seller and real estate agent to court claiming fraudulent misrepresentation. The lower court was not sympathetic and ruled that the seller and agent had no obligation to disclose ghostly presences. In other words, whether you had Banquo or Beetlejuice down in the basement, you didn't have to tell a buyer.

Stambovsky appealed the case in 1991 and got some sympathy from a New York Appellate Court that made the astonishing ruling that the house *was* haunted:

"Whether the source of the spectral apparitions seen by defendant seller are parapsychic or psychogenic, having reported their presence in both a national publication (*Readers' Digest*) and the local press (in 1977 and 1982, respectively), defendant is estopped to deny their existence and, as a matter of law, the house is haunted."

Apparently the seller had sold her story to the *Readers' Digest* for $3,000 and made a "verified" claim to the magazine that the house was haunted. As one contract lawyer pointed out, "If the seller now claimed in the litigation that the house wasn't haunted, the seller would have been caught in a $3,000 lie to *Readers' Digest*."

Having reached the conclusion that the house was haunted, the court asked what a buyer in Stambovsky's position was supposed to do:

"Applying the strict rule of caveat emptor to a contract involving a house possessed by poltergeists conjures up visions of a psychic or medium routinely accompanying the structural engineer and Terminix man on an inspection of every home subject to a contract of sale. It portends that the prudent attorney will establish an escrow account lest the subject of the transaction come back to haunt him and his client— or pray that his malpractice insurance coverage extends to supernatural disasters. In the interest of avoiding such untenable consequences, the notion that a haunting is a condition which can and should be ascertained upon reasonable inspection of the premises is a hobgoblin which should be exorcised from the body of legal precedent and laid quietly to rest."

The conclusion reached by the court—using no less than three references to the *Ghost Busters* song—was that when a seller creates a condition that materially impairs the value of the home (in this case, publicizing its ghost-iness), and that condition is unlikely to be discovered by a prudent buyer, the nondisclosure (or concealment) of that condition gives the buyer a basis to get out of (rescind) the contract.

In short, Stambovsky was allowed to back out of the $650,000 purchase. But don't feel bad for the sellers. Once word got out that the house was legally haunted, a new group of buyers were attracted to the property, including the well-known mentalist, The Amazing Kreskin.

So what's the rule for sellers? Do you have to tell people your belief that your house is haunted? Not exactly. It's true that nearly every U.S. state has passed laws to protect homebuyers from any sneaky sellers who might try to cover up a house's problems. These laws mostly require sellers to fill out a disclosure form, telling buyers about any material problems with the house. Some of these forms require disclosure of murders, suicides, and other deaths that took place on the property.

USA TODAY Snapshots®

Haunted houses, anyone?
In the USA, 37.2% agree or strongly agree that places can be haunted. By gender:

Male 32.2%

Female 45.5%

Source: The Baylor Religion Survey, a mailed survey of 1,721 Americans statistically representing a sampling of the USA by age, gender and race conducted in fall 2005 by the Gallup Organization; margin of error is ±4 percentage points.

By Tracey Wong Briggs and Alejandro Gonzalez, USA TODAY 2006

But don't expect to see a "haunted" box on any state's disclosure form. (That might be a hard one for any legislator to suggest with a straight face.) A few states have come bravely close, such as Minnesota, which requires sellers to disclose whether the home has been the site of any "perceived paranormal activity." (Minnesota Statutes § 513.56.)

Nevertheless, any honest seller who has observed certain, uh, oddities—such as plates flying around the kitchen or a bloodstain that reappears nightly on the back bedroom wall—should mention these to buyers. (Look for an "Other" box on the disclosure form.) No need to draw any conclusions; just state the facts, if they rise to the level of a material problem. In the meantime, you'd best keep those ghostly observations to yourself and avoid selling your tale to *Readers' Digest* or reality TV.

Ooh, You Could've Bought Madoff's Rolex!

L ike to bargain shop? Not getting the old buzz of excitement from discount malls and garage sales?

Maybe it's time to try a sheriff's auction: a sale of goods or property forfeited after a crime or nonpayment of debt, with proceeds in some cases going toward victim restitution.

Prices are cheap, and you never know what you'll find; household goods, jewelry, farm animals, exotic animals, and lots of cars. (You really never know what you'll find inside those cars: One buyer encountered a stash of marijuana, while another found a woman's body in the trunk. Aren't the police supposed to check for such things beforehand?)

Here are some items—whole houses, in some cases—that you could have snapped up for a song at past sales. To find future auctions, check the headlines or sheriff's office websites.

O.J. Simpson football memorabilia, 2009

Footballs, jerseys, and other memorabilia belonging to NFL great and convicted felon O.J. Simpson were among the items collected as evidence in the former NFL star's trial for armed robbery and kidnapping in Las Vegas.

Was he still carrying this stuff around? Not exactly: His conviction was actually for robbing the memorabilia, which was once his own, from two dealers he confronted at gunpoint in a hotel room.

The memorabilia were put up for auction by the L.A. County Sheriff's Office to satisfy part of Simpson's yet-unpaid $33.5 million civil judgment in the deaths of his exwife, Nicole Brown Simpson and Ronald Goldman.

Nicolas Cage's haunted mansion in New Orleans, 2009

No, Nick didn't get himself in trouble with the law—but he did get very behind financially, leading him to sue his former business manager and to the sale at foreclosure of two of his (many) homes around the world.

One, the LaLaurie Mansion in New Orleans' Garden District, was said by Cage to be one of the most haunted houses in the United States. Its one-time owners, Dr. Louis Lalaurie and his wife, Delphine, had a glittering social life but a horrific private world, keeping slaves in their attic in chains, and once chasing a girl with a whip to the roof of the house, where she jumped to her death. They're said to have buried her body in the back yard.

We're not sure if this lurid history drove the property's value up or down, but the auction ended with the bank buying the mansion and Cage's other New Orleans house (in the French Quarter) for a mere $4.5 million—two thirds their appraised value.

Bernard Madoff's Rolex, 2009

Victims of Madoff's investment Ponzi scheme, awaiting restitution, at least knew that shoppers at the New York auction didn't lack for choices: No fewer than 200 of Bernard and Ruth Madoff's possessions were on the block.

For the low-budget souvenir shoppers, there was a half-used office sticky pad, pens, stationery, and decoy ducks.

Moving on up, one could have bid on dishes, boogie boards emblazoned with Madoff's name, a blue satin N.Y. Mets baseball jacket with "Madoff" stitched on the back, a water-rescue ring buoy painted with "Bullship N.Y.," diamond and other jewelry, and—most valuable of all—a Rolex nicknamed the "Prisoner Watch."

Something for everyone! Auctioneers were disappointed, however, that the Rolex brought in only $65,000—at least $10,000 shy of the anticipated price.

A Cuban airplane, 2002

What were they supposed to do with a plane that was commandeered by Cuban migrants and flown across the straits to Florida? It was just taking up space at Key West International Airport....

Al Capone's former Wisconsin hideout, 2009

Yes, you read that right. This sheriff's sale of legendary gangster Al Capone's house just happened in 2009. But financial trouble had hit the current owners, who'd attempted to turn the place, with its machine-gun guard towers and 18-inch stone walls on 407 acres of wooded land, into a restaurant and tourist destination.

USA TODAY Snapshots®

Splurge?
How much money would you need to spend on yourself for it to be considered a splurge?

$0-$49   41%
$50-$99   32%
$100-$249   19%
$250-$499   5%
$500+   3%

Source: Shortcuts.com/AllYou.com survey of 5,250 women and 627 men by DMS Research conducted online June 12-22

By Michelle Healy and Keith Simmons, USA TODAY
2009

Capone reportedly bought the land during the Prohibition era of the late 1920s. He's said to have flown bootleg alcohol in on planes, then loaded it onto trucks bound for Chicago. Despite being suspected of many murders, the law didn't catch up with Capone until 1931, when he went to prison for tax evasion.

High Fences Make Spiteful Neighbors

B ack when people lived in caves, those who got angry at their neighbors probably built a high pile of rocks.

Today, with the advance of civilization, we don't do that. Instead, we build a high fence, a so-called "spite fence."

Spite fences are now illegal in most areas (and height limits on fences have also become common), but that didn't stop the sky-high neighbor disputes below.

The Crocker fence: *San Francisco, California*

Back in 1875, Charles Crocker, a railroad millionaire, moved to San Francisco and built a mansion on Nob Hill. The area had an expansive view of the Golden Gate Bridge and the surrounding bay. Apparently to impress others, Crocker planned to buy all the surrounding lots on the block to give his house a stunning stage.

Just one thing stood in his way: a small cottage owned by German undertaker Nicolas Yung. Depending on whom you read, Yung either refused to sell or kept upping the price to levels that Crocker considered unreasonable.

Crocker's response was to build a 40-foot, three-sided fence that towered over Yung's cottage, shutting out light and air.

At this point, you might have expected Mr. Yung to sue. But no, he had a more creative approach. He's said to have mounted a coffin on top of his house, facing Crocker's property, as if to curse him.

Crocker still wouldn't take the fence down. It stayed there for years—becoming a tourist attraction—until Yung's death. Crocker then bought the property and leveled it.

But perhaps the coffin had cursed Crocker after all: The Crocker Mansion burned to the ground during the 1906 San Francisco earthquake.

Forty-foot high fence—and growing! *Charlestown, Rhode Island*

Annoyed at his neighbor's opposition to his plans to build a home addition, Mr. Bloomquist planted four 40-foot Western Arborvitae trees on his side of the line separating their properties—thus blocking the neighbor's ocean view. When she sued, the court was forced to confront the highly complex question: Can trees constitute a fence? (This is what three tough years of law school trains people for, folks.) The answer: Yes. The court ordered Bloomquist to either remove the trees or keep them cut back to six feet high. (Poor trees.)

Chain-link spite fence: *Worcester, Massachusetts*

Here's a man who was willing to go to jail over his spite fence: Mr. Gencarelli reportedly bought plots of land and a house on Holden Street in Worcester. He proceeded to fill in wetlands on the property (triggering arguments with the neighbors), dump old cars there, sue neighbors over shrubs that were growing on his side of the boundary line, let the house decay until it was condemned, then decide he needed a chain-link fence to protect his little slice of Eden.

Next, he violated the city permit regarding the height and location of his fence, and ignored the subsequent court order to lower and move it. This finally led to two contempt of court convictions, a two-night stay in jail for the 77-year-old man, and an order to pay $35,000 so that the city could remove the fence. Restoring neighborly relations may take a little more work.

The "Redneck Stonehenge" car fence: *Hooper, Utah*

Utah farmer Rhett Davis actually offered to build a fence after neighbors who'd recently moved into nearby homes complained about the flies and dust. But the neighbors rejected that idea, because it would have blocked their pastoral view of horses and fields.

So Davis built what he calls a "humor fence," made of three cars salvaged from a demolition derby, stuffed into the ground nose first. He said it was a way to remind new neighbors that they've moved into an existing farming community. When last heard from, Davis and the neighbors were talking things out....

How about a spite house? *Boston, Massachusetts*

The "Skinny House," built over a century ago along the Freedom Trail on Hull Street in Boston, is just over ten feet wide and 30 feet deep— the thinnest house in Boston. Why build a house so thin that it must be entered from the side alley? Reportedly out of spite, to block a neighbor's view. But unfortunately no one sued, which would have been handy for giving us some written records on the matter.

And now, a word from a judge

The case under consideration by New York judge Daniel E. Fitzpatrick in 1971 wasn't itself all that interesting, but that didn't stop him from waxing poetic, rhapsodic, and downright dramatic on the matter of spite fences:

"[T]here is nothing more disturbing to a city dweller than having his neighbor erect a fence along the common lot-line. It is the equivalent to waving the proverbial flag at a bull and goading the daemon of rage into a seething frenzy. The trauma at first sight of the divisive wall gives rise to shrieks of unspeakable anguish and inflicts a psychic wound like that of a Spartan lance thrust firmly home in one's vitals. Fortunately, the insult to the ego while sometimes critical is seldom fatal. Once the initial shock has abated, several alternatives present themselves to the offended neighbor: the use of explosives to blow up the obtrusive structure; this is abandoned as having hazardous as well as undesirable New Left implications; set fire to it; but there are the laws against arson; with wire cutter and Stilson-wrench dismantle it; throw the pieces triumphantly onto the offending neighbor's property. Poetic Justice. Perhaps, but there are also laws against the malicious destruction of property to be considered. Such precipitate indulgence in self-help may also defeat any available legal or equitable remedy.

Calmer thoughts and the cooling winds of time convince that seeking out legal counsel is the best and wisest course. This brings on the petition in equity to remove the offending encumbrance by injunction, what common parlance with unerring accuracy calls 'an action to remove a spite fence.' It has always seemed to the court that the common tongue has a flair for intrinsic preciseness when it comes to inventing names for someone

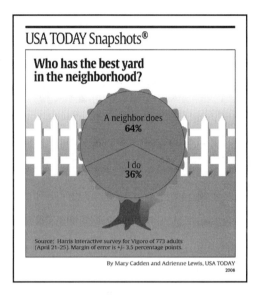

USA TODAY Snapshots®

Who has the best yard in the neighborhood?

A neighbor does
64%

I do
36%

Source: Harris Interactive survey for Vigoro of 773 adults (April 21-25). Margin of error is +/- 3.5 percentage points.

By Mary Cadden and Adrienne Lewis, USA TODAY
2008

or something. One might call it an 'offensive fence,' or a 'revenge fence,' or a 'nuisance fence'! These somehow are all flat and anaemic. What a world of hate, malice, and ill will is contained in that one word 'spite.' The last ounce of neighborliness has been squeezed out. The word has the ugly keen edge of the executioner's axe and nothing else can fill its place, so a 'spite fence' it is."

(*Kuczek v. Arpino*, 65 Misc.2d 935, 319 N.Y.S.2d 253, N.Y.Sup. (1971).)

Nuff said?

A DUI for Driving a *What*?!

No matter the law, there's always someone who thinks it doesn't apply to him or her—or who tries to wiggle out after getting caught, with an argument like, "How could I have been driving drunk, when I wasn't in a car, I was in a ... ?"

Maybe that's what the folks below were thinking when they chose to drive some rather nontraditional vehicles while under the influence of alcohol or drugs. Or maybe they weren't thinking at all.

Golf cart

Picture this scene: A woman named Tiffany holds a drink in her hand while trying to drive a golf cart around her Kentucky subdivision. A mixed drink, no less. After Tiffany admits to police that she's been consuming alcohol, another DUI conviction hits the books.

Motorized lounge chair

You've got to give credit to the 62-year-old Minnesota man who outfitted his lounge chair with a converted lawnmower motor, a radio, front and rear lights, and (what vehicle would be complete without it) a cup holder. Unfortunately, during the man's visit to a bar in the northern Minnesota town of Proctor, those cup holders saw no fewer than eight or nine beers—he seems to have lost count. After he crashed into a parked vehicle and was arrested, he pled guilty to drunk driving and forfeited the chair in order to avoid jail time.

But that's not the end of the story. The Proctor police now had a motorized chair to get rid of. So, they did what anyone else would probably do: put it up for sale on eBay. They called it a "La-Z-Boy," as the press had, until the La-Z-Boy folks themselves complained that this chair wasn't the real thing, and the listing had to be amended. Last we heard, the bidding was getting hot—right up into the $40,000 territory—until the demotion from La-Z-Boy status punched a hole in it.

All-terrain vehicle

A certain Arkansas man will think twice before he gets drunk and drives his 250 cc Suzuki three-wheeler in his and his adjoining neighbors' yards again anytime soon. Or ever.

A neighbor called police. The man got sentenced to 365 days in jail with all but sixty days suspended. Plus, he had his driver's license revoked for two years and was required to pay a $900 fine as well as court costs of $332.25. What's more, he was ordered to attend an inpatient alcohol treatment program of at least 28 days. And he must have spent some more money appealing this one all the way to the Arkansas Supreme Court, all to no avail.

Maybe a backyard trampoline would be a better idea.

Stand-up scooter

What's a stand-up scooter, you ask? Apparently (according to trial records), it's like a "skateboard with handlebars on the front," powered by an electric motor. In this North Carolina DUI case, a 20-year-old defendant and his buddy were driving their little scooters at a modest ten miles per hour. A police officer stopped them after watching them weave erratically and run a stop sign.

The defendant cried constitutional foul to an appeals court, claiming that North Carolina law wasn't clear on the meaning of "vehicle." He was basically told, "Tough luck."

Snowmobile

From Alaska to Connecticut to Minnesota, people have been convicted of DUIs while driving snowmobiles. At least no such cases have been reported in Florida. Or Texas.

Honda minibike

A Missouri man caught drunkenly driving his minibike probably thought he had a good shot at avoiding punishment. After all, Missouri law generally says that "motorized bicycles" aren't "vehicles." But no dice: The appeals court judges drew on the lofty words of a New Jersey court: "Although an intoxicated [motorized bicycle] driver may not have the same offensive striking power as does the intoxicated driver of the standard motor vehicle, the intoxicated [motorized bicycle] driver is a terribly serious danger to himself, to pedestrians and other cyclists."

USA TODAY Snapshots

Drinking five or more drinks in a day
Percentage of adults 18 and older who had five or more drinks in one day at least once in the past year:

21.4% (1997)
19.4% (2003)

Note: The 2003 figure is based on data covering January to September.
Source: National Center for Health Statistics

By Shannon Reilly and Julie Snider, USA TODAY 2004

Farm tractor

DUI charges against people driving tractors actually come along fairly regularly. We'll stay away from speculation as to the reasons.

In New Jersey, for example, a man was found guilty of a DUI after drunkenly driving a tractor on his own land. The police officer noticed that the man not only smelled of alcohol and had trouble getting off the tractor, but when instructed to stand on one leg, hopped around in a circle.

In Tennessee, a man driving his John Deere tractor at around 20 mph on the highway after picking up a six-pack at a convenience store attracted more attention than he anticipated when an off-duty police officer slammed into him from behind. Unfortunately, the officer was killed, so vehicular homicide got added to the man's DUI conviction.

Tricycle

Now we move to Pennsylvania, where a man was pedaling a tricycle when he smashed into the rear of a car. He was found to have a .142% blood alcohol content—nearly enough to render a first-time drinker unconscious. Yes, said the court (wearily, we imagine), a tricycle can be a "vehicle."

Motorized bar stool

This one has to take the cake: A 28-year-old Ohio man took a bar stool (chrome and red leather) and combined it with parts from a lawn mower to create his own, unique, motorized bar stool. We guess the idea was that he could leave his house and belly up to the bar without dealing with inconveniences like parking or finding an open seat.

After imbibing 15 beers, however, he crashed on the way home, and police charged him with a DUI.

Stationary bike at the gym

Okay, maybe this one takes the cake. (It doesn't matter, we don't really have a cake.)

After a call from the managers of a Tennessee gym saying one of its members reeked of alcohol and was having trouble pedaling a stationary bicycle, police arrested the woman for driving drunk. We wish we knew the end of that story, but it never got as far as any written court records.

Taking the Fifth: How "Funny Girl" Helped Popularize the Most Famous One-Liner in Criminal Law

Americans are so used to hearing of famous crooks "taking the Fifth," we tend to think that the magic words, "I decline to answer on the grounds that it may tend to incriminate me" have been used consistently since the Fifth Amendment was adopted back in 1791.

Not so. Although the principle against self-incrimination was tossed around before 1920 and was the subject of a few Supreme Court cases, the public really didn't become aware of it until 1920. That's when a con man and sometime gangster named Nicky Arnstein popularized it in a case that caused a media frenzy.

It all started in 1918, when a series of Wall Street robberies netted thieves $5 million in Liberty bonds. Some of the thefts had been prearranged with the couriers, and when police intervened, one of the crooks fingered a "Mr. Arnold."

Police were excited. They believed that they were on the way to nabbing Arnold Rothstein, the man credited with bankrolling organized crime and fixing the 1919 World Series. But when the turncoat courier looked at mugshots, it turned out the man he was really "singing" about was an associate of Rothstein's, Nicky Arnstein (who used the alias "Nicky Arnold"). Arnstein, a con man and gambler, was best known as the husband of Broadway star Fanny Brice (the inspiration for the movie *Funny Girl*).

Police proceeded to Ms. Brice's home and informed the singer that her husband was the brains behind "the Liberty Bond robberies." Concerned that the police would confiscate her valuables, Ms. Brice's close friend Hannah Ryan hid Brice's jewels in baby Frances's diaper. As police tore apart the apartment looking for evidence, Fannie brazenly stood by her man. (Brice later popularized the song "My Man" as an ode to Arnstein.) Meanwhile, Arnstein had disappeared, apparently last seen at Penn Station.

A few days later, attorney William Fallon got a mysterious phone call asking if Fallon wanted to take a case for a lot of money. What followed was a series of secret meetings in Pennsylvania and Chicago, in which the fugitive Arnstein engaged Fallon's services.

Arnstein's choice of Fallon was a no-brainer. Fallon was a brilliant orator with a quick wit and an apparently photographic memory. During the nine years he was in private practice, he didn't lose a single one of the 120 homicide cases he defended. Equally important, Fallon had represented several gangland legends, including Arnold Rothstein himself. Fallon's wisecracking demeanor and confident well-coiffed appearance—he reportedly would wear a shirt only once before discarding it in favor of a new one—became the model for the hundreds of media-savvy attorneys who followed. He earned many nicknames, including "Jail-Robber," "Eleven-to-One Fallon" (for his ability to get hung juries), and "The Great Mouthpiece," the moniker that became the title of his 1931 biography.

Over the next six months, Fallon—funded by Fanny Brice's payment of his fees—negotiated Arnstein's return to New York. On the day of his big comeback, Arnstein reportedly arrived in Fannie's Cadillac. (In an odd side note, the car had been stolen while the arraignment took place. But Fallon called his buddy Arnold Rothstein, who spread the word in the underworld; Brice had the car back within the hour.)

Most legal observers believed that Nicky Arnstein was actually taking the fall for Rothstein in the bond robberies. Even Fanny Brice acknowledged as much to the press, saying, "Nicky couldn't mastermind an electric bulb into a socket." Despite the suave portrayal of Brice's husband by Omar Sharif in the film *Funny Girl*, Nicky Arnstein was a low-level crook with friends in high—or high-rolling—places.

Rothstein's friendship extended to fronting Nicky's $60,000 bail (reportedly paid with Liberty bonds).

Back in New York, Arnstein had to face examination by a U.S. bankruptcy judge. The questions became more and more troublesome. Finally, Fallon instructed Arnstein not to answer 447 of the questions and to instead say: "I refuse to answer on the ground that to do so might tend to incriminate or degrade me."

The bankruptcy judge was unwilling to acknowledge the invocation. He maintained that since Arnstein was now bankrupt, he'd forfeited his right to invoke the Fifth. When Arnstein doggedly repeated his new mantra, the court committed him to jail for contempt. Fallon prepared a writ of habeas corpus—a request to free an unlawfully detained person—but ran into another problem. No federal judge in Manhattan would sign it. Fallon had no choice but to take the appeal directly to the U.S. Supreme Court.

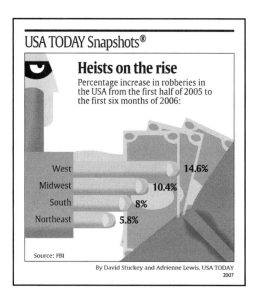

USA TODAY Snapshots®

Heists on the rise

Percentage increase in robberies in the USA from the first half of 2005 to the first six months of 2006:

West 14.6%
Midwest 10.4%
South 8%
Northeast 5.8%

Source: FBI

By David Stuckey and Adrienne Lewis, USA TODAY 2007

Fallon and Arnstein proceeded to Washington for a week of legal wrangling at the U.S. Supreme Court. The lawyer and his client turned their Washington sojourn into a series of wine-fueled, girl-crazy all-night parties, described by Fallon's biographer as a "Dionysian festival." The night before his court appearance, Fallon became obsessed with an actress he'd seen at a DC theater named Gertrude Vanderbilt. Inebriated and hopelessly in love, he begged Vanderbilt to attend the Supreme Court hearings the next day. She declined, but to Fallon's joy (and amazement) her chauffeur delivered her to the Supreme Court steps in time for Fallon's argument.

Despite having been in a pickled state the night before, Fallon proceeded brilliantly. (Fallon's love of firewater apparently had no effect on his skills. Once, a judge asked him if he smelled liquor on Fallon's breath. Fallon replied, "If Your Honor's sense of justice is as keen as your sense of smell, then my client need have no fear in this court.")

Later, Supreme Court Justice James Clark McReynolds read his findings in *Arndstein v. McCarthy* 254 U.S. 71 (1920) (Nicky's real name had a "d" in it). The Supremes ordered the U.S. District Court in Manhattan to issue the writ of habeas corpus and also ruled that a defendant has the right to assert the Fifth Amendment at any stage in the proceedings.

This ruling—though it focused primarily on Arnstein's bankruptcy status—was influential. The widespread coverage of the case—Brice was a big radio and Broadway star and the papers gobbled up any news about her husband's shenanigans—popularized the tactic for defendants. Soon after, "taking the Fifth," became standard operating procedure for high- and low-level criminal defendants. Enron President Kenneth Lay, for example, invoked it eight decades later when he testified to Congress.

Despite Fallon's brilliant new tactic, it didn't save Nicky Arnstein from spending a year and a half in Leavenworth prison. The lower court in New York still had to wrap up the Liberty Bond case, and by that time, Fallon was no longer by Arnstein's side. They'd argued about Fallon's girlfriend (Gertrude) and about his drinking. Maybe Fallon should have listened; he died in 1927 of alcohol-related causes.

Do You Know Enough About Law to Pass the U.S. Citizenship Test?

D o you know the first three words of the Constitution? Do you know how many Constitutional amendments there are? Can you name your U.S. representative? For some folks, knowing the answers to questions like these means the difference between becoming a U.S. citizen or remaining an immigrant (with a green card). That's because before applying for U.S. citizenship, immigrants to the United States must (among other things) pass an exam with 100 possible questions testing their knowledge of U.S. history and government.

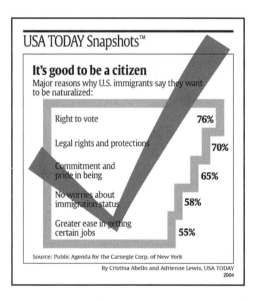

USA TODAY Snapshots™

It's good to be a citizen
Major reasons why U.S. immigrants say they want to be naturalized:

Right to vote	76%
Legal rights and protections	70%
Commitment and pride in being	65%
No worries about immigration status	58%
Greater ease in getting certain jobs	55%

Source: Public Agenda for the Carnegie Corp. of New York

By Cristina Abello and Adrienne Lewis, USA TODAY
2004

The funny thing is, many natural-born U.S. citizens freely admit to having no idea how to answer these questions—especially the 31 particularly challenging ones concerning the United States legislative and court systems and Constitutional law. What if retaining your citizenship meant you had to answer those 31 challenging queries correctly? How well would you do?

Oh, and by the way, it's not multiple-choice. So picture yourself having to come up with the answers in front of a stern immigration official. Good luck! You'll find the answers at the bottom.

Questions

1. What is the supreme law of the land?
2. What does the Constitution do?
3. The idea of self-government is in the first three words of the Constitution. What are these words?
4. What is an amendment?
5. What do we call the first ten amendments to the Constitution?
6. What is one right or freedom from the First Amendment?
7. How many amendments does the Constitution have?
8. What is freedom of religion?
9. What is the "rule of law"?
10. Name one branch or part of the government.
11. Who makes federal laws?
12. What are the two parts of the U.S. Congress?
13. How many U.S. senators are there?
14. We elect a U.S. senator for how many years?
15. Who is one of your state's U.S. senators now?
16. The House of Representatives has how many voting members?
17. We elect a U.S. representative for how many years?
18. Name your U.S. representative.
19. Who does a U.S. senator represent?
20. Who signs bills to become laws?
21. Who vetoes bills?
22. What does the judicial branch do?
23. What is the highest court in the United States?
24. How many justices are on the Supreme Court?
25. Who is the chief justice of the United States now?
26. What is one responsibility that is only for United States citizens?
27. Name one right only for United States citizens.

28. What are two rights of everyone living in the United States?

29. What is one promise you make when you become a United States citizen?

30. What happened at the Constitutional Convention?

31. When was the Constitution written?

32. The Federalist Papers supported the passage of the U.S. Constitution. Name one of the writers.

Answers

1. The Constitution

2. Sets up the government, defines the government, protects basic rights of Americans

3. We the People

4. A change (to the Constitution), an addition (to the Constitution)

5. The Bill of Rights

6. Speech, religion, assembly, press, petition the government

7. Twenty-seven

8. You can practice any religion or not practice a religion.

9. Everyone must follow the law. Leaders must obey the law. Government must obey the law. No one is above the law.

10. Congress, legislative; president, executive; the courts, judicial

11. Congress, Senate and House (of Representatives), (U.S. or national) legislature

12. The Senate and House (of Representatives)

13. One hundred

14. Six

15. [Depends on where you live]

16. 435

17. Two

18. [Depends on where you live]

19. All people of the state

20. The president

21. The president

22. Reviews laws, explains laws, resolves disputes (disagreements), decides if a law goes against the Constitution

23. The Supreme Court

24. Nine

25. John Roberts (John G. Roberts, Jr.)

26. Serve on a jury, vote in a federal election

27. Vote in a federal election, run for federal office

28. Freedom of expression, freedom of speech, freedom of assembly, freedom to petition the government, freedom of worship, the right to bear arms

29. Give up loyalty to other countries, defend the Constitution and laws of the United States, obey the laws of the United States, serve in the U.S. military (if needed), serve (do important work for) the nation (if needed), be loyal to the United States

30. The Constitution was written. The Founding Fathers wrote the Constitution.

31. 1787

32. (James) Madison, (Alexander) Hamilton, (John) Jay, Publius

Toupee or Not Toupee? All About British Barristers' Wigs

Some fashions are just too good to go out of style. Like the lovely black dresses—er, robes—worn by judges in the United States. But it's the members of the British legal establishment who can really strike a pose on the court catwalk. They've got wigs!

Who has to wear the wigs?

By tradition, British judges and barristers (trial court lawyers) wear wigs while in court or when carrying out related functions. No law actually requires it of them—wearing a dusty, unwashed old wig is considered a special privilege. In fact, British solicitors (lawyers who prepare legal documents and don't ordinarily appear in court) recently won the right to wear wigs, too.

Do the wigs come in different styles?

Yes, but it's all according to rank. (Guess where the word "bigwig" came from?) At the top of the legal pecking order are Queens Counsel (leading counsel), judges, and members of the House of Lords. On ceremonial occasions, they're entitled to wear a full-bottomed or "spaniel" wig (also called a peruke). It features thick curls that cover the ears and drop down to the shoulders.

On regular court days, judges wear smaller "bobwigs," identifiable by their frizzed sides rather than curls and a small, looped tail (queue) hanging down the back. Counsel wear "tiewigs," covering about half their head. These are fuzzy on top, with rows of curls along the side and back, and also a little tail or queue.

When did this wig-wearing thing begin?

In the mid 1600s, wearing fanciful, powdered wigs became all the rage among everyone in France and England who could afford them.

But the history of lawyers and judges wearing something on their head dates much further back. In medieval days, members of the legal profession wore coifs, which were pieces of white linen apparently first designed to cover the bald-topped tonsure of monks acting in a legal role. With the inevitable evolution of fashion, they began wearing round black skullcaps over the coifs, and then cornered hats over the skullcaps (going for the layered look, we presume).

Everyone else has stopped wearing wigs—so?

Ordinary people have long stopped wearing wigs of this style. Household servants have stopped wearing them, despite an elaborate hierarchy of traditional wigs. Even bishops of the Church of England, whom you might expect to hew to tradition longer than others, ceased to wear their traditional wigs around 1840. So, what's up with the legal profession? Actually, in 1992, there was great debate about potentially abolishing the wearing of court wigs. But nothing came of it.

One of the winning arguments seems to have been that wearing wigs and robes emphasizes the dignity and solemnity of legal proceedings. In vain, opponents argued that there's not much dignity to be had in wearing an anachronistic pile of horsehair on one's head. Another argument was that the wigs are useful in disguising the judges, therefore making it harder for criminals to come after them for revenge. Antiwiggites pointed out that the wigs don't really cover a lot of territory—you can still see the judges' faces and know their names.

What are the wigs made of?

Horsehair. Early on, it was black horsehair, which required regular attention, including curling, frizzing, and dressing with powder and a messy, scented ointment called pomatum.

Then, Humphrey Ravenscroft invented a more manageable wig made of grayish-white horsehair and requiring no curling, powdering, or pomading. In light of its relatively sterile qualities, he dubbed it the "forensic wig." The same style is worn today—and still sold by his company, Ede and Ravenscroft. (Why should we be surprised to discover that it has a website? It's www.edeandravenscroft.co.uk.)

Can you wash the wig?

Uh, no. When the wig is first made, it's boiled and then dried to keep its shape. After that, a lawyer is expected to wear it, without washing, for life. If another lawyer is lucky enough to inherit or buy a dead lawyer's wig, he or she can expect it to last for life, as well. But many have noted that the wigs start to yellow and smell bad with the passage of time. After two generations, it's probably time for the wig to retire.

Are the wigs expensive?

Hell, yes. Depending on style, they run anywhere from the equivalent of $800 to $4,000. Judges receive a stipend with which to purchase their wigs and other court attire, but barristers are on their own. Some say they've had to take out bank loans for this purpose. Fortunately, they can also rent (or "hire") a wig when needed.

Is there any way to buy a cheaper one?

You can buy one used. There's even said to be a black market in stolen barrister's wigs.

Do women wear the same style wigs as men?

Yes, they're just the same. One can choose from ten standard sizes, or order a custom-sized one.

Have fetishes developed around these wigs?

Good heavens, how would we know? But it is rather suggestive that in 2000, British fashion designer John Galliano produced a collection reportedly inspired by Freudian psychology, which included such items as surgical corsets, lace-up bondage boots, military uniforms over lace underwear, and a woman dressed as a "kinky barrister" in a corset and satin gown with a gold-thread noose, stiletto-heeled ballet boots in purple python skin, and a barrister's wig.

Worst Excuses Ever for Committing a Crime

"But Officer, I was just...."

Alright, let's hear 'em: Here are some of the worst excuses ever given for committing a crime. Some display a certain creativity, while others are just plain pathetic. All failed, proving once again that honesty is the best policy. The moral: If you can't tell the police the truth, keep your mouth shut.

My cat did it

A Florida man was arrested after police discovered over 1,000 images of child pornography on his computer. His excuse: His cat did it. He told the police that he would leave his computer on when he was away from home and the cat would jump on the keyboard, tap on the keys, and child pornography would mysteriously be downloaded to his hard drive. Maybe the cat was looking for kitty porn and got kiddie porn by mistake?

I wear Hilfigers

Actor Tom Sizemore was placed on probation after being convicted of illegal drug possession. A condition of his probation required that he undergo periodic urine tests for drugs. He ended up in jail after being caught using a prosthetic penis to cheat on his drug test. He attached the device—aptly named the Whizzinator—to his underwear and filled it with clean urine to use for the test. Unfortunately, Sizemore forgot that fresh urine is warm. His Whizzinator urine was too cold to pass for the real thing. His excuse: The underwear containing the Whizzinator were not his—they were Calvins, and he only wore Hilfigers.

I'm a performance artist

Irishman Michael Stone, leader of the Ulster Freedom Fighters, was arrested for attempted murder when he tried to enter the Northern Ireland Parliament with an imitation pistol, a knife, and eight explosive devices. His excuse: He had not intended to endanger anyone; rather, his act was a work of "performance art" replicating a terrorist attack. Unfortunately for him, neither the trial judge nor jury were convinced. The judge said that Stone's claim that he had been taking part in some sort of "comic parody" was "hopelessly unconvincing" and "self-contradictory." He was convicted and received a 16-year sentence.

Someone stole my marijuana

Police in Hazelton, Pennsylvania, pulled over a local man for speeding and switching lanes without using turn signals. During the traffic stop, they saw a glass bowl used for smoking marijuana in plain view on the front seat. They then searched the car and found 15 baggies of marijuana and 13 ecstasy pills. The driver's excuse: He had to drive extra fast because he was chasing someone who just robbed him of his Apple iPhone and three bags of marijuana. Needless to say, he was charged with drug possession. To add insult to injury, he was also cited for careless driving and failure to wear a seatbelt.

I don't know from metric

A California woman was stopped by Canadian police while driving through Windsor, Ontario, at almost 100 miles per hour. Her excuse: The Canadian speed limit signs were in kilometers per hour, but the speedometer in her Mercedes Benz only gave readings in miles per hour, and she didn't understand the metric system. She was fined $405.

It's for compost

Police in Iowa City, Iowa, caught a man with several large bags of marijuana. His excuse: He intended to use the marijuana for compost. Police didn't buy the story and he was arrested for possessing marijuana with intent to distribute.

I was up late counterfeiting

A Pennsylvania man was arrested and charged with causing an accident when he fell asleep behind the wheel of his car and crashed into a school bus. His excuse: He was very groggy at the time of the accident because he'd been up late the night before making counterfeit checks. He received a two-to-four year sentence.

USA TODAY Snapshots®

Stealing from stores
Shoplifting by the numbers:

Shoplifters in USA **23 million**
Amount retailers lose per year **More than $10 billion**
Percent of shoplifters who are adults **75%**

Source: National Shoplifting Prevention Coalition

By David Stuckey and Sam Ward, USA TODAY
2006

I kissed a girl

A French tennis player, while competing in Florida, tested positive for cocaine use. Facing a possible two-and-a-half year suspension, he and his attorneys fessed up to how he'd spent a recent evening: making out with a girl in a nightclub in Miami. Their theory was that she had being doing cocaine and some of it had literally rubbed off on him. To the surprise of many tennis watchers, the Court of Arbitration for Sport (CSS) bought the theory. It noted that the amount of cocaine found in the athlete's bloodstream was too tiny to have come from normal recreational use, and basically lowered his suspension to time served (a few months).

I kept one eye closed

Swedish police received a tip that a woman was driving erratically. They caught up with her car, which was swerving across all lanes, and attempted to effect a traffic stop. The woman at first ignored the officers' sirens and lights, but finally stopped at the side of the road after a three kilometer chase. A breath test revealed the woman's blood alcohol level was nearly ten times Sweden's legal limit of 0.02%. Her excuse: Her driving wasn't affected by her drinking because she'd been careful to keep one eye closed to prevent her from seeing double. She was sentenced to two months in prison for aggravated drunken driving.

I was researching a movie role

Actress Wynona Ryder was caught attempting to shoplift $5,560 worth of designer clothes and accessories from a Saks Fifth Avenue department store in Beverly Hills, California. Her excuse: Her director had told her to shoplift for an upcoming movie role she was researching. She was convicted of grand theft and vandalism and sentenced to three years' probation, 480 hours of community service, $3,700 in fines, and $6,355 in restitution to the Saks Fifth Avenue store. She was also ordered to attend psychological and drug counseling.

Ten Best Crime-Solving Lawyers in Mystery Series

There's nothing like a series of mysterious cases to test a lawyer's mettle and true grit. And there's nothing like writing a series of books to test a novelist's ability to keep the characters interesting, the plots surprising, and the readership steady. Below are ten of the more interesting lawyers who have succeeded in mystery novel series.

Alexandra Cooper

Fictional, sex crimes prosecutor Alexandra Cooper is the subject of 11 mystery novels by author Linda Fairstein, who until 2002 served as head of the sex crimes unit of the Manhattan District Attorney's Office (She prosecuted the "Preppy Murder" case in 1986.) One trademark of the Cooper novels is that Alex (as she's known to friends) explores different New York City landmarks, such as museums, art galleries, Poe's cottage, Lincoln Center, and even the New York Public Library, (where she learns the secret of the stone lions at the entrance)—places that, to Fairstein, "look so elegant and refined from the outside, but are seething with mystery and mayhem once you scratch beneath the surface." Do the fictional attorney and the real one have much in common other than hair color and professional resume? Fairstein told one interviewer, "[S]he's younger, thinner and blonder than I am, she's got that trust fund I never had, and still has a lively romantic set of interludes … And the girl has to eat somewhere, so why not let her dine at all my favorite restaurants?"

Recommended: *Bad Blood* (2007)—Alex takes on a secret brotherhood that rules the tunnels of the New York water system.

Andy Carpenter

Most judges would file lawyer Andy Carpenter under "W" … for wiseacre. Carpenter, a brilliant defense attorney whose father happened to leave him over $20 million, is a courtroom jester who somehow manages—throughout seven novels—to pull the mystery out of the fire. Series creator David Rosenfelt describes his similarities with the character as follows, "We share a warped perspective on life; a complete inability to understand women; a lack of physical courage; a devotion to logic, dogs and sports; and an inability to curb our obnoxious sarcasm." Having $20 million gives Carpenter the luxury of choosing only those cases he finds appealing while allowing him to spend the rest of his quality time with his beloved golden retriever Tara. And if you're wondering why Andy Carpenter owns a dog rescue operation, it might have something to do with the fact that author and former movie-executive Rosenfelt has rescued over 400 dogs (and owns 27). Woof!

Recommended: *Open and Shut* (2002)—Andy learns how his dead Dad amassed $22 million.

Barbara Holloway

Barbara is a compassionate criminal attorney who lives in Eugene, Oregon, likes to work on her laptop at the local café, takes those hard cases that other attorneys shun (a familiar trait amongst series lawyer-detectives), has a semiretired lawyer father who helps unravel legal issues (and occasionally appears as opposing counsel), and relies on the small town's sensibility for clues leading to solving her clients' dilemmas. Her creator—author and nonlawyer Kate Wilhelm—is celebrated for her award-winning science fiction (she's won Nebula and Hugo Awards), her speculative fiction (a literary genre in which the author speculates about worlds unlike the real world), and her mystery writing—she's also written a nonlawyer series, *The Constance and Charlie* series (Charlie is a former arson investigator, and his wife, Constance is a psychologist).

Recommended: *Sleight of Hand* (2007)—Barbara saves a former pick-pocket and Vegas star from a murder rap.

Dismas Hardy

John Lescroart (pronounced "less-kwah") debuted Dismas Hardy, a hard-drinking criminal defense lawyer, in his 1989 mystery *Dead Irish,* and has since published a dozen more murder mysteries set in modern San Francisco. Dismas—named after the patron saint of thieves and murderers—often solves cases with the aid of his friend and homicide detective Abe Glitsky, the protagonist in four Lescroart novels. Like Lisa Scottoline, Lescroart uses the law office—Dismas is the managing partner—as the source of revolving story lines. He often features different lead characters, including partners Wes Ferrell and Gina Roarke, junior partner Amy Wu, and chief investigator Wyatt Hunt. Hardy's deft skills in the courtroom lead many readers to believe that Lescroart, like his contemporaries, is an attorney—he's not. He relies on friend (and violent crimes prosecutor) Al Giannini for courtroom realism. Lescroart's dream casting for Dismas—Dennis Quaid.

Recommended: *A Plague of Secrets* (2009) Dismas sorts through murder, coffee beans, and a marijuana stash.

Horace Rumpole

Horace Rumpole loves cheap wines (Chateau Thames Embankment), adores his wife (who he refers to as "She Who Must Be Obeyed"), and thrives on cases that unravel by the application of his deft wit and skills of detection. Rumpole is a bit of an anomaly, not just because he's the only fictional lawyer in our group to wear a wig, but because all of the others started their career in print. Rumpole, the thick-jowled, cigar-chomping British barrister, first appeared in a stage play and then in a British TV series (*Rumpole of the Bailey*). The success of that show (1975–1992) led to a series of books that continues even though the TV show ended. Like many of the attorney-authors in this list, creator John Mortimer practiced law until the success of his series character made it possible to retire from practice. (Mortimer's barrister father had advised him to become a lawyer "because it gets you out of the house.") Despite being offered "large sums of money," Mortimer has resisted attempts to create an American version of the story, labeling such derivative attempts as "ridiculous."

Recommended: *Rumpole and the Reign of Terror* (2006)—The Brit barrister defends a Pakistani doctor accused of aiding al-Qaeda.

Mary DiNunzio

If legal mysteries had a "chick lit" section, then its biggest star might be attorney Mary DiNunzio, who struggles to get ahead at a Philadelphia firm where that glass ceiling always seems to be holding her down. A tough cookie with Italian–American origins, Mary has to deal with lost love, crazy friends from old South Philly, and a carousel of killers and criminals. Mary's background is not unlike that of her creator, exattorney Lisa Scottoline, herself a longtime Philadelphia resident. Although Scottoline studied creative writing at the University of Pennsylvania (Philip Roth was her instructor), she says she really learned how to write in law school, claiming that, "[T]he best lawyers make the best novelists." Scottoline also writes a lighthearted women's column for the *Philadelphia Enquirer*, a collection of which was released as *Why My Third Husband Will Be A Dog*.

Recommended: *Everywhere That Mary Went* (1993)—Uh-oh, Mary DiNunzio's got a stalker!

Nina Reilly

Fictional attorney Nina Reilly shuttles between Carmel, California, and South Lake Tahoe (with her young son, Bob) in this lively 13-book series written by sisters Pamela and Mary O'Shaughnessy (under the pen name, Perri O'Shaugnessy—the "Perri" is an homage to Perry Mason). Nina has come up the hard way, working as a paralegal and attending law school at night, dealing with a bad marriage, and all the while raising Bob (an amalgam of both authors' sons—although the authors note that their boys don't have Bob's secrets or mood swings).

Nina's clients—like the view out her Tahoe office window—reflect the rural northern California environment and include a lively cast of characters from barmaids to cyberpunks. Nina's practice parallels that of coauthor Pamela O'Shaugnessy, who practiced law with her mother in Monterey, and then later in Carmel and Tahoe. Nina's insightful sister-in-law Andrea is loosely based on the coauthor's psychologist sister.

Recommended: *Motion to Suppress* (1996)—Nina bonds with her client, a down-and-out bottle blond accused of murdering her missing hubby.

Paul Madriani

Fictional San Francisco attorney Paul Madriani lost his lucrative corporate gig when he partied with the wife of the firm's top partner. Then he defended her from murder charges when her hubby was iced. That's how Madriani's criminal law career kicks off in the 1989 best seller, *Compelling Evidence.* Madriani has appeared in eight more novels, two of which were made for TV (*The Judge,* starring Chris Noth as Madriani, and *Undue Influence,* featuring Brian Denehy). Although Madriani bears some similarities to his creator—San Francisco attorney Steve Martini (middle name Paul)—Martini maintains that he has more in common with Madriani's fictional partner, Harry Hinds.

Recommended: *The Judge* (1996)—Things get very judge-mental when Madriani defends a judge.

Perry Mason

Most lawyers agree that few cases ever have a "Perry Mason moment" —a truth-defying event within the courtroom that makes a witness suddenly blurt out, "Yes I did it!" But that didn't stop Erle Stanley Gardner from using the device in over 80 novels of courtroom mystery featuring the iconic Mason—and inventing the genre of American lawyer mysteries in the process. Mason, along with the series characters—sultry secretary Della Street (Mason's implied love interest), gruff Lieutenant Tragg, hangdog D.A. Hamilton Burger, and ever-cool investigator Paul Drake—have all become part of legal folklore (and have defined America's role-playing perception of the legal profession). The first Perry Mason novel, *The Case of the Velvet Claws*, appeared in 1933. The series became a quick success, enabling Gardner to stop practicing law in 1937. Perry Mason's name came from the publisher of Gardner's favorite childhood books (The Perry Mason Company).

But the rest of his origins or appearance are themselves a bit of a mystery: Gardner never provided any description or back story for the lawyer–detective. Although Perry is best remembered in his incarnation by actor Raymond Burr, the series was also a popular radio series and the subject of several movies as well as made-for-TV films. Although Gardner wrote dozens of other novels with other characters (including a crusading D.A.), his only Edgar

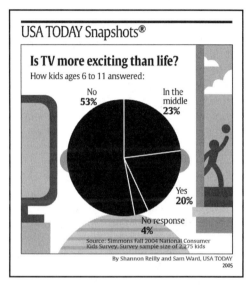

USA TODAY Snapshots®

Is TV more exciting than life?
How kids ages 6 to 11 answered:

No **53%**
In the middle **23%**
Yes **20%**
No response **4%**

Source: Simmons Fall 2004 National Consumer Kids Survey. Survey sample size of 2,275 kids

By Shannon Reilly and Sam Ward, USA TODAY 2005

Award—given in the field of mystery and crime writing—was for a nonfiction book in which he investigated miscarriages of justice against criminal defendants.

Recommended: *The Case of the Howling Dog* (1934)—Howling dogs, sexy housekeepers, a murderer's will; what's not to like?

Willa Jansen

Lawyer Lia Matera has created two successful series lawyers, Willa Jansen and Laura DiPalma (described by the author as "a litigator, and, like most trial lawyers, she's aggressive, Machiavellian, and vindictive.") Jansen deviates the most from standard fictional series lawyers in that—as described by Matera—she "was a red-diaper baby, raised by political activists who continue to cling to their Yippie ways. Willa finds herself justifying her increasingly bourgeois tastes to her parents while keeping her hippie attitudes in the closet at work." Willa works amidst labor law and corporate law firms, and much of the series subtext comes from the first-person narrator's politics and wit—the latter of which she often needs when dealing with San Francisco cases such as those in *Last Chants* (shamanism and computer technology) and *Star Witness* (alien abduction).

Recommended: *Star Witness* (2007)—Jansen's got her hands full when her client's alibi is alien abduction.

Wanna Play Auditor?

Like most everyone, small business owners feel like they end up paying a lot in taxes—and are always looking for a way to lower their bill. Luckily, the category of business expenses, which are deductible, is pretty broad: That trip to Hawaii where you attended a professional seminar? Deductible. Lunch with the accountant to talk over your business's numbers? Deductible. A new business laptop? Deductible.

But while there are legal limits on what a business owner can deduct, there are apparently no limits on human creativity in testing the boundaries. What if you were an IRS auditor and had to say yea or nay to the attempted deductions below—drawn from real-life cases. Which ones would you allow?

Here are the basic rules before you set to work. Business owners can't deduct just any expense. IRS rules say that, to be deductible, an expense must be (1) directly related to the business (something done to earn a profit), (2) "ordinary and necessary" for that business, and (3) reasonable in amount. That leaves out, for example, personal expenses such as movie tickets (unless the taxpayer is a screenwriter who needs to see movies for business reasons) and the salary of a child's nanny (even if having the nanny allows the businessperson to go to work every day).

Allow or not?

1. Dental expenses a professional actor incurred when his teeth were knocked out while making a boxing movie

2. Money an author paid to prostitutes while researching a book on legal brothels in Nevada

3. Flowers the president of a loan company sent to employees while they were in the hospital

④ A bar-mitzvah reception for a rabbi's son

⑤ High-protein foods a person with a rare blood type ate to maintain the quality of her blood so she could regularly sell it to a serological company

⑥ Parking fees a college professor paid to park on campus

⑦ Postage for postcards a doctor sent to his patients while on vacation in Europe

⑧ An aircraft controller's purchase of a small plane so she could learn to fly

⑨ The cost of an insurance agent's handgun collection

⑩ The cost of beer a gas station owner gave away to customers

⑪ Stage clothing used by a rock musician in Rod Stewart's band, including silk boxers, leather pants, men's underwear, hats, and a vest

⑫ Size 56-FF breast implants purchased by a Green Bay, Wisconsin, stripper with the stage name "Chesty Love"

Answers

1. *Allowed.* The court said that the dental expenses were deductible because they were directly attributable to the taxpayer's occupation as an actor.

2. *Disallowed.* The court said that sums spent on prostitutes were "so personal in nature as to preclude their deductibility." So business owners can forget about deducting that trip to the Mustang Ranch.

3. *Allowed.* The cost of the flowers was deductible because their purchase benefited the company, not the president personally.

4. *Disallowed.* Nice try Rabbi, but neither the IRS nor tax court would accept this as a business expense. Clearly, the reception was a personal, family event, not a deductible business meeting or business entertainment.

5. *Allowed.* The high-protein food sounds like a wacky deduction, but the court concluded that the taxpayer was in the business of selling blood

plasma and these were legitimate expenses for that business.

6. *Disallowed.* The parking fees were part of the professor's commuting expenses and therefore were personal, not business, expenses.

7. *Allowed.* The deduction for sending postcards to patients was allowed as a legitimate advertising expense for the doctor's medical business.

8. *Disallowed.* The IRS said that it was unreasonable for an aircraft controller to spend over $17,000 to buy a plane to learn to fly, when she could have learned to fly just as well (but far more cheaply) by renting a plane.

9. *Disallowed.* The insurance agent claimed that the handguns were a legitimate business expense because he had to go to "unsafe job sites" to settle insurance claims, and there was an unsolved murder in his neighborhood. The tax court didn't buy it, saying that, "A handgun simply does not qualify as an ordinary and necessary business expense for an insurance agent, even a bold and brave Wyatt Earp type with a fast draw who is willing to risk injury or death in the service of his clients."

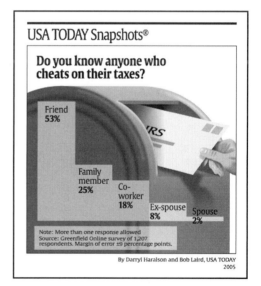

USA TODAY Snapshots®

Do you know anyone who cheats on their taxes?

Friend 53%

Family member 25%

Co-worker 18%

Ex-spouse 8%

Spouse 2%

Note: More than one response allowed
Source: Greenfield Online survey of 1,207 respondents. Margin of error ±9 percentage points.

By Darryl Haralson and Bob Laird, USA TODAY
2005

10. *Allowed.* The court said that a small business owner "can offer free beer to beer lovers" to improve business.

11. *Disallowed.* The rule is that business owners may deduct the cost of uniforms or special work clothes not suitable for personal wear, such as nurse's uniforms, theatrical costumes, and special sanitary clothing. But clothing that a person can wear on the street is not deductible—for example, one can't deduct the cost of business suits. The tax court rejected out of hand any deduction for the musician's silk boxers and underwear, declaring that underwear clearly could not qualify as a business expense. Most of the remaining clothes were likewise not deductible because they could be adapted for

street wear. However, there were some items that the court deemed too "flashy" or "loud" to be acceptable for ordinary wear and it allowed the musician a $200 deduction for them. The moral: Wear "loud" clothes on stage if you're a rock musician and want a tax deduction.

12. *Allowed.* A female Tax Court judge allowed a $2,088 deduction for the breast implant surgery. Noting that Chesty's tip income went up after she got the implants, the judge reasoned that they were similar to a stage prop and were a necessary expense for her to generate more income as a professional stripper. Moreover, the breasts were so large and cumbersome—about ten pounds each—that she could not derive any personal benefit from them. The moral: Breast implants are deductible if they are huge and you use them in your work.

Take Me Out to the Ball Game—But Don't Get Between Me and That Home Run Ball

B aseball is the great American pastime. Fans love the mellow pace, the beauty and symmetry of the field, the precision of the stats, and the many talents of the players—including the incredible skill it takes to hit a tiny, rotating sphere that's coming at you at high speed with a similarly tiny round wooden stick.

Hitting a baseball is a great feat, and seeing someone hit the ball a great distance is a thrilling experience for the fan, especially when it clears a fence and becomes the ultimate hit: the home run. The average distance for a home run in major league baseball in 2009 was 398.8 feet. The longest that season was 495 feet (Wladimir Balentein of the Reds, in case you're interested).

Yup, we love the home run. And that has led to a blending of baseball with that other great American pastime: the lawsuit. Baseball memorabilia has been big business since way back in 1887 when the first numbered set of baseball cards—sold along with tobacco—was printed. These days, signed balls, jerseys, and other items are highly prized. But nothing is more valuable than a historic home run ball. Someone paid over $800,000 in 2006 for a home run ball hit by Babe Ruth in the 1933 All-Star Game, and Hank Aaron's 755th sold for $650,000 in 1999.

Barry Bonds

A seven-time all-star named Barry Bonds hit a few historic home runs, too, creating some controversy. In 2001, Bonds hit a record-setting 73 home runs, and the 73rd generated a lawsuit between two men, Patrick

Hayashi and Alex Popov, who both claimed they caught the ball in the right-field arcade at Pacific Bell Park—Popov said he got to the ball first and that Hayashi grabbed it from his glove, while Hayashi claimed he found the ball rolling on the ground in the midst of the scrum of people trying to catch it.

After a 2002 court trial, San Francisco judge Kevin McCarthy ordered the two men to sell the ball and split the proceeds. He validated both men's claims, acknowledging that Popov had the ball, but that it was dislodged from his glove by a mob of fans, not including Hayashi, and that Hayashi's picking up of the ball from the ground was legitimate.

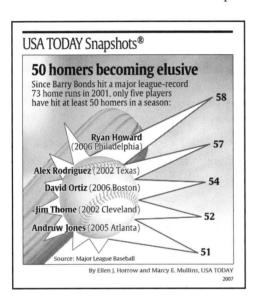

USA TODAY Snapshots®

50 homers becoming elusive
Since Barry Bonds hit a major league-record 73 home runs in 2001, only five players have hit at least 50 homers in a season:

58

Ryan Howard (2006 Philadelphia) — 57

Alex Rodriguez (2002 Texas) — 54

David Ortiz (2006 Boston)

Jim Thome (2002 Cleveland) — 52

Andruw Jones (2005 Atlanta) — 51

Source: Major League Baseball

By Ellen J. Horrow and Marcy E. Mullins, USA TODAY
2007

"Their legal claims are of equal quality, and they are equally entitled to the ball," McCarthy ruled. "The ball must be sold and divided equally between the parties." Comic book creator and film producer Todd McFarlane, who owns an enormous collection of sports memorabilia, bought the controversial ball for $450,000 in an auction.

Another Bonds home run was the subject of a lawsuit the season following his historic 73rd home run. During the 2002 season, Bonds hit his 600th career home run. Jay Arsenault caught the ball in the bleachers and held on to it—in violation of an agreement he made with others, according to three friends who sued him immediately in an effort to prevent him from selling the ball. They claimed that Arsenault received the tickets to the game in exchange for a promise that if he caught the 600th home run he would share the wealth and split any proceeds from selling it with his coworkers. The case settled when Arsenault agreed to sell the ball and split the money after all.

Ryan Howard

In 2008, Philadelphia Phillies slugger Ryan Howard hit his 200th career home run. Might not seem like that big a deal, with the 500-home-run club getting bigger with each passing year, but Howard reached the milestone faster than anyone in baseball history ever had before—it was only his 658th major league game. He hit the solo homer in the sixth inning of a game against the Florida Marlins at their Miami stadium, and a 12-year-old girl in the right-field stands picked it up when it landed there.

Jennifer Valdivia teased her older brother, who had attended many games but never grabbed a home run ball. She called her mom. The next thing she knew, Jennifer was being escorted away by Marlins personnel and taken to the Phillies' clubhouse, where a Phillies employee told her that if she gave up the ball right then, she could come back after the game and get it back, autographed by Howard himself. After the game, she was given a brand new ball instead—definitely not the one she had caught. Nor did Ryan Howard ever show up to meet her.

After Jennifer went home and told her mom what happened, her mother contacted the Phillies and asked for the ball back. She got the brush-off—and promptly hired a lawyer. It wasn't that the ball was worth much, but the family was upset about how Jennifer was treated, and Jennifer really wanted the ball. The Phillies finally told the Valdivias that Ryan Howard himself had the ball. The lawyers sued—and immediately received the ball. Jennifer keeps it near her bed and plans to show it to her children.

Ken Griffey

In June 2008, Ken Griffey became only the sixth major league player ever to hit 600 home runs when he sent one over the fence in Miami. Almost immediately, controversy ensued when 25-year-old Justin Kimball claimed he caught the ball and stuffed it into his wool cap—but that someone else them grabbed it from him and ran off with it. The Florida Marlins later announced major league baseball had authenticated the home run ball for a middle-aged male fan who would only give his first name as Joe. Although a lawsuit was predicted, it apparently never materialized and Joe is the keeper of the historic ball, at least for now.

Other famous balls and where they are now

Bill Mazeroski's 1960 walkoff homer in the World Series: A fan caught the ball and gave it back to Mazeroski in exchange for two cases of beer. The ball is now in the Baseball Hall of Fame in Cooperstown, New York.

Roger Maris' 61st home run: Maris hit the ball that broke Babe Ruth's record for single-season home runs on the last day of the Yankees' 1961 season. A Brooklyn truck driver named Sal Durante caught the ball and tried to return it to Maris after the game. Maris refused to take it, telling Durante he should make some money from it. Durante kept the ball for a while and then sold it for $5,000 to a man who then returned it to Maris. It's now in the Hall of Fame.

Hank Aaron's 755th home run: Aaron's final career home run was caught by a part-time member of the Brewers grounds crew, who intended to return it to Aaron—but when he couldn't return it to the star in person, he kept it. This got him fired, because the Brewers considered the ball their property, but he did keep the ball and later sold it for $650,000.

Kirk Gibson's walkoff homer in the 1988 World Series: Whereabouts unknown.

What's in a Name?

Just think how much power parents have when they give their helpless baby a moniker that's meant to stick for life. Plenty of kids grow up wondering whether mom was a little tipsy on anesthetic or dad was simply overwhelmed when it came time to fill out the birth certificate. Or for others, "Jane," "Percy," or "Sparkle" just turns out not to fit their personality.

Fortunately, there's a legal fix for such misnamings. By filling out some forms, submitting them to a local court, publishing notice in a local newspaper, and attending a brief court hearing, someone can trade in Adolf for Ace in a day.

The judge doesn't even need to ask about the reasons. "It's just not me," "I want to use my maiden name," "My name makes people think of a small furry rodent or a porn star," and "My new partner and I want to change our names to something new that we share" are among the many acceptable reasons.

The judges rarely blink an eye. They've said yes to people changing their name to Santa Claus, Sunshine, and Koriander.

But then there are the cases that do cause the judge to blink—or, possibly, stare in amazement.

For example, some people say they'd feel happier with their friends and family referring to them by numbers. Like the North Dakota man who wanted to do a switcheroo from Michael Herbert Dengler to "1069."

He'd apparently put a lot of thought into this, explaining that "a person's name should be a mark of indicium which corresponds to and is a verbal and graphic manifestation of the person's philosophy." Each character meant something to him: The number 1 reflected his existence as a single entity among millions of others, as well as the oneness of the universe; the number 0 demonstrated his status as "zero with respect to [his] march on the road of life;" the third character, 6, was the equivalent of his "relationship with the universe in my understanding of my spatial occupancy through this life;" and the fourth and final number, 9, was "like a string which surrounds the entirety of the previous three digits and explains the first three digits' concepts as they interact among each other to produce my philosophy." Oh, and here's the kicker: He proclaimed that "1069" was the only possible way he could express his identity.

The court said no go; a name must consist of words, not numbers. So Michael Herbert Dengler remained Michael Herbert Dengler.

Thomas Boyd Ritchie III was also destined to retain his name after the court refused to let him to shorten it to simply "III," pronounced "three." Having already convinced people in his daily life to refer to him this way, Mr. Ritchie wanted to make the change official. Too confusing, said the court.

Religious impulses prompt some name change requests. Tyler Joseph Chamberlain, an inmate in the Nebraska State Penitentiary, wanted to change his name to Farbauthi Grimnir Knapp Akihokas Darherjan, to reflect his status as a high priest of the Asatru religion. If you're wondering what the Asatru religion is, you're not alone; the court said no after Mr. Chamberlain couldn't prove that it existed, much less that he was one of its dedicated followers.

And Peter Robert Phillips will have to go through life without people calling him Jesus Christ. Freedom of expression is all well and good, according to the court, but some limitations are in order if a name change might "offend people or incite violence or protest." (The court also managed to squeeze into its opinion that "the name of the Lord is Holy.")

A Pennsylvania court likewise found that a name change to "World Saviour" was too much to ask for, despite Mr. Bethea's solemn intention to become "a vehicle for 'peace in the Middle East and the rest of the world.'" (That was in 1991, and given the state of Middle Eastern peace since then, Mr. Bethea is probably imagining the judge regretting his mistake.)

Finally, there are the cases that defy categorization. Darren Lloyd Bean was probably disappointed when the court refused to let him change his name to "Darren QX [pronounced 'Lloyd'] Bean!" All of the terms within the quotation marks were meant to be part of the name—hence the court's objection.

Mr. Snaphappy Fishsuit Mokiligon had better luck requesting a new name for himself (could it be this wasn't his first time in name change court?). But he had to go all the way to an appeals court to get the okay for his chosen new name, which was "variable." The courts were worried that he meant to use his new name literally, and vary up his identity at will. (Next thing you know, he'll be calling himself "1069"!) So the appeals court made a special note that he was thereafter "limited to actually using the word 'variable,' unless or until he changes his name again through a recognized legal process."

USA TODAY Snapshots®

Top baby names in 2006

Girls

1. Emily
2. Emma
3. Madison
4. Isabella
5. Ava

Boys

1. JACOB
2. Michael
3. Joshua
4. Ethan
5. Matthew

Source: Social Security Administration

By David Stuckey and Alejandro Gonzalez, USA TODAY 2007

How about this one: Mr. Alan Georges Temes asked for a switch to "Alan Georges Temes a.k.a. talks to trees." What Mr. Temes actually wanted was to be able to use the two names interchangeably—he didn't want to give up his birth name, but he used the name "talks to trees" professionally and personally and felt it "communicates more about who he is than his familial name." It was the "a.k.a." in the middle that stuck in the court's craw, so it denied the request.

Sometimes, however, a name change is an act of mercy. A New Zealand judge made a nine-year-old girl a ward of the court so that she could change her name from "Talula Does the Hula From Hawaii." Her parents were not happy, having given her the name at birth. (What was their second-choice name?)

But New Zealand judges lay limits, too. According to the BBC, they've drawn the line at "Yeah Detroit," "Stallion," "Twisty Poi," "Keenan Got Lucy," "Fat Boy," "Cinderella Beauty Blossom," and "Fish" and "Chips" (twins, of course).

Whose Sunken Treasure Is It?

ust when you think the world holds no more secrets, you hear a story like this one: In 2007, a fisherman in South Korea pulled up an octopus that was clutching a finely glazed greenish plate. Archaeologists followed this clue to a 12th century shipwreck containing hundreds of well-preserved celadon cups, bowls, plates, and other works meant for nobles and government officials in the Goryeo Dynasty.

What further treasures might lie in octopus's gardens in the sea? The United Nations estimates that more than three million shipwrecks remain to be found worldwide. Some hold little of value, unless your taste runs to old furnace oil and cooking pots.

USA TODAY Snapshots®

Leaving land

Number of adult boaters — 53.6 million

Amount spent of food and fuel during boating. — $16 billion

Note: Numbers from 2006
Source: National Marine Manufacturers Association

By David Stuckey and Sam Ward, USA TODAY
2008

But others look like a scene from *Pirates of the Caribbean*, with gold coins spilling out of sea chests—which makes sense when you realize that, in the days before electronic transfers and direct deposit, people had to pay for things using real coinage.

Some other recent finds:

- In 1985, Mel Fisher, an American, discovered a cargo of gold and silver coins, ingots, emeralds, and other jewelry worth an estimated $400 million in the wreck of the *Atocha*, a Spanish galleon sunk by a hurricane off the Florida Keys in 1622. (You can see some of what Fisher found at his Maritime Museum in Key West, Florida.)

- In February 2009, a U.S. salvage company called Odyssey Marine Exploration found the sunken *HMS Victory*, once the most powerful warship in the British navy. The ship had been mysteriously lost in the English Channel during a storm in 1744. Not only was the *Victory* carrying things you'd expect on a warship—like an impressive array of bronze cannons—but it also held great quantities of silver and gold (since warships then acted as "armored vehicles" for money transfers).

- In 2008, De Beers geologists prospecting for diamonds off Namibia found an unidentified ship that went down around the turn of the 15th century. It was carrying a hoard of Spanish and Portuguese coins, copper ingots, cannons, and ivory tusks, possibly heading to India for spice trading.

Are you digging through your closet for snorkel and flippers yet? Not so fast: Not only are there some practical concerns, but this would be a good time to have a talk with your maritime lawyer.

Don't forget:

September 19 is "International Talk Like a Pirate Day!" That's when you can roll out phrases like "Avast, me hearties," "Shiver me timbers," and the all-purpose "Arr!"

First, the field of treasure hunting is getting a little crowded, not to mention professionalized. Entire companies have formed comprising researchers, divers, archaeologists, navigators, and others in a united quest. Their research alone requires scouring libraries around the world in search of personal diaries or letters, old newspaper reports of sea battles and sinking ships, weather reports, insurance claims, and more. And they invest in state-of-the-art equipment, such as a device developed by the U.S. Navy, so sensitive that it can detect an individual gold coin buried two feet down in mud.

The at-sea work can also be a one-way trip to Davy Jones' locker. Just at the moment of triumph, having entered a sunken ship, many divers have lost their way and died deep in its hull. Others have succumbed to "the bends," a compression sickness that occurs at great depths. For example, at least 14 people have died exploring the wreck of the *Andrea Doria*, an Italian luxury liner that sunk to an especially deep 200 feet in the frigid waters near Nantucket, Massachusetts.

And there's one more reason you might want to stay on dry land. Unless you're content with the thrill of the find, you might spend a lot of money for little return. The law is getting mighty sticky regarding who owns the rights to the goodies.

At one time, maritime law regarding sunken treasure could basically be expressed as, "finders, keepers." But no more.

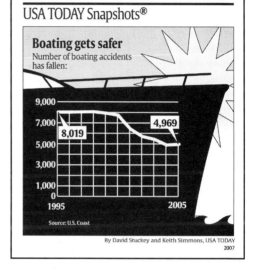

USA TODAY Snapshots®

Boating gets safer
Number of boating accidents has fallen:

8,019

4,969

1995   2005

Source: U.S. Coast

By David Stuckey and Keith Simmons, USA TODAY
2007

First off, a number of people might claim rights to the treasure, no matter how long it was sitting at the bottom of the sea. Governments are increasingly claiming ownership, either because it was actually their warship or because they fronted even a little bit of cash for the voyage. Insurance companies may also get into the act, claiming that if they paid out on the loss, they're now owed reimbursement.

What's more, UNESCO is asking countries to sign onto a treaty agreeing not to allow private plunder of important historical—and even burial (in the inevitable cases where crew went down with the ship) sites—but to preserve them as part of the public heritage. (Critics of this treaty point out that the public won't get much enjoyment out of underwater sites that are either rotting and rusting quickly or are in such deep water that they're practically inaccessible.)

The upshot is that, unless you can prove that a sunken ship has no owner with any continued interest in it (good luck) and no historic significance, you're unlikely to be able to claim "finder's rights"—that is, where you get to sift coins through your fingers muttering, "Mine, all mine." The best you might hope for is "salvor's rights," where you pull up and return the treasure in hopes of a reward from the owner.

A last warning: The law on the subject of undersea treasure is changing fast. Keep a sharp mariner's eye on the latest newspaper reports, and don't head out to sea without saying "Ahoy there" to your lawyer.

How Copyright Law Found Its Mojo

S ol Rabinowitz didn't know much about copyright law or running a record label when he founded Baton Records in the early fifties … but he learned fast. One of the songs he acquired for his label was *I've Got My Mo-Jo Working (But It Just Won't Work on You)* written by Preston Foster and performed by Ann Cole. (The "hook" for the song is the oft-repeated title.)

Rabinowitz had warned his artists not to perform songs before their releases—a practice that sometimes resulted in quickie covers that beat Baton's artists to the marketplace—but Cole performed the song regularly while on a tour with blues star Muddy Waters. Waters (aka McKinley Morganfield) loved the tune and when he returned to Chicago he recorded it for Chess Records, creating what many critics believe is one of the classic blues recordings.

In the studio, Waters couldn't remember all the Preston Foster lyrics, so he modified the final verses with what he thought were the correct words and claimed songwriting credits. Unbeknownst to Rabinowitz, Chess Records released their Muddy Waters version within one week of the Baton Records release. Although Ann Cole's version was the more popular release at the time (it went to #3 on the charts), the Muddy Waters version came into its own and eventually made it onto *Rolling Stone Magazine*'s list of top 500 songs of all time.

Both Waters and Preston Foster claimed copyright for the tune, and Rabinowitz had no choice but to hire lawyers to chase Waters and Chess Records. The result—Preston Foster was declared the sole songwriter and Rabinowitz's music publishing company, Dare Music, was the owner. A settlement for payment was reached between the parties.

That cleared the way for Foster and Rabinowitz to earn the songwriting income from Waters' version as well as the 150 to 200 versions by artists who later covered the song, (including The Zombies,

Jimmy Smith, Art Blakey, Canned Heat, Elvis Presley, B. B. King, Buddy Guy, Otis Rush, and Eric Clapton).

For almost two decades that income was unthreatened, until the early 1970s when a woman named Ruth Strachborneo, writer of a song entitled *Mojo Workout*, claimed that she was the originator of the phrase "got my Mojo working" and that she had sung a version for a television commercial in 1955 (although she hadn't recorded a version of her song until at least 1960). She claimed that Foster's song had been based on hers and that she was entitled to royalties from both Foster's song and from Muddy Waters's version.

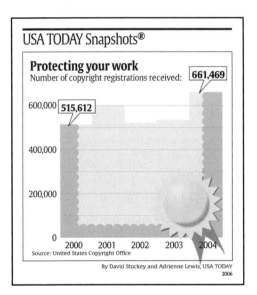

USA TODAY Snapshots®

Protecting your work
Number of copyright registrations received: 661,469

By David Stuckey and Adrienne Lewis, USA TODAY 2006

Rabinowitz hired a lawyer, but one of his concerns was whether Preston Foster should testify. According to Rabinowitz, Foster was "one of the shyest human beings I've ever met." Rabinowitz's lawyer told his client that Foster was so introverted, "We're gonna have to do something else. We can't put this guy on the stand."

The case had been assigned to the late district court judge Charles L. "Charlie" Brieant, Jr., known for his bowtie and Rollie-style mustache, as well as his ability to dispose of controversial cases—one angry defendant sent poisoned chocolates to the judge's wife (she survived the murder attempt).

To succeed on her copyright claim, Strachborneo would have to prove that Foster had access to her *Mojo Workout* and that the two songs were substantially similar. Brieant demonstrated that Foster had no access to Strachborneo's version of the tune before he wrote his song. And even if there had been access—and this is where the judge really showed his stuff—the songs were not substantially similar.

Before explaining his logic, Judge Brieant insisted that an understanding of the litigation required defining "MOJO," which he referred to as "a collective noun used to describe one or more talismanic objects believed to have power intrinsic to their nature, and believed able to impart power, or ward off evil or misfortune by being worn close to the body of, or possessed by, the person to whom the MOJO appertains. A simple example of MOJO would be a rabbit's foot. Other examples of MOJO, mentioned from time to time in the trial record, include such amulets as black cat bones, shrunken heads, lodestones, half dollar with seeds, four-leaf clover, ashes, blacksnake skin, strands of hair and teeth. MOJO is often worn around the neck in a leather bag or carried on the person. MOJO may, in a pastoral society, be taken into the fields with the cattle."

Having provided that background, Brieant noted, "Reliance on and belief in MOJO naturally leads to the conversational gambit, 'Have you got your MOJO working?' or 'I've got my MOJO working.' A person approaching a crisis, such as an examination at school, would be sure to have his MOJO with him, and working."

Then in a moment of judicial activism for which all MOJO holders will be forever grateful, Judge Brieant liberated and forever guaranteed the freedom of any songwriter to use the term.

"MOJO is a commonplace part of the rhetoric of the culture of a substantial portion of the American people. As a figure of speech, the concept of having, or not having, one's MOJO working is not something in which any one person could assert originality, or establish a proprietary right."

In short, Strachborneo lost.

Preserving Preston Foster's claim to copyright has been worth the effort. According to a recent interview, Sol Rabinowitz claims the song still earns $20,000 to $30,000 a year. "Every six months I send Preston a check," Rabinowitz wrote at his website, "He's basically still making a living from this song." And thanks to copyright law, his Mojo will continue to be working for him for many years to come.

Strachborneo v. Arc Music, 357 F. Supp 1393 (S.D. N.Y. 1973).

'Til Death—Or the Tabloids—Do Us Part: Messy Celebrity Divorces

I t's tough being a celebrity sometimes. Along with fame, money, and privilege comes the relentless attention to one's personal life, even something as personal as the end of a marriage. Or two.

Ike and Tina Turner

Ike and Tina Turner had a rock 'n' roll lifestyle from day one, when Tina pushed her way onstage to sing along with Ike's band in a bar, and they struggled to success together. They also had a bigger-than-life dynamic of jealousy, in which Tina's growing fame as a solo artist threatened Ike to the point that he began to control and abuse her. She eventually left after a violent incident, with no more than 36 cents in her purse.

The two fought over property rights in court until finally the case was resolved, if you can call it that—Ike kept all their monetary assets. (Tina said, "It's not about leaving with money. You leave with knowledge. Inner strength.") Ike may have had the last word in divorce court, but Tina has certainly had the last word in the world of fame and fortune, going on to an enormously successful solo career while Ike spent time in prison and had problems with drugs until his death in 2007.

Britney Spears and her first two husbands

In case you didn't know, pop star Britney Spears has had her share of marital issues. First, there was her marriage to Jason Alexander, which lasted only five hours before Spears filed for an annulment, claiming she lacked sufficient understanding of her husband's likes, dislikes, and desires to be capable of entering the marriage. The annulment was granted after 55 hours of marriage.

Nine months later, Spears married Kevin Federline. That marriage lasted just long enough for the pair to have two children together before separating in 2006. Their divorce became final in 2008, after two years of legal wrangling over money, prenups, and their children, who ended up in Federline's custody after Spears' bizarre behavior landed her in rehab and the hospital, as well as in a conservatorship proceeding through which her father sought (and got) control over her financial affairs.

Britney Spears' legal fees were more than $466,000 for her child custody dispute. She also pays Federline $20,000 a month in support, and on top of her own legal fees, she paid an additional sum of $250,000 to Kevin Federline's attorneys.

Spears got a happy ending though: By the end of 2009 she was back to sharing 50/50 custody with Federline, and even had permission to bring her tots along on her concert tour, as long as she pays for Federline to come along, too.

Ivana and Donald Trump

"Don't get mad, get everything." This divorce advice was dispensed by Ivana Trump following her famous divorce from billionaire real estate mogul Donald Trump. And she did, taking away a settlement that, while sealed, was rumored to include $20 million cash, the $14 million family estate in Connecticut, a $5 million housing allowance, $350,000 annual alimony, all of her jewelry, and a 49% interest in the couple's family home in Palm Beach, Florida. All of this despite a prenuptial agreement that was the source of enormous conflict during the parties' divorce.

In the divorce process, Donald denigrated Ivana's work as vice president of the Trump Organization—work that won her the title "Hotelier of the Year" in 1990, the same year that she famously confronted Donald's mistress, Marla Maples, on the ski slopes at Aspen. Ultimately, the divorce was resolved after Ivana's father died suddenly and Donald supported her at the funeral. Ivana and Donald both married twice more—and both are currently married to their third spouses—and their daughter, Ivanka Trump, married in 2009. So far, so good.

Shortest celebrity marriages

Wondering about the shortest celebrity marriages ever? You might think Britney set the record with her 55-hour nuptials, but you'd be wrong. Rudolph Valentino and Jean Acker had been married for all of six hours when she locked him out of their honeymoon suite. He knocked for 20 minutes before heading home; his bride later claimed the marriage was never consummated. And Zsa Zsa Gabor, something of a marriage expert given her nine tries, claims that she had one of the shortest celebrity marriages when her nuptials to Felipe de Alba were annulled after only one day.

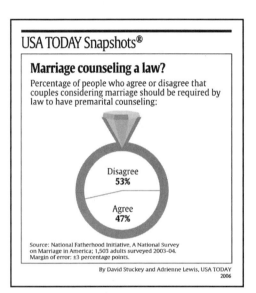

USA TODAY Snapshots®

Marriage counseling a law?

Percentage of people who agree or disagree that couples considering marriage should be required by law to have premarital counseling:

Disagree
53%

Agree
47%

Source: National Fatherhood Initiative, A National Survey on Marriage in America; 1,503 adults surveyed 2003-04. Margin of error: ±3 percentage points.

By David Stuckey and Adrienne Lewis, USA TODAY 2006

Dennis Hopper and Michelle Phillips made it all of eight days, but at least they had a sense of humor about it. Quipped Hopper, "Seven of those days were pretty good. The eighth day was the bad one," while Phillips remembered them as "the happiest eight days of my life." Then there were a couple of nine-day marriages, including Cher and Gregg Allman (Cher reportedly cried all the way home from the ceremony, though the two did reconcile after their divorce for a brief period) and Dennis Rodman and Carmen Electra.

Repetitive marriage syndrome

This next isn't necessarily about messy divorces; it's more about messy lives—the lives of celebs who marry the same person over and over again. We'll start with Marshall Mathers, also known as Eminem, and Kim Scott, who married on June 14, 1999, and divorced in 2001 (after separating and reconciling during 2000). After reconciling in 2004, they married again in 2006, then divorced again later the same year.

These youngsters followed in the great tradition of Elizabeth Taylor and Richard Burton, who married on March 15, 1964, and divorced in June 1974—then married again on October 10, 1975, and divorced again in August 1976. Taylor was married six other times, proving that hope really does spring eternal.

Divorces in fiction

And for those who like their divorces fictional—and who doesn't prefer that?—our discussion would not be complete without a look at Erica Kane, whose hope apparently springs even more eternal than Liz Taylor's. In 39 years as the main character in ABC's soap opera "All My Children," Erica has been married no fewer than ten times, to eight different men, as she married two of them twice (husbands four and seven and eight and nine, respectively). She remains married to husband number ten. And the actress who plays Erica Kane, Susan Lucci, has been married for 40 years to the same man. Truth is stranger than fiction.

Man's Best Friend?

There are big dogs and little dogs; jumpy dogs and lazy dogs; and helpful dogs and mischievous dogs. And then there are the dogs that go beyond mischief to commit actual crimes. The following doggy crime blotter might lead you to think twice about whether those big dark eyes are as innocent as they appear.

Shoplifting

Akira, an 11-year-old Siberian husky, escaped from her owner's home in Salt Lake City and headed to a local supermarket. She walked through the sliding doors and headed straight for the pet food aisle, where she stole a rawhide bone (worth $2.79). As she padded out of the store, she was confronted by the manager who told her to, "Drop it!" Ignoring the manager, Akira ran out of the store and headed for home. The entire incident was caught on the store's video camera. When her horrified owners brought her back to the store, she was easily identified as the shoplifting dog. Her owners bought her another bone and paid for two to make up for their dog's theft.

Auto theft

A California man left his Boxer, named Max, in the passenger seat of his pickup truck while he went inside a local mini-mart. When he came back out, he was astonished to find that both his pickup and Max were gone. He immediately called the police to report a stolen vehicle. Luckily, the pickup and Max were soon found in the parking lot of a fast food restaurant across the street.

Here's what happened: The man had left his manual transmission truck in neutral, but with the emergency brake on. Apparently realizing that this was a perfect opportunity to take his owner's truck and make a clean getaway, Max released the brake and the truck rolled out of the lot. Unfortunately, Max didn't think out his crime very well. He didn't know how to drive a truck (even assuming he could have placed two paws on the steering wheel and another two on the accelerator, brake, and clutch). As a result, the pickup rolled harmlessly across the street and came to a stop in the parking lot, where Max was easily nabbed.

Things could have been worse. A German Shepherd dog owned by a police officer in Ogden, Utah, was left alone in an idling Ford pickup when the officer had to leave the vehicle to respond to a police call. The dog jumped into the front seat and knocked the truck's automatic transmission into gear. The truck lurched forward. Unfortunately, at the same time Mary Stone was walking to her mailbox. She was struck by the pickup and ended up with a shattered tailbone and pelvis. The woman sued the city of Ogden for $580,000, but ultimately settled for $300,000.

Arson

A Reno man who lived in an old mobile home was left homeless after his three pet dogs started a fire. Apparently, while the man was away, the dogs turned on his stove's gas burners. A fire soon commenced and the arsonist dogs fled. The fire caused major damage to the home's kitchen and roof, and killed at least one cat. Why did the dogs cause the fire? Reno fire department investigators said it was an accident. They surmised that the dogs were trying to get something on top of the stove and pawed at the burners, accidentally turning them on. But how do they really know? Maybe the dogs were engaged in a nefarious conspiracy to get rid of the cat.

Assault with a deadly weapon

Iowan James Harris was out hunting pheasant with a pack of hunting dogs. Harris put his shotgun on the ground and started to cross a fence to pick up a fallen pheasant. As he crossed the fence, one of the dogs stepped on the shotgun's trigger, sending up to 120 birdshot pellets into Harris's left calf from three feet away. A local official said that the injury was "not life-threatening, but will give him trouble for a long time."

Toe removal

Terry Smith, a Lexington, Kentucky resident who was paralyzed from the waist down after an accident, owned a six-month-old pit bull named China. Smith's roommate came home one day to find him in bed with his sheets covered in blood. To his horror, the roommate discovered that four toes on Smith's left foot were missing. Apparently, China gnawed off the toes. Smith couldn't feel the dog's bites because of his paralysis. The dog may have been attracted to sores on Smith's feet. Pieces of the missing toes were found, but no complete toes could be retrieved. Smith was hospitalized, but expected to make a full recovery. China was placed in quarantine pending Smith's release.

USA TODAY Snapshots®

Watch where you lay things

Top five possessions dog owners said their dogs damaged because of chewing habits:

- Shoes — 39%
- Furniture — 38%
- Clothing — 26%
- Kids' toys — 20%
- Electronic equipment — 15%

Source: TheHealthyChew.com   By David Stuckey and Dave Merrill, USA TODAY 2006

Murder

A man who lived in London, England, was found slumped on his living room floor with horrific face and neck injuries. Scotland Yard was soon on the case, and immediately concluded that the man's dog, a Staffordshire Bull Terrier, was the culprit. Their deduction was doubtless aided by the fact that the dog's face was caked in his master's blood. Moreover, an autopsy revealed that the man died from a neck injury consistent with a dog bite. The motive for the crime was unclear. Police suspect the man was epileptic, and may have had some sort of seizure that frightened his dog. Staffordshire Bull Terriers were originally bred for fighting and have incredibly strong jaws. A Scotland Yard spokesperson said that Bull Terriers are known to have a tendency to attack other dogs, but are generally good natured with humans. However, "If you were to get one on a bad day then you'd have a problem." Apparently, the dog in question had a really bad day. So did his owner.

Best Scenes From Movie Courtrooms

L ooking for courtroom drama? You won't necessarily find it in a courtroom, where moments of grinding tedium and fumbling ineptitude occur at least as often as those of eloquence and glory.

But, for inspiring discourses on justice, there's always the silver screen. Hollywood loves a good courtroom scene almost as much as it loves scripted first kisses, weddings, and car chases. Here are some of our favorites.

Twelve Angry Men, 1957

This celluloid classic stars Henry Fonda as "Juror #8," a man fighting to uphold the principle of reasonable doubt in the trial of a Latino boy, who faces death for allegedly killing his father. Here's his moving appeal to fellow jurors during a deliberation that occupies most of the movie:

> *I don't really know what the truth is. I don't suppose anybody will ever really know. Nine of us now seem to feel that the defendant is innocent, but we're just gambling on probabilities—we may be wrong. We may be trying to let a guilty man go free, I don't know. Nobody really can. But we have a reasonable doubt, and that's something that's very valuable in our system. No jury can declare a man guilty unless it's SURE. We nine can't understand how you three are still so sure.*

And Justice for All, 1979

Al Pacino plays the defense attorney in a high-profile rape trial. He delivers this biting commentary during the final courtroom scene:

> *What is justice? What is the intention of justice? The intention of justice is to see that the guilty people are proven guilty and that the innocent*

are freed. Simple, isn't it? Only it's not that simple. . . . [I]t is the defense counselor's duty to protect the rights of the individual as it is the prosecution's duty to uphold and defend the laws of the state. Justice for all. Only we have a problem here. You know what it is? Both sides want to win. We want to win. We want to win regardless of the truth; and we want to win regardless of justice; regardless of who's guilty or innocent. Winning is everything.

Bananas, 1971

In Woody Allen's comedy, he plays Fielding Mellish, a hapless nebbish of a New Yorker (of course) whose political activist girlfriend recently dumped him. Mellish tries to redeem himself by traveling to a Latin American country and joining the revolution. Upon returning to the United States, he's put on trial as a subversive. Here's what Woody Allen has to say at his trial:

I object, Your Honor, this trial is a travesty, it's a travesty of a mockery of a sham of a mockery of a travesty of two mockeries of a sham. I move for a mistrial.

The People Vs. Larry Flynt, 1996

Ed Norton plays a smart young attorney named Alan Isaacman who defends the First Amendment rights of *Hustler*-magazine publisher Larry Flynt, who is played by Woody Harrelson. Here's his appeal to the jury during one of Flynt's many trials:

I'm not trying to convince you that you should like what Larry Flynt does. I don't like what Larry Flynt does. But what I do like is that I live in a country where you and I can make that decision for ourselves. I like that I live in a country where I can pick up Hustler *magazine and read it if I want to or throw it in a garbage can if that's where I think it belongs. Or better yet, I can exercise my opinion and not buy it. I like that I have that right. I care about it. And you should care about it too.*

A Time to Kill, 1996

Matthew McConaughey plays the lawyer hired to defend Carl Lee Hailey, a poor Southern farmer played by Samuel L. Jackson. Hailey has been accused of murdering the men who kidnapped, raped, and killed his ten-year-old daughter.

I set out to prove that a black man could receive a fair trial in the South, that we are all equal in the eyes of law. That's not the truth. Because the eyes of the law are human eyes. Yours and mine. And until we can see each other as equals, justice is never going to be evenhanded. It will remain nothing more than a reflection of our own prejudices. So until that day, we have a duty under God to seek the truth, not with our eyes, not with our minds, where fear and hate turn commonality into prejudice, but with our hearts, where we don't know better.

Anatomy of a Murder, 1959

Based on a true case, this film is the story of how the temporary insanity defense originated. In a colorful sequence, and after repeated questioning by his lawyer, Paul Biegler (Jimmy Stewart), the defendant (Ben Gazzara), explains his excuse for a murder of passion: "I must have been crazy." What adds to the legal realism is that after all his great legal work, the client skips town and blows off Biegler's bill. One of the best moments of the film occurs when Stewart discourses on juries:

Twelve people go off into a room: twelve different minds, twelve different hearts, from twelve different walks of life; twelve sets of eyes, ears, shapes, and sizes. And these twelve people are asked to judge another human being as different from them as they are from each other. And in their judgment, they must become of one mind—unanimous. It's one of the miracles of Man's disorganized soul that they can do it, and in most instances, do it right well. God bless juries.

The Ox-Bow Incident, 1941

When a rancher is found dead, a local posse decides that it's not worth waiting to bring the villains back for a trial. Stringing them up on the spot seems more fitting unless it's after dark. Or as a local storekeeper played by Henry Fonda puts it, "I got nothin' particular against hangin' a murderin' rustler; it's just I don't like doin' it in the dark. There's always some crazy fool who'll lose his head and start hangin' everybody in sight." Unfortunately, that's exactly what happens and this dark, powerful Western ends with Carter's reading one of the hanged men's final letter to his wife:

> *A man just naturally can't take the law into his own hands and hang people without hurtin' everybody in the world, 'cause then he's just not breaking one law but all laws. Law is a lot more than words you put in a book, or judges or lawyers or sheriffs you hire to carry it out. It's everything people ever have found out about justice and what's right and wrong. It's the very conscience of humanity. There can't be any such thing as civilization unless people have a conscience, because if people touch God anywhere, where is it except through their conscience? And what is anybody's conscience except a little piece of the conscience of all men that ever lived? I guess that's all I've got to say except kiss the babies for me and God bless you."*

The Verdict (1991)

Though short on legal reality—attorney Paul Galvin (Paul Newman) is far too boozed up to lead a major medical malpractice case like this— *The Verdict* is an entertaining courtroom melodrama with a knockout supporting cast (Milo O'Shea, James Mason, Charlotte Rampling, Lindsay Crouse, and Jack Warden). David Mamet's screenplay crackles as Galvin attempts to recover his courtroom balance after a nefarious opposing counsel and judge block his evidence. Galvin puts down the bottle long enough to deliver a stirring summation:

> *You know, so much of the time we're just lost. We say, "Please, God, tell us what is right; tell us what is true." And there is no justice: The rich win, the poor are powerless. We become tired of hearing people lie. And after a time, we become dead... a little dead. We think of ourselves as victims... and we become victims. We become... we become weak. We doubt*

ourselves, we doubt our beliefs. We doubt our institutions. And we doubt the law. But today you are the law. You ARE the law. Not some book... not the lawyers... not the, a marble statue... or the trappings of the court. See those are just symbols of our desire to be just. They are... they are, in fact, a prayer: a fervent and a frightened prayer. In my religion, they say, "Act as if ye had faith... and faith will be given to you." IF... if we are to have faith in justice, we need only to believe in ourselves. And ACT with justice. See, I believe there is justice in our heart.

"Monty Python's Flying Circus," Season One

Okay, it's not Hollywood, and it's not even a movie, but we couldn't resist this inspiring interchange between Eric Idle as the plaintiff and Terry Jones as the bewigged British judge:

Judge: *Mr. Larch, you've heard the case for the prosecution. Is there anything you wish to say before I pass sentence?*

Mr. Larch: *Well... I'd just like to say, m'lud, I've got a family ... a wife and six kids ... and I hope very much you don't have to take away my freedom ... because ... well, because m'lud, freedom is a state much prized within the realm of civilized society. It is a bond wherewith the savage man may charm the outward hatchments of his soul, and soothe the troubled breast into a magnitude of quiet. It is most precious as a blessed balm, the savior of princes, the harbinger of happiness, yea, the very stuff and pith of all we hold most dear. What frees the prisoner in his lonely cell, chained within the bondage of rude walls, far from the owl of Thebes? What fires and stirs the woodcock in his springe or wakes the drowsy apricot betide? What goddess doth the storm-toss'd mariner offer most tempestuous prayers to? Freedom! Freedom! Freedom!*

Judge: *It's only a bloody parking offence.*

Take My Wives, Please: Polygamy Law FAQ

S o, you're showing a group of tourists around the United States, and they ask you, "What's the story—can you marry more than one person in this country or not?" Would you know how to answer? We're here to help.

U.S. laws against polygamy began appearing in the second half of the nineteenth century, apparently aimed at curtailing the growth and expansion of the Church of Latter-Day Saints, which prior to 1890 had endorsed polygamous marriages. The passage of the Morill Anti-Bigamy Act in 1862 was the first major anti-Mormon statute—federal legislation to prohibit bigamy and limit property ownership by a church or nonprofit. (Enforcement of the law was delayed for several years because Abraham Lincoln promised not to prosecute anyone if Mormon leader Brigham Young agreed not to become involved in the Civil War.)

Despite many challenges over the last 150 years, polygamy remains verboten. Here are the FAQ.

Is polygamy legal anywhere in the United States?

No. It's a crime under federal and state laws.

If it's a crime, how come so many people get away with it?

It's estimated that 30,000 to 60,000 people are practicing polygamy right now, most of them living either in the Salt Lake City area (the location for the "Big Love" TV series), or near the Utah-Arizona border in Colorado City and Hildale (formerly Short Creek). Enforcement of antipolygamy laws is usually lax unless law enforcement is required because of reports of abuse. Attempts at cracking the whip—as was done in the ill-fated Short Creek raids of 1953—often end up turning public sentiment against the authorities, because the typical raid results in separation of children and parents.

If it's a crime, what's the danger? Who is the victim?

The primary dangers of polygamy, as practiced in the United States, are that it (1) exploits underage girls married to much older men (statutory rape), (2) according to evidence, leads to trafficking in wives across state lines (violation of the Mann Act), and (3) includes situations where polygamous husbands have married their own daughters or nieces (incest). In a 2001 crackdown by Utah authorities, evidence was found for all of these abuses along with claims that teenage boys (dubbed "lost boys") were abandoned by the church elders (often dumped in Salt Lake City) in order to create a surplus of potential brides.

Aren't laws against polygamy a violation of religious freedom?

Not according to the Supreme Court. In an 1878 case, George Reynolds, a member of the Church of Latter-Day Saints argued that it was his religious duty to marry multiple times and therefore the federal prohibition (instituted in 1862) was a violation of his freedom to practice religion. The Supreme Court disagreed. What if someone claimed that human sacrifice was necessary for a religion? Such an interpretation would "make the professed doctrines of religious belief superior to the law of the land, and in effect permit every citizen to become a law unto himself." In other words, the government cannot intrude on religious opinion but it can legislate the actions that result from those opinions. The Court denied Reynolds' appeal.

Are prohibitions against polygamy a violation of laws that prohibit discrimination based on status (equal protection laws)?

No, not according to attorney and law professor Marci Hamilton. "Anti-polygamy statutes draw the line at the number of spouses, not their characteristics or status."

Is it true Justice Scalia wants to legalize polygamy?

No. Scalia has said he expects challenges to antipolygamy laws. But questions about Scalia's beliefs have arisen based on two of his statements; one in his dissent in *Romer v. Evans* (1996) and the other in *Lawrence v. Texas* (2003). In *Romer*—in which the Supreme Court overturned a Colorado law because it had "impermissibly targeted" homosexuals—Scalia argued that states should be free to target sexual practices; after all polygamists had already been a targeted class, "unless," he stated, "polygamists for some reason have fewer constitutional rights than homosexuals."

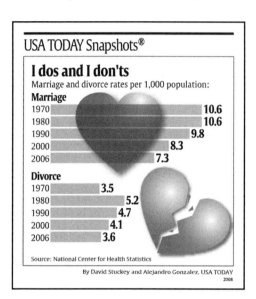

USA TODAY Snapshots®

I dos and I don'ts

Marriage and divorce rates per 1,000 population:

Marriage
1970 — 10.6
1980 — 10.6
1990 — 9.8
2000 — 8.3
2006 — 7.3

Divorce
1970 — 3.5
1980 — 5.2
1990 — 4.7
2000 — 4.1
2006 — 3.6

Source: National Center for Health Statistics

By David Stuckey and Alejandro Gonzalez, USA TODAY 2008

In *Lawrence,* the Supreme Court declared a Texas antisodomy law to be unconstitutional and reversed a case, *Bowers v. Hardwick*, that previously held that states could determine what forms of sexual behavior are "immoral and unacceptable." Justice Scalia lamented, "This effectively decrees the end of all morals legislation." Taken together, these two statements have encouraged hopes for some polygamists who view the battle for legal polygamy as a civil rights struggle.

What's polygyny, and is that illegal?

Polygyny is the practice of having more than one wife at one time; polyandry is the flip—having more than one husband at one time. Both practices are illegal in the United States. In 1903 Senate hearings, Joseph F. Smith, president and prophet of the LDS, supposedly testified to the Senate that Mormons were not practicing polygamy (personally believing that it was polygyny and, therefore, distinguishable from what was prohibited). Like similar uses of linguistic technicalities ("I have never had sexual relations with Monica Lewinsky"), his deception was a failure.

How can antipolygamy laws be enforced if they were originally intended to discriminate against Mormons?

Although today's laws are derived from a discriminatory approach to legislation, that does not make antipolygamy laws unconstitutional. That's because these laws are considered "facially neutral"—that is, anti-polygamy laws apply equally to all people, including Hindus, Mormons, Jews, and Muslims, all of whom once practiced polygamy.

Is there a difference between bigamy and polygamy?

Yes and no. Many antipolygamy laws are titled as antibigamy laws since both bigamy and polygamy involve being married to more than one person at the same time. A misconception also arose that the distinction has something to do with the number of spouses (not true). The *Model Penal Code* (*MPC*)—a guide for drafting state laws—attempts to distinguish them as follows: If multiple spouses form a family, it's polygamy (a felony); if they don't—for example, the traditional scenario in which a man has two wives and neither wife knows of the other—it's bigamy (a misdemeanor). In other words, under the *MPC*, it's better to hide multiple spouses than to flaunt them.

How Robert Crumb Almost Lost "Keep on Truckin'"

H ard as it may be for some people to believe (everyone under 30, raise your hands), there was a time in American commerce when we did not buy merchandise emblazoned with licensed cartoon, movie, and other characters. In the 1950s, Walt Disney created the first market for kids' merchandise, initially with Mickey Mouse, but even more so with the surprisingly successful Davy Crockett craze.

But aside from kids buying lunchboxes and coonskin caps, Americans did not adorn their apartments and homes with image-laden posters, bathmats, towels, and sheets and did not declare their identity by wearing trademark-adorned T-shirts, hats, and sweatshirts.

Then along came the 1960s counterculture, and the kids who grew up with Mickey and Davy wanted merchandise to reflect their current lifestyle. The image that initially drove this new merchandise market was a cartoon panel entitled "Keep on Truckin," created by cartoonist Robert Crumb.

In 1968, "Keep on Truckin'" debuted in *Zap No. 1*, an underground comic, and Crumb was surprised by the wild popularity that followed. (He believed "Keep on Truckin" to be "the dumbest page in the whole comic.") Within months, the imagery and phrase was being hawked on T-shirts, posters, patches, stickers, and bathmats, none of which were authorized by Crumb.

A fellow artist persuaded Crumb to get a lawyer. "I just never thought that I could ever get myself in a position where I could actually have a lawyer to protect me," he later said. "So it sounded good to me, you know. You have to have somebody in the legal business on your side."

One of the companies he pursued was A.A. Sales. Initially, the parties reached a settlement and $750 was paid to Crumb, but there was confusion as to the payment and A.A. Sales continued to sell unauthorized posters, puzzles, and patches. In 1973, Crumb's lawyers filed suit in federal court. The judge, Albert Charles Wollenberg, a 73-year old Eisenhower appointee, was no stranger to underground comics—he had previously ruled in the infamous *Air Pirates* case in which he halted Mickey Mouse's use in a risqué comic.

A.A. Sales decided to dig in its heels. At first it argued that the

cartoon did not contain sufficient originality, and alternatively that Crumb abused copyright. When those defenses didn't fly—Crumb had borrowed the phrase, but his drawing of the zoot-suited, big-footed walking characters was his own—A.A. Sales trudged out a defense that was available only in the United States. Known as "notice omission," the defense was essentially that Crumb lost his copyright ownership because he had published his work without the little "C" in the circle with the date and Crumb's name.

The only problem with A.A.'s defense was that it didn't know of any omission and had no proof that there ever was an omission. So it did what many copyright defendants did at the time—it went on a fishing expedition.

Fortunately, Crumb had included the copyright notice when he published *Zap No.1*. He did so more out of attention to detail than for any legal reason, since he thought it was "traditional." The notice had also been included in *Head Comix* (when the cartoon was including a book published by Viking Press). Lacking proof, A.A. Sales continued to pursue discovery and Crumb lamented the whole process and expense:

"Morally, I feel that—I mean in 1967 when I was drawing this stuff, to me it was all a mater of morality because I just didn't develop an awareness of where this is the hard, cold facts of business life in America, the way it works, you know, like the whole principle that you can be starving in the gutter and somebody could be getting rich off your work, and not paying you a cent because you didn't put a little C with a circle next to your work is a reality of life in American which I was not that keenly aware of when I did the work. But now I am, obviously, because here we are arguing about it."

USA TODAY Snapshots®

Kids wear sports on their sleeves

Sports-related clothing that kids age 7-11 own:

NFL	37%
Major League Baseball	27%
NBA	23%
College football	19%
NASCAR	13%

Source: ESPN Sports Poll, a service of TNS Sport

By Ellen J. Horrow and Bob Laird, USA TODAY
2006

A.A. Sales discovered many copies of "Keep on Truckin'" without notice—but none were admissible, because they were all unauthorized infringements. It looked like the defense would fail ... until the deposition of Robert Rita, owner of the Print Mint, a company that printed underground comics. Rita had used the "Keep on Truckin'" image on a 3 x 6-inch business card with Crumb's permission. About 15,000 to 20,000 cards were said to have been printed (although that number was later recalculated as less then 6,000 copies). Rita stated that Crumb had never required notice on the card. Crumb, on the other hand stated that he didn't recall anything about the cards and didn't remember seeing them.

Under the 1909 Copyright Act, which was in effect at the time of the case, any authorized publication of a work without notice resulted in a loss of copyright—a fate that had previously befallen a wide variety of works ranging from primitive computer games to the Danish Troll dolls. (The principle of notice omission favors big business over artists since artists are more likely to forget about notice and big businesses are more likely to discover those failures.) Although every other nation had abandoned the defense, the United States refused to change its approach, a fact that kept it from becoming a member of important international treaties such as the Berne Convention.

In 1975, using the Print Mint business cards as evidence, Judge Wollenberg granted A.A. Sales' motion for summary judgment. "Keep on Truckin'" then fell into the public domain. In other words, Crumb's image, which had spawned the first adult merchandising boon was now free for anyone to commercialize.

Fortunately, in 1977 the Ninth Circuit determined there was a relevant factual question as to whether Crumb had authorized publication of the cards. The summary judgment was reversed and "Keep on Truckin'" was pulled back from the public domain. The case with A.A. Sales was settled prior to trial and Crumb now retains copyright ownership of the work.

The case was a bitter experience for Crumb, who later documented his feelings about Judge Wollenberg in one of his comics. And in his comic book, *Home Grown Funnies*, Crumb also reflected his bitterness (as well as creating the precursor to today's Creative Commons copyright license) when he inserted the following notice: "All material herein may be reprinted for free by any underground publication or other small enterprise. All fat capitalists who reprint without permission will be sued for breech [sic] of copyright! Nyahh."

The Copyright Act of 1976 (enacted in 1978) attempted to correct the problems experienced by Crumb with a more forgiving notice omission law, but Congress finally threw in the towel with a law effective March 1, 1989, that ended penalties for notice omission. Works published after that date no longer require notice and the failure to include notice will never result in loss of copyright ownership.

Trials of the Centuries

oes every century contain a trial that stands out from the millions of others because of its historical importance, political impact, public attention received, courtroom drama involved— or all of these?

Well, no. But many do, and their names alone are burnt into the memory of subsequent generations. Here is our list of the trials of the centuries, beginning in the time of ancient Greece.

Fourth century B.C.E.

Who was tried: Socrates

When: 399 B.C.E.

Where: Athens, Greece

Criminal charges: Disbelief in orthodox religion, corrupting the youth of Athens

Verdict: Guilty

Sentence: Death

In one of the most famous trials in all of history, the great classical Greek philosopher Socrates was accused by Athens's leaders of corrupting the minds of the youth of the city—namely, his many students. A charge of impiety was thrown in for good measure. The real reason for the charges was revenge for Socrates' scathing criticism of the city's oligarchy and the desire to use him as a scapegoat for the city's problems.

Socrates was found guilty and sentenced to death by drinking hemlock. He could have escaped Athens and avoided punishment, but chose not to because he believed it would show he feared death, a fear he believed no true philosopher could hold. His trial and death were immortalized in works written by his leading disciple: the philosopher Plato.

First century C.E.

Who was tried: Jesus of Nazareth

When: 33 C.E.

Where: Jerusalem, Roman province of Judea

Criminal charges: Blasphemy, treason

Verdict: Guilty

Sentence: Death

According to the Christian Gospels, Jesus was tried by Pontius Pilate, governor of Judea, after being accused of blasphemy and treason against Rome by Jewish priests. Although Pilate did not believe Jesus' alleged crimes merited execution under Roman law, he ordered him crucified after the Jerusalem mob refused to call on the Romans to free him, choosing that Barabbas be freed instead. Without this trial, there may have been no Christian religion.

Fifteenth century

Who was tried: Joan of Arc

When: 1431

Where: Rouen, France

Criminal charges: Heresy

Verdict: Guilty

Sentence: Death

Joan of Arc was a 19-year-old, illiterate French peasant girl who led French armies to several important victories over the British during the Hundred Years War after claiming to hear voices from God. She was captured and tried for blasphemy by the British. The charges were politically motivated and a guilty verdict a foregone conclusion. However, Joan's extraordinary display of dignity and intellect during her trial would inspire people for centuries and be immortalized in numerous works of art, including the play *Saint Joan* by George Bernard Shaw. Joan was burned at the stake and later made a saint by the Catholic Church.

Sixteenth century

Who was tried: Martin Luther

When: 1521

Where: Worms, Germany

Criminal charges: Heresy

Verdict: Guilty

Sentence: Excommunication, banishment, death

Martin Luther, the German Catholic priest who spearheaded the Protestant Reformation that changed European and world history, was charged with heresy and summoned to appear before the diet (formal assembly) of German electors in Worms, a town on the Rhine. At a dramatic trial before the emperor of the Holy Roman Empire, the local Catholic archbishop, and other officials, Luther was presented with copies of his writings and asked whether the books were his and whether he stood by their contents. Luther famously declared, "Here I stand. I can do no other." He was found guilty of heresy and ordered arrested and executed. Luther escaped punishment when friends spirited him off to a remote castle in the Thuringian Forest. He went on with his work and founded the new religion that came to be known as Lutheranism.

Seventeenth century

Who was tried: Galileo Gallilei

When: 1633

Where: Rome, Italy

Criminal charges: Heresy

Verdict: Guilty

Sentence: Abjuration, lifelong house arrest

The Renaissance Italian Galileo Galilei was a seminal figure in the history of science. The first man to use a telescope to observe the heavens, his discoveries helped confirm that the Sun, not the Earth, was the center of the solar system. His outspoken public support for a heliocentric universe met with bitter opposition from some philosophers and clerics. In 1632, he was tried by the Roman Inquisition and found guilty of heresy. To save his life, he recanted his support of Copernicus and spent the rest of his days under house arrest. Galileo's trial is seen as a sign that it might not be possible for science and religion to peacefully coexist.

Eighteenth century

Who was tried: Louis XVI, Marie Antoinette
When: 1792
Where: Paris, France
Criminal charges: Treason
Verdict: Guilty
Sentence: Death

King Louis XVI and his queen, Marie Antoinette, ruled France at the time of one of the greatest cataclysms in history: the French Revolution. Louis and Marie at first attempted to deal with France's revolutionary forces and accept a constitutional monarchy. However, they later tried to escape the country to lead foreign armies against France. They were caught while attempting to flee, then arrested and imprisoned. In what amounted to show trials, they were found guilty of treason by the Convention (the revolutionary assembly) and ordered executed. Both were guillotined. It was the first and only time French monarchs were executed. Their death marked the end of the old regime in France and helped pave the way for Napoleon, world war, and the modern world.

Nineteenth century

Who was tried: Alfred Dreyfus
When: 1894, 1899
Where: Paris and Rennes, France
Criminal charges: Treason
Verdict: Guilty
Sentence: Life in prison, later pardoned and declared innocent

Alfred Dreyfus was an unknown young captain in the French Army. He was charged with treason when the French discovered that military secrets were being communicated to the German embassy in Paris.

Army investigators concluded that the secrets must have come from an artillery office assigned to the General Staff. Dreyfus met both requirements; moreover he was a Jew, spoke German, and was generally disliked by his fellow officers, most of whom were Catholics and anti-Semitic. Dreyfus was court-martialed and convicted of treason largely on the basis of documents that were later proved to have been forged by army investigators. He was sentenced to life in prison and sent to the notorious French penal colony on Devil's Island.

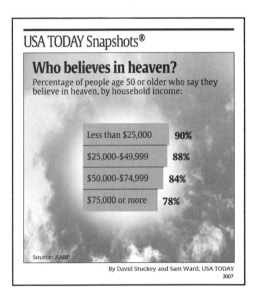

USA TODAY Snapshots®

Who believes in heaven?
Percentage of people age 50 or older who say they believe in heaven, by household income:

Less than $25,000	**90%**
$25,000-$49,999	**88%**
$50,000-$74,999	**84%**
$75,000 or more	**78%**

Source: AARP

By David Stuckey and Sam Ward, USA TODAY
2007

Eventually, the truth came to light. Documents showed that the actual spy was a French Army major named Ferdinand Esterhazy. However, the leaders of the French Army refused to admit that Dreyfus had been framed. The great French author Emile Zola published a famous denunciation of Dreyfus's conviction and the French General Staff that helped stoke a national outcry. Dreyfus was brought back from Guiana in 1899 to be tried again. He was again found guilty, but was soon pardoned by the French government. He was later fully exonerated and reinstated in the French Army.

The "Dreyfus affair" bitterly divided France and led to an upsurge of anti-Semitism and the founding of the modern Zionist movement. The undercurrents of hate and xenophobia unleashed by the affair would later become a maelstrom in the twentieth century, resulting in two world wars and the Holocaust.

Twentieth century

Who was tried: Herman Goering, Albert Speer, Rudolf Hess, Karl Donitz, Martin Bormann, Hans Frank, Wilhelm Frick, Hans Fritzche, Walther Funk, Alfred Jodl, Ernst Kaltenbrunner, Wilhelm Keitel, Gustav Krupp, Robert Ley, Franch von Pappen, Erich Raeder, Joachim von Ribbentrop, Alfred Rosenberg, Fritz Sauckel, Hjalmar Schacht, Baldur von Schirach, Arthur Seyss-Inquart, Julius Streicher

When: 1945–1946

Where: Nuremburg, Germany

Criminal charges: Crimes against humanity, waging aggressive war, war crimes, conspiracy to commit crimes against peace

Verdict: Guilty

Sentence: Death, various prison terms

Many famous trials took place during the twentieth century (such as that of the Gang of Four after China's Cultural Revolution), and many at the time were called the "trial of century," but none equal the Nuremburg Trial in importance. At the close of World War II, the victorious Allies chose to try 22 surviving top leaders of Nazi Germany before an international military tribunal in Nuremberg, Germany. The Nazis were charged with (1) crimes against peace, including planning and waging aggressive war; (2) war crimes; and (3) crimes against humanity, including murder, extermination, enslavement, persecution on political or racial grounds, involuntary deportment, and inhumane acts against civilian populations.

Most of the defendants claimed they knew nothing about the Nazi's crimes, or were simply following orders—what came to be known as the "Nuremberg defense." However, the evidence against them was monumental, including the Nazi's own propaganda films and extensive paperwork documenting mass murder and other crimes. The evidence even included the shrunken head of a concentration camp inmate and tattooed human skin from camp inmates used to make lampshades.

All but three of the defendants were found guilty of one or more of the charges. Some were sentenced to death, others to prison terms. The most famous defendant was Hermann Goering, the head of the Nazi air force and Hitler's Number Two man and heir apparent. He was found guilty of all counts and sentenced to death. However, he cheated the hangman by poisoning himself in his cell.

The Nuremberg Trial established for the first time that a nation's leaders can be held accountable under international law for their actions during wartime.

Twenty-first century

Who was tried: Saddam Hussein

When: 2004–2006

Where: Baghdad, Iraq

Criminal charges: Murder

Verdict: Guilty

Sentence: Death

It's too soon to say which trial will be the trial of the twenty-first century, but the trial of the first decade of the twenty-first century was that of Iraq's former dictator Saddam Hussein. After being captured by the American Army in 2003, Hussein was tried by the Iraqi Interim Government for crimes against humanity, including the killing of 148 Shiites in retaliation for an assassination attempt on him in 1982. After a contentious trial that lasted almost one year, he was found guilty and sentenced to death. Hussein was executed by hanging on December 30, 2006.

"Oops" Headlines About Law and Crimes

L ate night efforts to get the paper out sometimes lead to hilarious blooper headlines (now referred to as "crash blossoms"). And tales of law and criminals are well represented among them.

Here are some of our favorites:

Lawmen from Mexico Barbecue Guests

Dead Man Ignored Police Order

Defendant's Speech Ends in Long Sentence

DEAF MUTE GETS NEW HEARING IN KILLING

Man Robs, Then Kills Himself

Doctor Testifies in Horse Suit

Legalized Outhouses Aired by Legislature

Farmer Bill Dies In House

JUVENILE COURT TO TRY SHOOTING DEFENDANT

Silent Teamster Gets Cruel Punishment: Lawyer

Police Union to Seek Blinding Arbitration

Bar Trying to Help Alcoholic Lawyers

POLICE KILL MAN WITH AX

City May Impose Mandatory Time for Prostitution

Police Begin Campaign to Run Down Jaywalkers

Police Discover Crack in Australia

Two Convicts Evade Noose; Jury Hung

S. FLORIDA ILLEGAL ALIENS CUT IN HALF BY NEW LAW

Man Held in Miami after Shooting Bee

Thugs Eat Then Rob Proprietor

Hershey Bars Protest

LAWYERS GIVE POOR FREE LEGAL ADVICE

Stolen Painting Found by Tree

Killer Sentenced to Die for Second Time in 10 Years

Enfield Couple Slain; Police Suspect Homicide

WOMAN ARRESTED IN DEATH OF NEWBORN FOUND
IN TRASH BIN

How Rich People Avoid Getting Beaten Up in Prison

W ere you losing sleep over whether Martha Stewart would have to share an open toilet, Bernie Madoff would be forced to join a prison gang, and Michael Vick would get kicked across the prison yard by every dog-loving inmate? Well, rest your fears. Unlike the average person sent upriver, the rich and privileged have access to an unusual form of help: prison and sentencing consultants.

That's right. Even after the judge has sent the jury home, there's a cadre of professionals offering all manner of assistance with, in the words of one of their ads, "mak[ing] the transition from your yard to the prison yard easier and less traumatic."

Below are some of the ways a consultant may help the client—at a price, of course. For just the basic "prison prep," the cost is about $3,500. But a convicted felon seeking the deluxe package of sentencing and facility placement services could pay well over $10,000.

A shorter sentence

The Marthas, Bernies, and Michaels of the world may hire a sentencing specialist to help the defense attorney craft an argument with which to bargain with the prosecutor or persuade the judge to go light on the actual time to be served. Depending on the defendant's life history, the specifics of the crime, and the legally possible sentence, they may bargain for mental health or substance abuse treatment or push for restitution, community service, or other alternatives in lieu of a long stay.

In Martha Stewart's case, for example, they argued that her sentence should be reduced in exchange for a promise to do community service at the Women's Venture Fund, which teaches urban women entrepreneurial skills. Given that the range of possible sentences for Stewart's crime was ten to 16 months, but she was sentenced to only five months in a federal women's prison camp in West Virginia plus five additional months of home detention, the argument seems to have had some effect.

Placement at the best possible prison

Like hotels, prisons can be ranked in terms of milieu, amenities, and even recreational opportunities. Instead of a star rating, however, federal convicts are concerned with whether they're assigned to a minimum-, medium-, or high-security prison.

Minimum security can be almost cushy, especially at prison "camps," which are not surrounded by fences, and tend to house first-time, nonviolent offenders who aren't looking for fights.

Consultants always make sure to emphasize that prison is never "easy." But the prison Martha Stewart went to is widely known as "Camp Cupcake," and she described it as, "like an old-fashioned college campus—without the freedom, of course." Like a college, inmates there have roommates and can go out to run the track or play basketball, volleyball, or softball, as well as visit the library.

Medium- security prisons are more restrictive. Inmates are held behind a double-layered, razor-wire perimeter with electronic detection systems. Guards regularly search cells and pat prisoners down in a search for weapons and other contraband.

But even that looks cushy next to high-security prisons—some of which live up to the worst stereotypes or movie dramatizations, with

USA TODAY Snapshots®

Corporate crime and punishment

Should corporate officers and members of boards of directors who are convicted of practices harmful to employees, investors and the public be sent to jail?

Yes **89%**

No **7%**

Don't know **4%**

Source: Pepperdine University Graziadio School of Business and Management Corporate Board survey of 482 adults 18 and older. Margin of error ±5 percentage points.

By Jae Yang and Adrienne Lewis, USA TODAY 2007

rampant gang and racial violence interspersed with long hours locked in a cell with nothing to do. Michael Vick, the former Philadelphia Eagle convicted of dogfighting, spent 22 months at Leavenworth, a high-security prison in Kansas.

Which type of prison a convict gets sent to depends on how he or she scores on a U.S. Bureau of Prisons system known as Form BP-337. This calculates an inmate's "Security Point Total" by measuring such factors as age, health, history of violence and escape, likelihood of attempting to escape (perhaps because of a lengthy sentence), nature of the offense, and whether the person surrendered voluntarily or not.

The lower the score, the better the placement. The prison consultant coaches the attorney on how to push a marginal score toward a lower-security one by asking for consideration of extraordinary factors like a medical history or family concerns. For example, Martha Stewart pointed out—in vain—that her 90-year-old mother would have trouble traveling all the way from Connecticut to West Virginia for visits. In the case of someone like Bernard Madoff, they'll also point out the safety risks arising from being so well-known.

After help from his consultant, Madoff—who, you may remember, was sentenced to 150 years for masterminding one of the largest Ponzi schemes in U.S. history—is doing his time in the medium-security wing of the Butner Federal Correctional Complex near Raleigh, North Carolina.

Which other famous criminals have used prison consultants?

Michael Milken (securities law violations), Ivan Boesky (insider trading), Mike Tyson (sexual assault), Michael Vick (animal abuse), and Leona Helmsley (tax evasion). And a criminal background doesn't preclude a career as a prison consultant—in fact, it may enhance it. Many prison and sentencing consultants have done time themselves.

Advice about navigating the prison system

A prison consultant can prepare the defendant for life on the inside by reviewing the rules and regulations of a specific prison and providing information about prison culture. For example, all federal prisoners can spend a maximum of $290 a month at the prison commissary, which sells snacks, stamps, and some toiletries. Many of them can work at menial jobs within the prison, but the pay is usually less than $1 an hour.

Family orientation

The consultant may also work with the defendant's family to prepare them for the realities of having a family member in prison. The consultant will tell them about visiting hours, telephone access, and strict prohibitions on sending money and gifts.

Advice on steering clear of trouble

New inmates must navigate some treacherous waters. Those who think it's wise to chat up the guards, for example, might find themselves branded as snitches. Those who try to get friendly by sitting at a lunch table with members of another race may provoke suspicion and anger. Those accustomed to ordering their corporate minions around will have to drop the attitude and get friendly with others, perhaps by joining card games and talking sports. As Bernie Madoff's prison consultant, Herb Hoelter, advised him, "It's a matter of keeping your space and having respect for other people." Oh, and watch out for the TV room—that's where most altercations arise.

How Much Can a Fake Lawyer Earn?

When people visit a lawyer, they rarely check that he or she is for real. (Too much trouble? Not really; all you have to do is contact the state bar association to make sure that the lawyer is on file and hasn't been disbarred.) But why bother, when the supposed lawyer looks so professional, in that pressed wool suit, sitting in a leather chair in a twentieth floor downtown office?

For the con artists of the world—and the wannabe lawyers too lazy to go to law school—this presents one big profit opportunity. Fake like a lawyer!

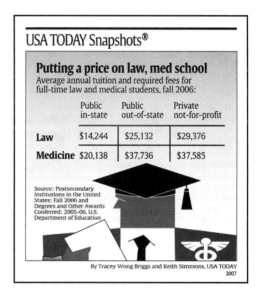

USA TODAY Snapshots®

Putting a price on law, med school
Average annual tuition and required fees for full-time law and medical students, fall 2006:

	Public in-state	Public out-of-state	Private not-for-profit
Law	$14,244	$25,132	$29,376
Medicine	$20,138	$37,736	$37,585

Source: Postsecondary Institutions in the United States: Fall 2006 and Degrees and Other Awards Conferred: 2005–06, U.S. Department of Education

By Tracey Wong Briggs and Keith Simmons, USA TODAY 2007

Now, given that law can actually be rather difficult, you'd think such less-than-thrilling theater wouldn't be worth the cost of dry cleaning and office rental. Until, that is, you take a look at the numbers. (And these are only the fake lawyers who got caught....)

Fake immigration attorney

One fake attorney earned $129,000 by offering to sell green card extensions to immigrants who believed he could help them avoid deportation. It was easy to fall for the scam: The nonlawyer had a lavish office in Los Angeles, told people he used to be a judge, also ran a fake traffic school, and stole the identity of (and $80,000 from) one of his traffic school customers. But the gravy train came to a quick stop when, in 2008, he was charged with 31 counts of fraud.

Fake DUI attorney

In 2008, a man paid a fake attorney $18,000 to help him get out of a drunk-driving charge. The pseudo-attorney took the matter to court, where his bizarre questioning during jury selection ("Do you like animals?") didn't apparently raise any eyebrows. But he lost the case.

USA TODAY Snapshots®

The lies have it

Overall, 42% of high school students think a person has to lie or cheat sometimes to succeed. By gender:

Male **50%**

Female **33%**

Source: Josephson Institute's 2006 Report Card on the Ethics of American Youth, a questionnaire survey of 36,000 high school students ages 14-19 from 114 schools, January-June; margin of error is ±1 percentage point.

By Tracey Wong Briggs and Alejandro Gonzalez, USA TODAY 2006

Fake criminal defense attorney—and fake man!

A Union, South Carolina, woman came up with a clever idea while serving time in jail. She'd call the parents of a fellow inmate, pretend to be a male attorney named Billy Whitney, and offer them legal services with the goal of springing their daughter. For a while, it worked: She scammed the couple out of $8,000.

Not surprisingly, however, the parents became suspicious when they came to pick up their supposedly released daughter and she was still behind bars. They'd also been planning to thank Whitney, but he didn't show up to meet them. When they called the office of the real Whitney, they realized there was something, uh, different about the sound of his voice.

Bad luck for the scam artist: She ended up back in jail.

Fake big-firm attorney

A Manhattan white-shoe law firm billed $300 an hour for the work of a paralegal who fooled the firm by pretending to be an "unduly aggressive" attorney. The fake attorney participated in several lawsuits, including a product liability case over the drug Oxycontin. He impersonated a lawyer in New York, New Jersey, and Connecticut, a misdemeanor in all three states.

Bonus question: How many lawsuits can a fake attorney win in eight months?

Twenty-five, according to a fake lawyer operating out of Newport Beach, California, who managed to prevail in that many matters before his ruse was discovered. "I lied about being a lawyer but other than the lie, everything else was totally legit," he said.

Can You Name That Supreme Court Case?

T he Supreme Court decides upwards of 100 cases every year, and we don't hear about most of them.

But then there are the REALLY BIG cases—the ones that become pillars of U.S. law (or hurdles, depending on your views). Many are known by name to almost every American. Okay, maybe to every law student.

How many of these biggies have you heard of? Try matching the case names below with the right summary of the Court's decision or "holding."

Case Names

New York Times Co. v. Sullivan, 1964

Mapp v. Ohio, 1961

Plessy v. Ferguson, 1896

Loving v. Virginia, 1967

Gideon v. Wainwright, 1963

Marbury v. Madison, 1803

Regents of the University of California v. Bakke, 1978

Plyler v. Doe, 1982

Sony v. Universal City Studios, 1984

Bowers v. Hardwick, 1986

Brown v. Board of Education of Topeka, 1954

Miranda v. Arizona, 1966

Roe v. Wade, 1973

Dred Scott v. Sandford, 1857

What the court decided

1. The Sixth Amendment right to a fair trial means everyone should have a lawyer, even if they can't afford one—so states must provide free lawyers for them in the latter case.

2. Undocumented alien children must be allowed to attend public schools, as a matter of equal protection under the Fourteenth Amendment.

3. Neither the Constitutional rights of privacy nor liberty protect homosexuals against state laws prohibiting sodomy, even if the acts occur in a private home between consenting adults. Justice Powell, who after much agonizing cast the swing vote, commented to one of his clerks that he'd never met a homosexual—not realizing that the clerk himself was a closeted homosexual. He was later quoted as saying he'd made a mistake on this vote. In fact, the Court overturned this decision in the case of *Lawrence v. State of Texas*, abolishing all U.S. sodomy laws.

4. Reserving admission slots for minority students violates the 1964 Civil Rights Act, which prohibits excluding anyone—even white men— from federally funded programs on the basis of race. (And so, the white male plaintiff gained admission to med school.)

5. Before questioning suspects in custody, police must, in keeping with the Fifth Amendment right against self-incrimination, tell them that they have the right to remain silent, that anything they say may be used against them in court, that they have the right to have a lawyer present, and the right to a free lawyer if they can't afford one. (If you can practically recite these phrases by memory, chances are you watched the TV shows "Adam 12" or "Dragnet" in the 1960s.)

6

A woman has a right, under the Fourteenth Amendment, to choose an abortion within the first trimester of her pregnancy, though states may legally restrict this right during later trimesters.

7

States can't ban interracial marriage—such race distinctions violate the Fourteenth Amendment. (The couple in this case, a white man and a woman who was part black and part American Indian had traveled to a state that allowed them to marry, but after returning home was arrested for violating their state's law against miscegenation.)

8

States can't maintain racially segregated schools for blacks and whites; it violates the Fourteenth Amendment's guarantee of equal protection under the law. (Certain Southern states were seriously displeased at having to desegregate their schools and referred to the date of this decision as "Black Monday.")

9

Public officials can't sue the media for libel unless they can prove that the media acted with "actual malice." This is part of the First Amendment's protection of freedom of the press.

10

No fair trying to introduce evidence against a criminal defendant if it was obtained through an illegal search and seizure—such evidence is inadmissible in court. (This case is credited with transforming police practices across the United States— waving around a piece of paper and pretending it's a search warrant no longer cuts it.)

11

This case legalized time-shifting of TV shows (taping shows for the purpose of watching them later). Because of the vast consumer interest, this case attracted a record number of friends-of-the-court briefs.

⑫

This case made three holdings that stained the Court's history. It held that persons of African descent who were slaves in the United States could never be citizens (and could therefore not bring lawsuits); that such people were the private property of their owners and only through due process could they be taken from their owners; and that Congress had no authority to prohibit slavery in federal territories. The decision was a contributing cause for the Civil War.

⑬

Although we now take for granted the Supreme Court's ability to declare laws unconstitutional, this was the first case in which the Court actually flexed its muscle and did so. The 4-0 decision (prior to the decision, the Supreme Court's numbers had been reduced from five to four justices) held that the Court must provide a judicial review of any law that conflicts with the Constitution.

⑭

In a 7-1 decision, the Court upheld racial segregation in public accommodations— an African-American man sought to board a whites-only train—and permitted the "separate but equal" standard. The case was overturned sixty years later in *Brown v. Board of Education*.

Answers

1. *Gideon v. Wainwright*, 1963
2. *Plyler v. Doe*, 1982
3. *Bowers v. Hardwick*, 1986
4. *Regents of the University of California v. Bakke*, 1978
5. *Miranda v. Arizona*, 1966
6. *Roe v. Wade*, 1973
7. *Loving v. Virginia*, 1967
8. *Brown v. Board of Education of Topeka*, 1954

9. *New York Times Co. v. Sullivan*, 1964
10. *Mapp v. Ohio*, 1961
11. *Sony v. Universal City Studios*, 1984
12. *Dred Scott v. Sandford*, 1857
13. *Marbury v. Madison*, 1803
14. *Plessy v. Ferguson*, 1896

Most Creative Jail Breaks

You marveled as Johnny Depp, playing John Dillinger in *Public Enemies*, shot his way out of an Indiana prison; you cheered when Tim Robbins, playing Andy Dufresne, escaped through the tunnel he'd been digging for the last 19 years in *The Shawshank Redemption*; your kids may have even rooted for Bolt, the animated Disney stunt dog, as he busted his cat-friend Mittens out of the pound.

USA TODAY Snapshots®

The time for crime
Average sentence length by top offenses:
(in months)

Murder
𝖎𝖎𝖎𝖎𝖎𝖎𝖎𝖎𝖎𝖎𝖎𝖎𝖎𝖎𝖎𝖎𝖎𝖎𝖎𝖎𝖎𝖎𝖎𝖎𝖎 189.3

Kidnapping/hostage taking
𝖎𝖎𝖎𝖎𝖎𝖎𝖎𝖎𝖎𝖎𝖎𝖎𝖎𝖎𝖎𝖎𝖎𝖎𝖎𝖎 149.3

Robbery
𝖎𝖎𝖎𝖎𝖎𝖎𝖎𝖎𝖎𝖎𝖎 79.6

Drug trafficking
𝖎𝖎𝖎𝖎𝖎𝖎𝖎𝖎𝖎𝖎𝖎 76.4

Sexual abuse
𝖎𝖎𝖎𝖎𝖎𝖎𝖎𝖎𝖎𝖎𝖎 75.4

Source: U.S. Sentencing Commission

By David Stuckey and Alejandro Gonzalez, USA TODAY 200?

Jailbreaks make great material for movies and television, because the stakes are high and the planning and execution must be perfect.

But what about real-life jail breaks? The results in those cases are less fun to contemplate, but many do involve notable planning, innovation, and determination. Here are a few that, although they'll never win an Oscar, warrant a nod for creativity.

 ## Use of a Bathroom

Who: Alfie "Houdini" Hinds

When: 1956

Where: Old Bailey Criminal Court, England

How: Locked prison guards in the bathroom of the courthouse after they uncuffed him to use the toilet. (This was the second of three successful escapes.)

Break-In

Who: Ted Bundy

When: December 1977

Where: Garfield County Jail, Colorado

How: Squeezed through a hole in the ceiling of his cell and made his way through the crawlspace to the jailer's quarters. He broke through the ceiling of the jailer's apartment and walked out the front door.

Display of Patience and Planning

Who: Tim Jenkin, Stephen Lee, and Alex Moumbaris

When: December 1979

Where: Pretoria Prison, South Africa

How: Spent 18 months planning and practicing their escape through 14 locked doors

Aerial Drama

Who: John Killick

When: March 1999

Where: Silverwater Jail, Austrailia

How: Picked up from the prison courtyard by a helicopter commandeered by his librarian girlfriend

Impersonation

Who: Charles Victor Thompson

When: November 2005

Where: Harris County Jail, Texas

How: Walked out of jail by posing as a district attorney

Use of the Mail

Who: Richard Lee McNair

When: April 2006

Where: United States Penitentiary Pollock, Louisiana

How: Hid himself among mailbags that were then shipped out of the facility

Use of a Kitchen Tool

Who: Ralph "Bucky" Phillips

When: April 2006

Where: Alden Correctional Facility, New York

How: Escaped from the prison kitchen by cutting through the ceiling with a can opener

Homage to a Great Story

Who: Jose Espinosa and Otis Blunt

When: December 2007

Where: Union County Jail, New Jersey

How: Dug a hole in the jailhouse wall by scraping away the mortar and smashing and hiding the cinderblocks, while covering the hole with pin-up pictures. Perhaps an approach borrowed from *The Shawshank Redemption*?

The United States Constitution— Not Written in Stone (Sort Of)

The U.S. Constitution was adopted in 1787 and—if you don't count the first ten amendments, which were enacted four years later (the Bill of Rights)—has been amended only 17 times since then. That's over two centuries of being governed by the same basic document.

Have you ever wondered why, in a society that needs to change its automobile models, skirt lengths, and president every one to four years, so few changes have been made to the Constitution?

It's not because the Constitution is perfect. The fact that a civil war had to be fought to keep the union together some 70 years after its adoption shows that our founding document left much to be desired. (Its provisions permitting slavery ultimately led to the Civil War.) And it's not because there was a dearth of ideas for amendments—over 10,000 amendments have been proposed and never made it.

No, the reason for the lack of tinkering is that it's extremely difficult to amend the Constitution.

There are two ways to do it. The first method has never been used, and it's unlikely it ever will be. It's a special constitutional convention, which can be called at the request of at least two-thirds of the states. At such a convention, the Constitution can be changed in any way desired. Indeed, an entirely new Constitution could be adopted. Any changes made at the convention would then need to be approved by three-fourths of the states.

The second method for changing the Constitution—and the only one ever actually used—is the adoption of individual amendments. For an amendment to take effect, it must be approved by a two-thirds vote of the Congress and then ratified by three-fourths of the state legislatures—both high hurdles to clear. Of the 33 amendments that have received the required two-thirds Congressional vote, only 27 (including the Bill of Rights) were ratified by three-fourths of the states.

The following list describes some of the better-known proposed amendments to the Constitution. Do you know which of these were ultimately ratified by Congress and the states and became part of the Constitution?

1 **Flag desecration amendment:** Allows the Congress to enact laws prohibiting all forms of flag desecration, including burning the flag or using it for clothing or napkins

2 **Balanced budget amendment:** Requires Congress to enact a balanced budget each year—that is, a budget in which the total outlays are no greater than the total receipts taken in by the government

3 **Every vote counts amendment:** Does away with the Electoral College and provides that the president and vice president should be elected by a direct popular vote—in other words, the person with the most votes from the people gets elected

4 **Victims' rights amendment:** Gives the victims of crimes of violence and other serious crimes the right to be present when the alleged offender is tried and to present an oral or written statement to the court before the defendant is sentenced or released on parole

5 **Reservation of rights amendment:** Provides that the powers not granted to the national government nor prohibited to the states by the Constitution are reserved to the states or the people

6 **Christian amendment:** Rewrites the preamble to the Constitution to recognize the law of God as supreme authority and Jesus Christ as the Messiah and Savior

7 **Trial by jury amendment:** Guarantees the right to a jury trial in all civil cases

8 **Federal marriage amendment:** Limits marriage to unions of one man with one woman

9 **Direct election of senators amendment:** Provides that all U.S. senators must be selected by popular election by the people of each state instead of by the state legislatures

10 **District of Columbia presidential election amendment:** Permits DC residents to vote for the president and vice-president and grants three electoral votes

11 **District of Columbia voting rights amendment:** Grants DC residents the full voting rights in Congress of a U.S. state

12 **Bricker amendment:** Provides that no treaty can be made by the United States with a foreign country or international agency such as the United Nations that conflicts with the Constitution

13 **Common property amendment:** Guarantees the right of the people to use and enjoy common property, including air, water, wildlife, and other renewable resources

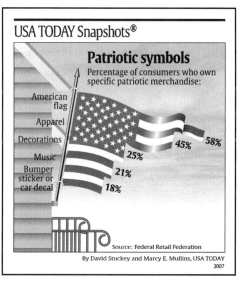

USA TODAY Snapshots®

Patriotic symbols

Percentage of consumers who own specific patriotic merchandise:

American flag 58%
Apparel 45%
Decorations 25%
Music 21%
Bumper sticker or car decal 18%

Source: Federal Retail Federation

By David Stuckey and Marcy E. Mullins, USA TODAY
2007

14 **Income tax amendment:** Allows the Congress to levy an income tax without apportioning it among the states or basing it on U.S. Census results

15 **Equal opportunity to govern amendment:** Permits foreign-born individuals to serve as president and vice president provided they have been U.S. citizens for 20 years

16 **Titles of nobility amendment:** Provides that if a U.S. citizen accepts a title of nobility from a foreign nation, his or her U.S. citizenship must be revoked

⑰ **Equal rights amendment:** Provides that "Equality of rights under the law shall not be denied or abridged by the United States or by any state on account of sex"

⑱ **Congressional pay raises amendment:** Provides that any law raising or lowering Congress members' pay may not take effect until the beginning of the next set of terms for the House of Representatives

⑲ **State sovereign immunity amendment:** Prevents states from being sued in federal court by someone of another state or country unless they consent

⑳ **Presidential succession amendment:** Provides that the vice president becomes president if the president dies, resigns, or is removed from office; establishes procedures to remove a sitting president from office if he or she becomes unable to serve

---

Answers

The proposed amendments listed above that were never ratified and did not become part of the Constitution are: 1, 2, 3, 4, 6, 8, 11, 12, 13, 15, 16, and 17. Of these, the Equal Rights Amendment and District of Columbia Voting Rights Amendment were both approved by Congress, but were not ratified by the required three-fourths of the state legislatures.

The following amendments were ratified by Congress and the states and are part of the Constitution:

5. Reservation of rights amendment—the Tenth Amendment to the Constitution, adopted as part of the Bill of Rights in 1791

7. Trial by jury amendment—the Seventh Amendment, also part of the Bill of Rights

9. Direct election of senators amendment—the Seventeenth Amendment, adopted in 1913

10. District of Columbia presidential election amendment—the Twenty-third Amendment, adopted in 1961

14. Income tax amendment—the Sixteenth Amendment, adopted in 1913

18. Congressional pay raises amendment—the twenty-seventh Amendment, adopted in 1992 and the last time the Constitution was successfully amended

19. State sovereign immunity amendment—the eleventh Amendment, adopted in 1795

20. Presidential succession amendment—the twenty-fifth Amendment, adopted in 1967

You Can Have the House and Kids, But Not the Dog!

A s if divorcing couples didn't have enough to get riled up about, the recent trend toward treating dogs as kin rather than property is making for some rough custody battles.

You may have seen the headlines when, for example, divorcing Hollywood stars Drew Barrymore and Tom Green argued for rights to their yellow Labrador-Chow, Flossie, the dog who saved them from a burning house by barking until they awoke. (Barrymore got to keep Flossie.)

Similar battles are taking place across the United States, as couples untying the knot scoff at legal formulae saying that dogs should be treated as just another item of property to be divvied up along with the sofa and SUV. In fact, surveys show that 83% of pet owners now refer to themselves as the animal's "mom" or "dad." (That may explain why Americans spent $38.4 billion on pets in 2006 alone. That's a lot of rawhide and kitty litter!)

Here are some actual cases in which a court had to decide who got custody of (or visitation with, or the right to support) a dog:

Barney: *Dog with a complex social schedule*

While they were married, Anthony Desanctis and Lynda Hurley Pritchard got Barney the dog from the SPCA. When they decided to divorce, the couple agreed that Barney would be Lynda's property, and came up with a visitation arrangement for Anthony to see the dog. But then Lynda moved and stopped making Barney available for Anthony's visits. Anthony filed a lawsuit trying to get joint custody of Barney.

The judge (in 2002) tossed the suit, finding that dogs are to be treated as property, not children. Trying to arrange dog custody, the judge said, was like trying to arrange "a visitation schedule for a table or a lamp." The judge found that the couple had agreed that Barney, "and his social schedule," would belong to Lynda.

Roddy: *Christmas means a car trip!*

The former Mr. and Mrs. Bennett did a remarkable job agreeing on who'd get what during their divorce—except when it came to their dog, Roddy. The judge initially decided that Mr. Bennett would get the dog, and Mrs. Bennett would have the right to take Roddy every other weekend and on Christmas.

But the couple couldn't make that work. They soon returned to court, Mr. Bennett to argue that his wife shouldn't have any visitation rights, and Mrs. Bennett to argue that Mr. Bennett should have to share custody because he wasn't letting her visit Roddy. The judge entered a second order, this time requiring shared custody, with Roddy switching homes once a month.

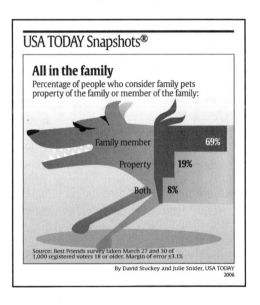

USA TODAY Snapshots®

All in the family
Percentage of people who consider family pets property of the family or member of the family:

Family member 69%
Property 19%
Both 8%

Source: Best Friends survey taken March 27 and 30 of 1,000 registered voters 18 or older. Margin of error ±3.1%

By David Stuckey and Julie Snider, USA TODAY
2006

Mr. Bennett didn't like that either and appealed the order. The appeals court (in 1995) found that Roddy should be awarded, as property, to one spouse or the other. While the appeals court sympathized with the judge's efforts to come up with a fair solution, it found, "Our courts are overwhelmed with the supervision of custody, visitation, and support matters relating to the protection of our children. We cannot undertake the same responsibility as to animals." Roddy may have been feeling a little overwhelmed by now, too.

The dog who liked Bible study *and* motorcycle rides

A divorcing couple in Tennessee actually found a judge who was interested in the dog's best interests (similar to what judges consider in child custody cases) and they revealed that their dog had a broad range of interests indeed. According to the wife, the dog enjoyed the Bible study meetings she had at her house. The husband countered that the dog enjoyed riding on the back of his motorcycle. After hearing all of the evidence, the judge ordered joint custody. The judge also found that the dog should not be required to wear a helmet while riding on the motorcycle, the dog should be allowed to continue attending Bible study, the dog should not be in the presence of people who had been drinking alcohol, and the dog should not be allowed to spend time with "ill-bred or mongrel-type dogs."

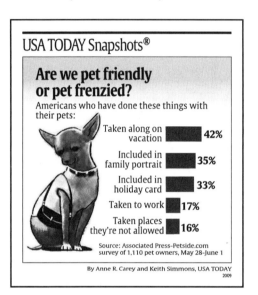

USA TODAY Snapshots®

Are we pet friendly or pet frenzied?

Americans who have done these things with their pets:

Taken along on vacation — 42%
Included in family portrait — 35%
Included in holiday card — 33%
Taken to work — 17%
Taken places they're not allowed — 16%

Source: Associated Press-Petside.com survey of 1,110 pet owners, May 28-June 1

By Anne R. Carey and Keith Simmons, USA TODAY 2009

Sable and the Solomonic judge

A Maryland couple asked a court to resolve their custody dispute over Sable, their dog. The wife had spent more than $20,000 trying to keep custody of Sable, then the court granted her former husband visitation rights. When the couple returned to court to argue over the dog some more, the fight came to an abrupt end when a judge threatened to sell the dog and let the couple split the proceeds unless they could agree on a reasonable visitation schedule for Sable.

Gigi: *Who's your mama?*

When Stanley and Linda Perkins divorced, they spent up to $150,000 litigating custody of their dog, a Pointer/Greyhound mix named Gigi. The judge considered, among other things, the results of a "bonding study" conducted by an animal behaviorist and a "day in the life" video, presented by Linda's divorce lawyer, showing Gigi romping at the beach and sleeping under Linda's chair at work. Linda got custody of the dog.

Who gets Dexter's costumes and portrait gallery?

Doreen Houseman and Eric Dare never married—but that didn't stop them from having a doozy of a custody battle over their pug, Dexter. When Doreen moved out of the couple's shared home, she took Dexter and all of his paraphernalia—including the professional photographs they'd had taken of him, as well as his collection of costumes. She allowed Eric to take Dexter for visits, but then Eric refused to give Dexter back.

Doreen sued, claiming that Eric had promised to let her keep Dexter. Eric countered that he'd paid for the pug ($1,500) and for most of his food and vet bills over the years. (No word on who paid for the costumes, photos, and elaborate events they'd thrown for this four-footed party animal.)

In a groundbreaking opinion, the court awarded shared possession of Dexter, who is to alternate homes every five weeks. The judge didn't accept that he has to use a "best interests of the pet" standard (used in child custody cases), but he did find that, unlike other property, such as a sofa, a pet is unique.

Five Defective Products That Changed the Law

••

Back in 1918, a Mississippi man, Bryson Pillars, became ill after chewing on tobacco. The cause: A "human toe with flesh and nail intact" had ended up in his package of Brown Mule Chewing tobacco. According to the Pillars, the toe "crumbled like dry bread" and caused him to "foam at the mouth." His doctor determined that Pillars was suffering from ptomaine poisoning (no pun intended). He sued R.J. Reynolds and won. The judge, presumably a tobacco chewer, established a simple standard: "We can imagine no reason why, with ordinary care, human toes could not be left out of chewing tobacco." (*Pillars v. R. J. Reynolds Tobacco*, 78 So. Rprtr 365 (1918).)

Nowadays we take it for granted that if a product causes an injury, the manufacturer is going to be responsible. But there was a time, not that long ago, when consumers—other than those who chewed "toe-bacco"—lived in a caveat emptor world. If you were injured using a defective handsaw or suffered vision loss from chemicals in your eye makeup, you lived with it and didn't expect a check from the manufacturer. Below are some of the defective products that helped to change legal rules—and consumers' expectations.

The broken-spoked 1916 Buick Coupe

Donald C. MacPherson, a stonecutter who specialized in tombstones, purchased a Buick coupe (with rumble seat) from a dealership in Schenectady, New York. He used his new car—powered by a one-half horsepower engine—from May through November. (The rest of the time it was stored in his barn.) One summer day, while driving to Saratoga Springs, a defective hickory-wood spoke in the Buick's rear wheel buckled and broke, causing the car to roll over and pin MacPherson.

Two months, later MacPherson's vision had deteriorated—he was having trouble identifying people—and he was enduring sharp pains in his broken right arm and wrist while cutting gravestones. He sued the Buick Motor Company for negligence, claiming that Buick owed him a duty of care to inspect the components used in the automobile.

At that time, the duty of care—the modern standard for negligence—was said to exist only if there was a direct contractual relationship ("privity") between the customer and the maker of the defective product. In other words, in order to bring the claim, MacPherson would have had to have purchased the car directly from Buick, not a retailer.

(Making it more complicated, Buick had contracted with a third-party to purchase the wheel—further distancing MacPherson from the source of the accident.)

Despite initial setbacks—the case was thrown out and then reinstated by an appellate court—MacPherson prevailed and was awarded $5,025. Buick appealed, and in 1916, Justice Benjamin Cardozo changed the law of manufacturing and sales when he held that Buick could not hide behind the façade of its dealership to avoid its obligations to consumers.

Cardozo wrote that Buick "was not at liberty to put the finished product on the market without subjecting the component parts to ordinary and simple tests.... The more probable the danger, the greater the need of caution." With his holding, Cardozo extended the duty of care to all auto manufacturers—a standard previously limited to inherently dangerous products, such as poisons and explosives. (*MacPherson v. Buick Motor Company*, 217 NY 382 (1916).)

The killer antibiotic—"Elixir Sulfanilamide"

In 1937, Harold Watkins, chief chemist for the Massengill Company, was attempting to produce a version of sulfanilamide—the revolutionary new antibiotic—in liquid form so that it would be more palatable for kids. The drug wouldn't dissolve in water or alcohol, but it was soluble in diethylene glycol, an industrial solvent. Watkins tested the solution on rats (who developed kidney failure and died), and he tested it for taste and fragrance on humans (it had a raspberry flavor). But he never tested the product—which was 24 times stronger than the version tested on rats—for safety on humans.

Within four weeks of its release, Massengill's Elixir Sulfanilamide had killed 105 people, a third of whom were children. The company "regretted" the error, but claimed that the manufacturing process followed standards of the time. Aside from a $26,100 fine (the largest fine ever issued by the FDA at the time), the company had no other legal liability. The following year—as a result of the public outcry—Congress passed the Food Drug and Cosmetic Act of 1938, a landmark law that for the first time required that drug companies test drugs for safety before releasing them. (Federal Food, Drug, and Cosmetic Act 1938. Public Law 717,52, Stat. 1040; 25 June 1938.) Eventually, the scandal claimed its 106th victim when Harold Watkins—the chemist who invented the elixir—killed himself.

By the way, diethylene glycol continues to cause injuries. In 1986, 14 deaths in India were attributed to the substance after an error was made substituting industrial glycerine (18.5 % diethylene glycol) for medicinal glycerine, and in 1990, 40 children died in Nigeria when diethylene glycol was substituted for propylene glycol in a cough syrup. The solvent's cousin, ethylene glycol—which is used as auto antifreeze—also is a problem for health officials because it's sometimes consumed accidentally by children, or deliberately by folks on a "'Lost weekend" (who seek out its alcohol content). More than 3,000 cases of such poisoning are reported each year.

The exploding Coca-Cola bottle

Gladys Escola was working as a waitress in Madera, California, moving bottles of Coca-Cola from their case to an open refrigerator, when one bottle exploded. According to Gladys, there was a loud "pop" and the bottle was in two pieces; the top still in her bloody hand, and the lower portion on the floor. She looked down at a five-inch gash that had severed nerves, tendons, and muscles in the palm and thumb.

Escola retained a local lawyer, Melvin Belli, who was not deterred by the lack of evidence (the broken bottle had been tossed by a restaurant employee). Even though there seemed no way to prove *why* the bottle had exploded or that the Coca-Cola Company was responsible for the damage—negligence is never presumed—Belli believed that it was enough to demonstrate that the bottle had been produced by the company and that nobody else had interfered with it once it left Coca-Cola's control.

Belli asserted a theory of negligence known as *res ipsa loquitor* (in Latin, "the thing speaks for itself"). Under this theory, if the manufacturer had exclusive control over the product, negligence can be based on circumstantial evidence. The jury sided with Gladys Escola, as did the California Supreme Court. Equally important in the Supreme Court's decision was the concurring opinion of Justice Roger Traynor who argued that, as a matter of public policy, "a manufacturer incurs an absolute liability when an article that he has placed on the market, knowing that it is to be used without inspection, proves to have a defect that causes injury to human beings." Nineteen years later, Traynor's then-radical concurring opinion became California law (see the very next case described). (*Escola v. Coca-Cola Bottling Co.*, 24 Cal.2d 453, 150 P.2d 436 (1944).)

The Shopsmith five-in-one tool

It was Christmas 1955, and Bill Greenman's wife gave him a gift that any handyman would covet: the Shopsmith Mark 5, a machine that functioned as a table saw, lathe, disc sander, horizontal drill, and drill press.

Two years later when Bill tried to create a chalice using an oversized piece of lumber, a large chunk of wood flew off the machine and struck him on the forehead, causing a head injury. He sued, and the case proceeded along two legal theories: first, that the manufacturer had breached its warranties (contractual promises that the machine would work as advertised in its brochure) and second, that the manufacturer was negligent.

The jury awarded Greenman $65,000. The manufacturer, Yuba Power Products, appealed, claiming that Greenman had waited too long (over ten months) before reporting the breach of warranty (the brochure had required prompt notice).

For most of the twentieth century, product liability had been tied to contractual relationships, whether it was the "privity" of purchase or the contractual promise of a warranty. But all that changed when California

Supreme Court Justice Roger Traynor established a rule of strict liability for defective products. Traynor held that when a manufacturer puts a product into commerce, it has an obligation to make that product safe for normal use. If the product is defective, there's no need to prove fault.

As a result of Greenman's case about the Mark 5, most states followed California's lead and began to enforce strict liability principles for physical injuries caused by products. (The resulting economic shift sent manufacturers scurrying for product liability insurance. No wonder that when—in a 1996 poll—personal injury lawyers voted for the top cases in their field, *Greenman v. Yuba Power Products* was Number One. (*Greenman v. Yuba Power Products*, 59 Cal.2d 57, 27 Cal.Rptr. 697 (1963).)

The 190 degree McDonald's coffee

When Stella Liebeck ordered a coffee from the drive-through window at her local McDonald's in Albuquerque, New Mexico, the 79 year old had no idea that she was soon to become the linchpin for a product liability movement. Chris, her grandson was driving, and he pulled the car over so that Stella could add cream and sugar. With the coffee cup held between her knees, Liebeck pulled the far side of the lid toward her, accidentally spilling the coffee on her cotton sweatpants. For approximately a minute and half, she endured direct scalding on her thighs, buttocks, and groin. At  a nearby hospital, doctors reported that 6% of her skin had third-degree burns, while 16% of her skin had lesser burns. A week of painful skin grafts followed (during which time Liebeck lost 20% of her weight). Medical treatments continued for another two years. The injuries were unfortunate, but was McDonald's at fault? After all, as Elaine asked on the "Seinfeld" show—in an episode in which Kramer was considering a lawsuit over spilt coffee—isn't coffee supposed to be hot?

Liebeck had not wanted to sue McDonald's. She asked for a payment of $20,000 (she had incurred over $11,000 in medical bills). McDonald's offered her $800. Liebeck sued—the first lawsuit of her life—and the court apportioned her liability at 20%. (Under a principle known as comparative liability, a victim who contributes to her injury will have any resulting damages reduced by a percentage attributable to her own negligence). The jury awarded her $200,000 in compensatory damages (reduced to $160,000) and punitive damages of $2.7 million (equivalent to two days of McDonald's coffee sales revenue). After a series of appeals, the parties settled out of court for what was reported to be less than $600,000.

So what made a jury of reasonable citizens award millions of dollars for some spilled coffee? According to the evidence, McDonald's kept their coffee at 30 to 50 degrees hotter than competitors (approximately 190 degrees). The Shriner Burn Institute had previously warned McDonald's not to serve coffee above 130 degrees—primarily because it took only two to seven seconds to cause a third-degree burn at that temperature. A McDonald's quality assurance manager testified that the company knew of the risk but decided against turning down the heat or posting a warning about the possibility of severe burns. And previous to Liebeck, the company had responded to over 700 incidents of scalding coffee injuries.

The case provided fodder for many opponents of tort lawsuits—by manufacturers, doctors, insurers, small business owners, and others—all of whom wanted to reduce the ballooning size of awards, limit personal injury lawsuits, and modify the cultural perspective that all injuries demand compensation.

Leibeck's predicament was mocked on national TV and became a platform for Republican legislators, including presidential candidate George W. Bush. (Ironically, many people attribute Bush's victory to the vote splitting caused by Ralph Nader, who made his name with product liability claims against the Chevrolet Corvair and Ford Pinto.)

Despite a great of deal of misinformation about Liebeck's case—she died in 2004 at the age of 91—her spilled cup of coffee provided the perfect public relations element to swing the pendulum of product liability. Tort reformers seized on her story and continue to use it to push legislators to modify laws affecting personal injury lawsuits. (*Liebeck v. McDonald's Restaurants*, CV-93-02419, 1995 WL 360309 (Bernalillo County, N.M. Dist. Ct., August 18, 1994).)

Biggest U.S. Family Legal Feuds

The nineteenth century Hatfields and McCoys may be the most famous family feuders, but they didn't often resort to lawyers and litigation. (They were too busy with homemade methods of dispute resolution like arson, kidnapping, and murder.)

Not so the families below, who represent either progress toward more civilized forms of settling arguments or a colossal waste of social resources and the U.S. court system. You be the judge.

The Koch family of Kansas: *Talking through lawyers*

If your family owned Koch Industries, one of the nation's largest privately held companies (up there with the likes of Cargill), wouldn't having several billion dollars of your own be enough to ease your worries about whether one of your siblings got a little more? No! (Thinking along these lines may explain why the authors of this book are toiling at desk jobs rather than running multinational corporations.)

It all goes back to the early 1980s, when brothers Charles and David bought William (David's fraternal twin) and Frederick out of Koch Industries for about $1 billion. The latter two soon decided they'd been duped, and the lawsuits began—no fewer than 25 of them, brought before various courts, on charges ranging from fraud to mismanagement to corruption. Bill and Fred even sued their mother about her distributions of money from a family foundation.

All 25 suits were dismissed except two: one alleging withheld information regarding oil output on a family refinery, and one claiming misleading accounting practices.

If the allegations sound a bit dry, the trial that took place in 1998 certainly wasn't. Various brothers flew in by private jet, mounted PR campaigns with TV commercials and public surveys, refused to speak as they passed each other in the courthouse hallways, spilled stories of family grief describing who made Mom cry and who returned whose Christmas presents unopened, and generally created a public spectacle for the people of Kansas.

At the end of it all, William and Frederick walked away with nothing. Appeals and other lawsuits are no doubt pending.

Doris Duke's heirs: *Fighting for million-dollar scraps*

Hey look, you can have a family feud without a family! By the time of heiress Doris Duke's death in 1993 at age 80, she was divorced and had no friends or family to whom she felt close—the legacy of a lifetime of suspicion of fortune hunters. Duke left most of her $1.2 billion estate to various charities, for the "improvement of humanity." She also set aside $100,000 in trust for the care of her dog.

Unfortunately, certain members of humanity felt they deserved a more personal share—in particular, Chandi Heffner. Duke had adopted Heffner as an adult (35 years old). Heffner was a Hare Krishna devotee whom Duke apparently believed to be the reincarnation of her only natural-born daughter, who'd died after a premature birth. Duke took Heffner with her on world travels and bought her a $1.5 million horse ranch in Oahu, until the two became estranged.

Duke explicitly cut Heffner out of her will. Undaunted, Heffner filed three lawsuits and finally got a $65 million settlement out of the Duke estate.

Meanwhile, Duke's alcoholic butler, Bernard Lafferty, and her doctor, Harry Demopoulos, filed suits over who was the rightful executor of the estate. And no wonder, since the role was worth millions of dollars in executor's fees. The butler won the right to be coexecutor for awhile—despite allegations that he'd conspired to administer final doses of morphine that hastened Duke's death—but he was finally persuaded to step down in return for a cool $4.5 million.

Winemaker family feuds

Is it something in the grapes—or maybe the phrase "sour grapes" applies extra to those who toil in the vineyards? Three major California winemaking families have experienced family feuds of major proportions. In brief, it looks something like this.

The Gallos

Ernest and Julio Gallo played a large part in the growth of California's wine industry; when Ernest Gallo died in 2007, he was the renowned patriarch of three generations of winemakers. But although wine and cheese are generally thought to mix well, the winemaking Gallo brothers weren't willing to see their family name on a line of gourmet cheese that their younger brother Joseph, Jr., planned to market in the 1980s. They successfully sued to prevent him from using the family name. Joe, Jr., sued back, claiming that he was cheated out of his part of the family legacy after both parents of the three brothers died—in a 1933 murder-suicide.

Robert Mondavi

Another patriarch (or two), another set of brothers (or two), another feud (or two). Anyone see a pattern emerging? This time, it's Robert Mondavi, the son of an Italian immigrant father who invited Robert and his brother to go into the wine business in hopes that the two would work together. Mondavi was the driving force behind both the family's 1943 purchase of a then-floundering winery called Charles Krug and a vision of selling not only wine but a lifestyle in which wine and food were central—a vision in which California wines rivaled the best wines of Europe.

But not everyone in the family was in agreement with Mondavi's vision for Krug, and in 1965, a feud erupted between Robert and his mother and brother, leading Mondavi to start his own winery five miles down the road from Charles Krug. Thus began a court battle between the two brothers that created a decades-long split. Mondavi built his new winery into an enormously successful business and brought his own two sons into the business.

In yet another generation, after years of infighting, one brother was ousted from the business in 2004. In other words, not a decade went by without some conflict in the Mondavi family. Robert Mondavi died in 2008, but Mondavi wine lives on.

The Korbel champagne feud

The Korbel winery was the first to prove that California can produce high-quality champagne—but has also been the scene of generations of legal battles. First, Adolph Heck, of Bohemian lineage, spent most of the 1970s in a legal tug-of-war with his own brothers for ownership of the winery that they'd inherited from their father. The case settled in 1984 with Adolph Heck gaining control. After Adolph died in 1984, his son Gary Heck took over.

USA TODAY Snapshots®

All in the family
Do you plan to bring your children into the family business?

No **43%**
Undecided **31%**
Yes **26%**

Father & Son PIZZERIA

Source: SunTrust Bank Private Wealth Management survey of 201 business owners of companies with revenue of $10 million or more.

By Jae Yang and and Bob Laird, USA TODAY 2007

Some years went by in relative peace—until 2006. That's when Heck and his daughter, Richie Ann Samii, began the lawsuits, filing no fewer than nine legal actions against each other over the years following. Heck accused Samii and her then-boyfriend of assaulting a winery visitor, Samii accused Heck of misusing trust funds, and so on and so on. The nastiness between them included death threats and other inappropriate postings on a website.

In 2009, the parties settled all outstanding lawsuits just before trial, agreeing to release each other from every "action of every nature… throughout the universe and in perpetuity," in a settlement that covers conduct "from the beginning of time." Guess they really, really mean it.

Herbert H. Haft's discount drugstore empire: *Medicines to cure everything but family strife*

Herbert Haft was an enormously successful businessman who started with a single drugstore in Washington and ended up with a chain of 77, as well as a multitude of other discount businesses, including Crown Books and Shoppers Food Warehouse. He always involved family members in his ventures—for better and for worse. He battled with his brother-in-law over the latter's investments in the drugstore chain, and then with his own brother when his brother sided with the brother-in-law. He was estranged from his brother for 15 years.

Both of Haft's sons, and his wife, worked for him—at least until he fired his oldest son from leadership of the family's largest company, Dart, and also removed his wife of 45 years from the Board of Directors, claiming the two were acting in concert against him. Self-fulfilling prophecy, anyone? His wife sued for divorce, his son sued for wrongful discharge, and the 1990s saw the entire family embroiled in suits and more suits. Finally, in 1997 Haft gave over control of the business in exchange for a payout of $50 million.

This wasn't the end of the fighting, though. Just weeks before his death in 2004, Haft's daughter sued to prevent him from marrying his longtime companion, alleging that he wasn't competent to make the decision to marry. The last-minute bid failed, and Haft did marry—in his hospital bed. He died before a court could rule on his daughter's petition to determine his competency.

There's no Band-Aid for this boo-boo:
J. Seward Johnson's children fight with his wife

John Seward Johnson was the son of Robert Wood Johnson, the founder of the Johnson & Johnson family of companies—you know, the Band-Aid people. J. Seward Johnson was a businessman and a philanthropist, who founded the Harbor Branch Oceanographic Institute. He had four children with his first wife and then two more with his second wife, to whom he was married for more than 30 years.

Eight days after their divorce was final, the 76-year-old Johnson married a maid in his household, 34-year-old Barbara Piasecka.

Apparently the kids weren't too keen on Barbara, and when Johnson left her his entire fortune—north of $400 million—they objected. The kids argued that Johnson was bullied and coerced by Piasecka and was not of sound mind when he signed the will less than six weeks before he died in 1983. They say that, left to his own devices, he never would have excluded the children and the Oceanographic Institute, which he loved. They also accused Johnson's lawyer, Nina Zagat, of being complicit in influencing Johnson improperly.

The case went to trial, with both sides putting on witnesses who testified about Piasecka's relationship with Johnson—her witnesses saying she was a tender, loving wife, and those on the other side painting a picture of a tantrum-throwing shrew who abused her frail, elderly husband.

In the end, the case settled with the children receiving a collective $42.5 million to add to their existing fortunes, created by their father through trust funds when they reached adulthood. They always contended it wasn't about the money.

It never is, is it? And we could go on and on, adding the contest over Ike Turner's will, the battle over Michael Jackson's estate, the fight over Anna Nicole Smith's money and the future of her small child, or the family fight to control Michael Crichton's trust. Sadly, space does not permit a complete rundown of every tawdry family story involving lots and lots of money.

Off to Court in a Chicken Costume

est you doubt that court cases can be found on every theme imagined by man or woman, we bring you a series centering around people (mostly defendants) dressed up like chickens.

Chicken for religious reasons

After being arrested for tampering with utility metering devices in Tennessee, Mr. Hodges appeared in court dressed like a chicken.

At least, that was the judge's description of his "grossly shocking and bizarre attire," which consisted of "brown and white fur tied around his body at his ankles, loins and head, with a like vest made out of fur, and complete with eye goggles over his eyes. He had colored his face and chest with a very pale green paint or coloring. He had what appeared to be a human skull dangling from his waist and in his hand he carried a stuffed snake."

The judge cited Hodges for contempt of court.

But wait, there's another side to the story! Hodges explained that, "This is a spiritual attire and ... I have never worn anything else in court but this when I am on trial." In light of that statement, an appeals court granted him the right to a new trial.

(*State v. Hodges*, 695 S.W.2d 171, Tenn., 1985.)

Chicken with a wig

Meanwhile, in Ohio, a Worthington Kroger store was being plagued by robberies. First, a man hit the store up while dressed in a Santa Claus suit. Then about a month later, the store was robbed by a man dressed as a chicken—and with a voice sounding suspiciously like that of an ex-employee named Haines.

The evidence against Haines mounted: A video surveillance tape of the second robbery showed the robber wearing a yellow wig with his costume. Investigators learned that Haines had a band. They checked its website, and there was Haines wearing the same yellow wig! Oops.

Haines was convicted of aggravated robbery plus a few other crimes.

(*State v. Haines*, Not Reported in N.E.2d, 2005 WL 2789065; Ohio App. 10 Dist., 2005.)

Chicken with a mean right hook

Ted Giannoulas created a sports mascot called "The Famous Chicken" in which he appeared in costume at games to make fun of celebrities, ballplayers, umpires, and others. And so, (in the words of the court that had to deal with the eventual fallout), "inevitably, the Chicken's beady glare came to rest on that lovable and carefree icon of childhood, Barney."

Giannoulas dressed someone else up in a dinosaur costume, and developed a routine where he would "flip, slap, tackle, trample, and generally assault" the dinosaur.

When the owners of the rights to the Barney character (Lyons Partnership) heard about this, they sued for copyright and trademark infringement.

Emotions in the court room ran high as Lyons presented tales of children who'd seen the performance and, according to the court's account, "honestly believed that the real Barney was being assaulted. In one poignant account related by Lyons, a parent describes how the spectacle brought his two-year-old child to tears. In fact, we are told, only after several days of solace was the child able to relate the horror of what she had observed in her own words—"Chicken step on Barney"—without crying."

Giannoulas defended himself with the argument that he was "engaged in a sophisticated critique of society's acceptance of this ubiquitous and insipid creature."

The appeals court went with Giannoulas's argument. It said the use of the Barney look-alike was a mere parody and wouldn't confuse any consumers sufficiently to infringe on Lyons's rights in the character.

(*Lyons Partnership v. Giannoulas*, 179 F.3d 384, C.A.5 (Tex.), 1999.)

Chicken gone freelance

Hey look, another case with Ted Giannoulas! Back in the 1980s, he had a job in California as the costumed chicken mascot at a radio station. After leaving that job, he continued making his way in the world as a costumed chicken—but the radio station sued, alleging he was breaching his employment contract and unfairly competing with it, plus infringing on its service mark.

The court didn't want to mess with Giannoulas's chosen method of making a living, so they said he could still appear in a chicken suit—just not one bearing the station's specific ensemble, suit, or logo.

(*KGB, Inc., v. Giannoulas*, 104 Cal.App.3d 844, 164 Cal.Rptr. 571, Cal.App. 4 Dist., 1980.)

Free-range, free-speech chicken

Wild Wings 'n Things, a restaurant franchise based in Colorado Springs, asks its franchisees to hire someone in a chicken suit to wave at people driving on nearby roads, in some cases carrying a sign pointing people to the nearest restaurant. They call him "Chicken Man."

Unfortunately, Chicken Man ruffled feathers in the town of Woodland Park, Colorado, where city officials worried that he was a safety hazard and an aesthetic blight. They announced that Chicken Man was violating a city ordinance against posting unauthorized signs and then set to work to make the ordinance even more applicable. Chicken Man began waving a flag instead of a sign, awaiting the outcome of the city council's efforts.

But approximately one in eight citizens of Woodland Park signed a petition in support of Chicken Man's right to free speech (even though he doesn't talk, or even cluck). When last heard from, the ordinance was mired in bureaucracy, and Chicken Man was still roaming freely in Woodland Park and elsewhere.

For the record, there don't seem to have been any lawsuits brought by people dressed as turkeys.

When Judges Get Fed Up

J udges see the full panoply of human folly—and sometimes wish they didn't have to. Such as, perhaps, in the cases below.

Has anyone seen my nameplate?

Like many celebrities in Los Angeles, Judge Lance Ito—who became known as the world's most-watched judge when he presided over the 1995 O.J. Simpson murder trial on live television—has had to deal with unwanted public attention. The intrusions on his privacy have ranged from presentations of satirical skits on Jay Leno's "Tonight Show" to raids on his home trash cans by souvenir hunters.

But the circus all died down eventually, right? Apparently not. As late as 2009, Judge Ito told the press that he'd given up on replacing nameplates stolen from his courtroom. Every time he'd get a new one, someone—most likely another souvenir hunter—would filch it. So now his ninth floor courtroom has no nameplate.

Silence in the court!

At a preliminary hearing, Ohio Municipal Court Judge Stephen Belden was getting fed up with the interruptions, complaining, and arguing by the robbery defendant before him. He ordered the defendant to be silent, but that didn't work. Finally, the judge improvised, using everyone's favorite tool for improvising: duct tape.

Yes, Judge Belden ordered the defendant's mouth to be sealed shut. No word on why the courtroom had a supply of duct tape at hand.

You put your underwear on *how*?

Florida state judge Pat Kinsey was trying her best to understand plaintiff

Albert Freed's claim that his new Hanes underwear ruined his "dream trip to Hawaii" because the fly "'gaped open and acted like a sand belt on [his] privates,' causing personal injury."

But when the argument started coming down to whether Freed's method of putting on his underwear—by placing it inside the pants he planned to wear that day and then pulling both on together, without adjusting himself to get comfortable—the judge apparently reached the limits of her expertise, judicial or otherwise.

Fortunately, a male attorney awaiting a hearing on his next case happened to be in the courtroom. He agreed to serve as an expert witness.

Later, in a footnote to her opinion (which rejected Freed's claim), the judge thanked the attorney for "testifying about his sensitivity to penile discomfort" and for offering "surprisingly candid testimony despite the intimate nature of the questions."

Don't mess with a judge!

In case anyone was wondering, judges do wear pants under their robes—which makes it perhaps understandable that Washington, DC, Administrative Law Judge Roy L. Pearson was upset when the dry cleaners lost his favorite pair.

Very upset. He sued the Korean-immigrant owners of the dry cleaning establishment, Jin and Soo Chung, for fraud, demanding a cool $67 million in damages.

The Chungs were so intimidated, they offered the judge various settlements; first $3,000, then $4,600, then $12,000. And this for a pair of pants worth an estimated $395. The judge wouldn't touch such paltry sums, but he did reduce his claim to $54 million. What a relief! Nevertheless, the dry cleaning business owners weren't ready to settle, and the case went to court.

Despite Judge Pearson's breathless, emotional testimony about the mental anguish he had suffered—not to mention his careful trial preparation, involving more than 1,400 hours of work—Pearson lost the case.

In fact, the judge in charge of the case, Judith Bartnoff, seemed to have been pretty fed up with Pearson by the end of the trial, for example admonishing him to refer to himself as "I" rather than "we." Judge Bartnoff ordered Pearson to pay the Chung's court costs and attorneys' fees.

Pearson later lost his job for lack of "judicial temperament."

And don't be yawning in my courtroom, either

Circuit Judge Daniel Rozak, in Joliet, Illinois, has seen plenty of instances of contempt of court—swearing, use of cell phones in court, and more. In fact, he's known for bringing a third of all contempt charges in the twelfth Circuit.

So he was, once again, not amused when Clifton Williams, in court for his cousin's drug hearing, "raised his hands while at the same time making a loud yawning sound."

The judge sentenced Williams to six months in jail—the maximum contempt penalty without a jury trial. Meanwhile, Williams's cousin, the actual defendant, didn't have to do any jail time—he got two years' probation.

Five Strange But True Butt-Related Inventions

When our Founding Fathers wrote the Constitution back in 1787, they had no idea that the patent system they initiated would someday be used to protect a method for revealing butt cleavage. (In fact there's more than one patent addressing the issue). Sound strange? Butt wait, there's more. Below are patents focused on the human rear end.

PATENT NO. 6,473,908: "Garment having a buttocks cleavage revealing feature"

What's buttocks cleavage? It's when a little bit of the buttocks (and the cleft between them) is exposed. Some people find this type of exposure unappealing—in the United States it's disparagingly referred to as plumber's crack, in Britain it's builder's bum, and in Brazil, call it cofrinho. Even with this negative rap, apparently there are those among us who like to expose their gluteal cleft. For those folks, inventor Thomas A. Bontems created a method for affixing a strategically placed see-through material allowing for ideal butt cleavage exposure. One nice feature is that the see-through portion of the invention is not limited to a basic heart-shaped peek-a-boo cutout;

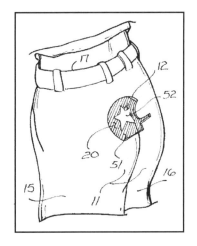

wearers can also expose themselves through flower-shaped, butterfly shaped, and football-helmet shaped windows of opportunity. (We're not sure if the football helmet is for fans or players occupying center position). There's even a "logo" view that presumably allows for unlimited corporate licensing opportunities—for example, you can expose yourself within the Apple logo or Chevrolet "bowtie." Since inventors create things that solve problems, one may wonder what problem Bontems' invention solves? According to the inventor, many people like to expose portions of their anatomy but they're not comfortable wearing tight fitting or low-cut jeans. This invention "incorporates a revealing feature that does not detract from or govern the overall structure of the garment." In other words, Bontems has leveled the playing field and liberated butt cleavage from the thin, the sexy, and the good-looking. Free at last!!

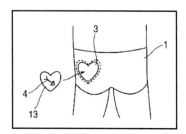

If you liked this invention you might also like: Patent No. 5,970,516, "Article of clothing for making a patterned sunburn." This invention allows the user to swap out an interchangeable see-through portion of a bathing suit to create tanning tattoos.

PATENT NO. 6,012,168: "Privacy accessory for use with hospital gown"

Even exhibitionists would probably like to avoid one situation of butt cleavage exposure—the use of an old-fashioned, posterior-exposing hospital gown. Laurie Hutton and Lois Histopad came up with a temporary-albeit worky solution as shown in their 1998 patent—a flap-and-strap garment that can be worn underneath the gown to guarantee "practical modesty coverage." Much as we may support the concept, this flapping backside accessory seems like a stopgap measure. Sure enough, a better solution arrived in 2001 with Sarah Bowens' Patent No. 6,237,153, "Hospital Garment," which featured three panels, one of which was an overlapping back panel.

Despite the obsolescence of their invention, we support Histopad and Hutton because as lawyers, we can relate to the need for covering your backside.

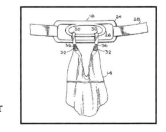

If you liked this invention you might also like: Patent No. 4,028,740, "Convertible beach attire." Speaking of hiding your butt, perhaps you'd like a nice "pair of modesty panels" to cover your skimpy swimwear while walking from your car to the beach. These panels come with a complex-looking belt and loop combo that makes you wonder why the wearer doesn't just drape a towel around the overexposed area.

PATENT NO. 4,151,613: "Protective device for the buttocks and hips of a person for use in skateboarding"

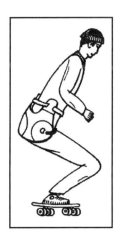

Skateboarding is all about style, and what could be more stylish than wearing a plastic and foam portable seat on your butt? Now, that should impress your boarding buds. No doubt, inventor Jhoon Rhee had the noblest intentions: to shield skateboarders from hip and butt damage. After all, skateboarding injuries account for 50,000 emergency room visits per year. And since 90% of the skateboarding victims are under 15, it makes a lot of sense that kids should wear this "butthelmet," although getting them to comply should be about as easy as getting them to clean out the septic tank. And here's some good news for manufacturers: Rhee's patent expired in 1995, so anyone can sell and use this shielding device.

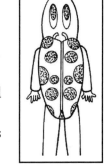

If you liked this invention you might also like: Patent No. 5,913,405, "Ladybug (child protector)." Apparently influenced by Kafka's *The Metamorphosis*, inventor Francisco Bordier has designed a polyurethane bug-styled protective covering for use by children learning to walk.

NOLO   *Keep Up to Date*

 Go to **Nolo.com/newsletters/index.html** to sign up for free newsletters and discounts on Nolo products.

- **Nolo Briefs.** Our monthly email newsletter with great deals and free information.

- **Nolo's Special Offer.** A monthly newsletter with the biggest Nolo discounts around.

- **BizBriefs.** Tips and discounts on Nolo products for business owners and managers.

- **Landlord's Quarterly.** Deals and free tips just for landlords and property managers, too.

 Don't forget to check for updates at **Nolo.com.** Under "Products," find this book and click "Legal Updates."

Let Us Hear From You

 Comments on this book? We want to hear 'em. Email us at feedback@nolo.com.

US-TRIV1

NOLO® *Online Legal Forms*

Nolo offers a large library of legal solutions and forms, created by Nolo's in-house legal staff. These reliable documents can be prepared in minutes.

Create a Document

- **Incorporation.** Incorporate your business in any state.
- **LLC Formations.** Gain asset protection and pass-through tax status in any state.
- **Wills.** Nolo has helped people make over 2 million wills. Is it time to make or revise yours?
- **Living Trust (avoid probate).** Plan now to save your family the cost, delays, and hassle of probate.
- **Trademark.** Protect the name of your business or product.
- **Provisional Patent.** Preserve your rights under patent law and claim "patent pending" status.

Download a Legal Form

Nolo.com has hundreds of top quality legal forms available for download—bills of sale, promissory notes, nondisclosure agreements, LLC operating agreements, corporate minutes, commercial lease and sublease, motor vehicle bill of sale, consignment agreements and many, many more.

Review Your Documents

Many lawyers in Nolo's consumer-friendly lawyer directory will review Nolo documents for a very reasonable fee. Check their detailed profiles at **Nolo.com/lawyers/index.html**.